FILM NOIR

The term "film noir" still conjures up images o   ....an malaise: hard-boiled detectives, fatal women, and the shadowy hells of urban life. But, from its beginnings, film noir has been an international phenomenon, and its stylistic icons have migrated across the complex geo-political terrain of world cinema. This book traces film noir's emergent connection to European cinema, its movement within a cosmopolitan culture of literary and cinematic translation, and its postwar consolidation in the US, Europe, Asia, the Middle East, and Latin America.

The authors examine how film noir crosses national boundaries, speaks to diverse international audiences, and dramatizes local crimes and the crises of local spaces in the face of global phenomena like world-wide depression, war, political occupation, economic and cultural modernization, decolonization, and migration. This fresh study of film noir and global culture also discusses film noir's heterogeneous style and revises important scholarly debates about this perpetually alluring genre.

Key films discussed include:
- *The Maltese Falcon* (Huston, 1941)
- *Stray Dog* (Kurosawa, 1949)
- *Aventurera* (Gout, 1950)
- *Out of the Past* (Tourneur, 1947)
- *Ossessione* (Visconti, 1943)
- *La Bête humaine* (Renoir, 1938)
- C.I.D. (Khosla, 1956)
- *The Lady from Shanghai* (Welles, 1947)
- *The American Friend* (Wenders, 1977)
- *Chungking Express* (Wong, 1994)

Jennifer Fay is Associate Professor of English and Director of Film Studies at Michigan State University and is the author of *Theaters of Occupation: Hollywood and the Re-education of Postwar Germany* (2008).

Justus Nieland is Associate Professor of English at Michigan State University and the author of *Feeling Modern: The Eccentricities of Public Life* (2008).

Routledge Film Guidebooks

The Routledge Film Guidebooks offer a clear introduction to and overview of the work of key filmmakers, movements or genres. Each guidebook contains an introduction, including a brief history; defining characteristics and major films; a chronology; key debates surrounding the filmmaker, movement or genre; and pivotal scenes, focusing on narrative structure, camera work and production quality.

Bollywood: a Guidebook to Popular Hindi Cinema
Tejaswini Ganti

James Cameron
Alexandra Keller

Jane Campion
Deb Verhoeven

Horror
Brigid Cherry

Film Noir: Hard-Boiled Modernity and the Cultures of Globalization
Jennifer Fay and Justus Nieland

Film Noir

Hard-Boiled Modernity and the Cultures of Globalization

JENNIFER FAY AND JUSTUS NIELAND

Routledge
Taylor & Francis Group

LONDON AND NEW YORK

First published 2010
by Routledge
2 Park Square, Milton Park, Abingdon, Oxon OX14 4RN

Simultaneously published in the USA and Canada
by Routledge
270 Madison Ave, New York, NY 10016

Routledge is an imprint of the Taylor & Francis Group, an informa business

© 2010 Jennifer Fay and Justus Nieland

Typeset in Joanna by Swales & Willis Ltd, Exeter, Devon
Printed and bound in Great Britain by TJ International Ltd, Padstow, Cornwall

British Library Cataloguing in Publication Data
A catalogue record for this book is available from the British Library

Library of Congress Cataloging in Publication Data
Fay, Jennifer.
Film noir : hard-boiled modernity and the cultures of globalization / Jennifer Fay
and Justus Nieland.
    p. cm.—(Routledge film guidebooks)
    1. Film noir—History and criticism.   I. Nieland, Justus.   II. Title.
    PN1995.9.F54F39 2009
    791.43'655—dc22
    2009022509

ISBN10: 0–415–45812–9 (hbk)
ISBN10: 0–415–45813–7 (pbk)
ISBN10: 0–203–86968–0 (ebk)

ISBN13: 978–0–415–45812–2 (hbk)
ISBN13: 978–0–415–45813–9 (pbk)
ISBN13: 978–0–203–86968–0 (ebk)

CONTENTS

LIST OF FIGURES

PREFACE

Down these mean streets, again . . .

When we think of film noir, we tend to picture the uniquely American features of this perpetually alluring genre: the hard-boiled detective conversant in local customs, the sultry femme fatale, and a disintegrating American city filled with violent crime, seedy nightclubs, and psychological distress. But, from its beginning, noir has been an international phenomenon. This book traces noir's emergent connection to European cinema, its international culture of literary and cinematic translation, and its postwar consolidation in the US, Europe, Asia, and Latin America. Because we are interested in the way that cinema circulates as a global commodity, especially after World War II, we will examine how noir is capable of crossing national boundaries, speaking to diverse international audiences, and dramatizing the crises of local spaces. These local "crimes" are bred by global phenomena like world-wide depression, war, political occupation, economic and cultural modernization, and migration. This book argues that film noir is best appreciated as an always international phenomenon concerned with the local effects of globalization and the threats to national urban culture it seems to herald.

For a good example of noir's internationalism, consider the many adaptations of James M. Cain's hard-boiled American novel *The Postman Always Rings Twice* (1934), a slim and lurid thriller written during the throes of the Depression, and long considered a signature of the hard-boiled novel's tough diction and cynical moral vision. For literary critics, *Postman*'s sex and violence in the American grain exemplifies a broader turn in American literature of the 1930s to local, regional realities. Yet the novel has circulated widely in translation and in far-flung cinematic adaptations dating from the 1930s. Before relaxed censorship codes and the box-office success of Billy Wilder's *Double Indemnity* (an adaptation of the Cain novel of the same name) finally cleared the way for the first Hollywood version of the novel in 1946, *Postman* had already been twice adapted in Europe, first in France (*Le Dernier tournant/The Final Turn*, 1939) and then in Italy (*Ossessione/Obsession*, 1943). Following Tay Garnett's Hollywood version (1946), another loose adaptation appeared in Norway (*Døden er et Kjertegn/Death Is a Caress*, 1949). And, since Garnett's version was itself remade in Hollywood (*The Postman Always Rings Twice*, 1981), the novel has been adapted in Hungary (*Szenvedély/Passion*, 1998), Malaysia (*Buai-laju laju/Swing My Swing High, My Darling*, 2004), and most recently Germany (*Jerichow*, 2008).

We say more about this novel and its adaptations below, but here we want to signal two important arguments that we develop throughout the book. The first is that noir lends itself to domestication in different national contexts, in part because it is concerned with the local and for this reason travels well and endures historically. Indeed, noir's international circulation has been historically linked to the problem of national culture and the status of national cinema in an era of increasing global interconnectedness, for better and for worse. This link makes noir an especially attractive object of study for film scholars and students interested both in older questions of film genre and in newer questions about cinema's international contexts of production, distribution, and reception. From the 1930s to the present, film noir has, we argue, repeatedly been connected to anxieties about the boundaries of national culture – about the fixity or integrity of national culture in a world of more fluid identities and economies in which national boundaries are increasingly irrelevant.

The second key argument concerns film noir's international networks of affinity and influence. *The Postman*'s circulation in global cinema also demonstrates that, while the "original" source is an American novel, the films above are not necessarily responding to or imitating American culture. *Ossessione*, as we discuss below, is influenced as much by French and Italian cinema of the 1930s as well as cinematic adaptations of French realist novels as it is by American film and hard-boiled fiction. Further, the cinematic movements with which *Ossessione* and *Le Dernier tournant* are associated, Italian neorealism and French poetic realism, respectively, would later influence some of the most canonical post-World War II American noirs. Thus noir's artistic translations and appropriations extend across the Atlantic in both directions. We will find similar instances of mutual influence across the Pacific, and other noir examples in which the American context recedes altogether. Though we are attentive to such histories when they are available, our book is less interested in "proving" influence than in explaining through case studies some of the historical and geo-political forces that give rise to film noir's rich culture of exchange and translation.

In this respect, this book proposes an understanding of film noir as a fully international phenomenon, and as an expression of disquiet with the conditions of a modern, globalized age. In doing so, we are indebted to some important work produced over the last decade or so regarding the nature of noir's internationalism, including: "European Precursors of Film Noir," a 1996 special issue of the journal *Iris*; David Desser's groundbreaking essay "Global Noir: Genre Film in the Age of Transnationalism" (2001); the growing body of work on film noir's culture of exile (Koepnick, 2002; Kaes, 2003; Isenberg, 2007); and Andrew Spicer's invaluable recent collection *European Film Noir* (2007).[1] In our own discussion of film noir, we privilege three related but distinct modes of internationalism: cosmopolitanism, Americanization, globalization. This is how we tend to use them in the pages that follow:

- **Cosmopolitanism** has a long philosophical history, originating in the eighteenth-century Enlightenment to describe a universal law and government that could lead to a global world order and

perpetual peace. We prefer a more equivocal, less idealized definition of the term that describes a culture that, in theory, belongs to
all parts of the world and not just one country, city, or locality.
Often cosmopolitan culture is associated with urban centers
whose residents may feel a greater affinity with people living in
other big cities than with fellow citizens living in more provincial
areas, because urban dwellers the world over may share a common education, access to art, and, of course, a taste for international films only shown in cities. Film noir is a symptom of
cosmopolitanism insofar as it is international and describes a relationship to locality that people all over the world (especially in
urban centers) may recognize as their own. We say more about
(and critique) cosmopolitanism below, especially as it is related
to other international cultures of modernism, occupation, and
cinephilia.

- **Americanization** describes the process by which the US imposes
  its cultural, economic, and political norms onto other countries
  as a quasi-cosmopolitanism, especially after World War II. In the
  most pejorative sense, Americanization is an unwanted culture
  foisted upon countries whose economies and armies simply cannot compete with American power and whose citizens act more
  like consumers. In more positive terms, it may describe how people around the world are seduced not only by American goods
  and films, but also by the American model of democracy. Since
  Hollywood was initially the cultural engine of Americanization,
  this term has particular relevance for our discussion of American
  film noir.

- **Globalization**, for some of its cheerleaders, names a process of
  world-wide economic interconnectedness and free, unregulated
  markets; for other supporters, it promises to be the engine of a
  renewed political enfranchisement and world understanding.
  While attentive to the promises of globalization, we also use the
  term to describe a more recent phenomenon in which transnational corporations, and especially giant media conglomerates,

do not necessarily promote one national culture over another but instead produce a homogenized, bland, consumer culture that threatens the longevity of local customs and languages, as well as eroding the uniqueness of urban and rural lifestyles.

These three big terms allow us to demonstrate that films noir have always been transnational objects of art, commerce, and critical fascination. As such, films noir have consistently raised questions about national authenticity and distinctiveness, and have activated the crises and promises suggested by the terms outlined above. Noirs have been often read as symptoms of the health, sickness, or decay of nations either corrupted or reinvigorated by foreign influences and perspectives. And they have functioned for critics and scholars as celluloid clocks telling the time of national life (its rootedness in tradition, or its movement into the future, or its traumatic upheavals, displacements, and confusions) and keeping pace with global movements that may render that life a phenomenon of the past.

Our story of noir's internationalism is thus linked to the broader condition of global disquiet with the mobile and dislocated social and cultural relations of modernity itself: of rootless and wandering desire; of chance, accident, and class instability; of local traditions and spaces either imperiled or energized by global flows of culture and capital; and of homelife across the world that has become unsettled, uncanny, or newly foreign. While film noir tends to respond to modernity in its traumatic, catastrophic, or irrational registers, noir has itself been produced and circulated in a modern global culture of translation, transfer, and traffic across national borders. In this sense, we also intend our picture of film noir to underscore the invigorating potential of thinking and feeling beyond the national boundaries that have long delimited the study of film noir as a great American phenomenon. In keeping with film noir's own penchant for moral and political ambiguity, this book's pedagogical lessons about noir's vital internationalism in a globalized age are neither utterly despairing nor particularly hopeful. Instead, our story is decidedly ambivalent – shot through, like the best noirs, with complexity and shades of grey. Film noir is at once one of cultural globalization's most eloquent critics and one of its very best examples. Such is noir's ambiguous modernity, and ours.

NOTE

1 See "European Precursors of Film Noir," *Iris* 21 (Spring 1996), ed. Janice Morgan and Dudley Andrew; and David Desser, "Global Noir: Genre Film in the Age of Transnationalism," in *Film Genre Reader III*, ed. Barry Keith Grant (Austin: University of Texas Press, 2003), pp. 516–536. On noir's culture of exile, see Koepnick's *The Dark Mirror: German Cinema between Hitler and Hollywood* (Berkeley: University of California Press, 2002); Anton Kaes, "'A Stranger in the House': Fritz Lang's *Fury* and the Cinema of Exile," *New German Critique*, No. 89, Film and Exile (Spring–Summer, 2003), pp. 33–58; Noah Isenberg, "Permanent Vacation: Home and Homelessness in the Life and Work of Edgar G. Ulmer," in *Caught by Politics: Hitler Exiles and American Visual Culture*, ed. Sabine Eckmann and Lutz Koepnick (London: Palgrave Macmillan, 2007). See also *European Film Noir*, ed. Andrew Spicer (Manchester: Manchester University Press, 2007), as well as the essays on international neo-noir (of France, Britain, and Asia) forthcoming in *Neo-Noir*, ed. Mark Bould, Kathrina Glitre, and Greg Tuck (London: Wallflower Press, 2009).

ACKNOWLEDGMENTS

This book began in the classroom at Michigan State University when we co-taught "Film Noir and the Cultures of Globalization." We were lucky to have a group of students willing to watch crime thrillers and melodramas from around the world and indulge our hunches about noir's internationalism. Our class both studied and performed noir style. Aaron Berton, Ryan Gafke, Cory García, Lisa Gibes, Tristan Johnson, Kyle Lilek, Sara Molnar, Kiersten Paine, Zach Paul, Rahul Ragunathan, Alex Reyme, Kaitlyn Rich, Madeline Schichtel, Kyle Surma, and Thomas Wilcox all helped us to refine our ideas and clarify our claims. Cory gets special props for the "noir noise" mix and extra credit for the secret film graffiti that turned our campus into a noir wonderland.

We are grateful to our outside readers for supporting this project, especially Mark Bould, who provided insightful feedback and generously made available his own work in progress. While writing, we relied on the smart, attentive comments from Andrew Nieland, and our colleagues Patrick O'Donnell, Karl Schoonover, and Scott Juengel, who all graciously read our drafts. A grant from the Global Literary and Cultural Studies Center at Michigan State University enabled us to complete the book.

Justus would like to extend personal thanks to Jim Naremore, for sparking his interest in film noir, and for still having written the best book on the subject. And Jen thanks David Bordwell for being an inspiring historian of international film style.

Love to Sarah Wohlford, Lila Nieland, Iris Nieland, and Scott Juengel for suffering through our year (plus) of darkness, and brightening it along the way.

1

FILM NOIR AND THE CULTURE OF INTERNATIONALISM

In this chapter, we track noir's relationship to the idea of national culture in three broad historical moments. First, we discuss noir's internationalism in the interwar period that followed the world-wide
depression. We begin here because this era was marked by intense
debate about the fate of Western democracies and individual freedom
itself in a climate of radical politics, rising fascisms, and restrictive,
often violent versions of national community in the US, France, and
Italy. Second, we examine noir's global currency in the wartime and
immediate postwar period, when American films noir became
forcibly linked to a culture of political occupation in France, Germany,
and Japan, and to an ambiguous critique of the new, postwar global
order dominated by America and its linked midcentury promises of
democratic and economic freedoms. Third, we discuss the longer
postwar period (from midcentury to the present) in which so-called
"historical" film noir was made new as it circulated globally – as both
a commercial product and a beloved critical object – in a range of
countries (Mexico, Spain, Italy, France, Germany, India, Iran, and
Hong Kong) that were becoming "modern" at different speeds, and
under the pressure of the monolithic American example.

PART I: DISLOCATING JAMES M. CAIN'S *THE POSTMAN ALWAYS RINGS TWICE*

In the Preface to this book, we listed the surprising iterations of Cain's novel. This section concerns a more restricted ambit of *Postman*'s global travel, discussing Cain's original novel, its relationship to French film-maker Jean Renoir and his 1938 noir *La Bête humaine/The Human Beast*, and Luchino Visconti's adaptation *Ossessione* (1943), a film whose sensibility is indebted both to Renoir and to Cain. By examining Cain's dislocations in the interwar period, we begin to sketch a more accurate picture of the phenomenon of film noir as heterogeneous, polyglot, and, indeed, cosmopolitan. We see this in the way a noir sensibility has, from the 1930s to the present, articulated forms of emotional attachment beyond one's country of origin, and in its special relationship to a putatively universal "modern man" forged in the shadow of global catastrophe – the mass destruction of world war and the new "shared" global reality of atomic annihilation. But we also see it in the particular international movements and imaginative scope of its central artists and artworks. Even in seemingly modest cultural products like *The Postman Always Rings Twice*, then, we begin to observe how the noir sensibility's particular traits and local visions are pro-duced in a culture of translation, transnational cultural flows, and cross-cultural imaginings.

Pulp Modernism in the 1930s: Between the New and the Real

In making this sort of a claim about a novel like Cain's, we draw on a growing body of scholarly work that has recast American hard-boiled writers as "modern" experimentalists steeped in the highly innovative aesthetic cultures of early-twentieth-century modernity.[1] Because so many canonical films noir were adaptations of these novels, the new critical picture of novelists like Cain, Dashiell Hammett, and Raymond Chandler has enabled film historians to demonstrate noir's privileged relationship to aesthetic modernism – a broad and politically diverse explosion of experimentation across the arts from the late nineteenth century through World War II and beyond. The 1930s were a period of crisis in the history of modernism, as the formal experiments of its high period in the 1910s and 1920s were increasingly seen as insufficiently populist, realist, or local to document the dark and desperate realities of a world-wide depression. So-called "high modernism" in the West was a cosmopolitan phenomenon, hatched in major metropolitan centers like New York, Paris, and London, where artists of various nationalities flocked and enjoyed access to cultural products from around the globe. Because "high" modernist art tended to be quite allusive, abstract, and stylistically challenging, it was often just plain difficult to read and comprehend, and therefore frequently dismissed as elitist or apolitical. However, rather than think about the urgent political demands of the 1930s as the cause of modernism's exhaustion, it is more accurate to understand the decade as host to modernism's transformation as it converged with a range of documentary, "realist" artistic practices. As a result, the cosmopolitan vision of Anglo-European modernisms became more realist and preoccupied with the local, and various realisms became imbued with a spirit of cosmopolitan innovation. In the process, both modernism and realism became acutely noir in tone.

The Postman's migrations in the 1930s exemplify these sorts of convergences. In Visconti's Ossessione, Postman is at the heart of a modern and cosmopolitan mode of Italian realism. Renoir's interest in Cain is part of a heady intermingling of noir realisms and modernisms in the politicized French film culture of the 1930s. And Cain's original novel is a particularly good example of modern American writing's turn toward vernacular, realist style in the name of a hard-boiled nationalism. Cain desired what we might call an "organic" national culture, a form of cultural expression rooted in the people, surging naturally from and reflecting an authentic, national spirit.[2] Yet the very noirness of Postman stems from the way the lure of some vital common expression finds itself confronted with the phantom of national culture, a specter that haunts the book's transnational travel. The "Americanness" of Cain's novel is challenged not only by the novel itself, but also in the way the book travels as a sign of both cosmopolitan liberation and worldly corruption in France and Italy.

Noir's Displaced Persons

Despite Cain's efforts to ground national culture in the "authentically" American vernacular of tough-guy prose, the social world of *Postman* is decidedly uncertain and unstable. This, perhaps, is why Cain's story has traveled so well and so widely, and why his particular noir sensibility has been so given to global translation and local inflection. Cain's lean and speedy plot itself eschews stability. Frank, a vagabond and petty hustler, and Cora, the proprietress of a roadside tavern in California, fall hard for each other. The lovers plot to kill Cora's husband, Nick, a Greek immigrant, for his insurance policy, and eventually succeed after an initial botched attempt. The authorities are suspicious, and eventually manage to turn the couple against each other before the pair is saved, inheritance intact, by the wiles of a savvy defense attorney. Having pulled off their risky plan, the pair is unhappy and more insecure than ever: Cora wants a home and business, and Frank longs for his life on the road. When Cora discovers she is pregnant, the lovers reignite their passion and plan a life together, but their future is scrapped when Cora and her unborn child are killed in a car accident, and Frank, wrongly convicted of Cora's murder, is sentenced to die at the hands of the state.

The plot makes clear that *Postman* is a story about rootless people and, more importantly, a restless modern existence pervaded by chance and desire, risk and accident. This is most obvious, of course, in Frank's itinerant hustling. Frank's vagabondage and his sexual appetites are metaphors for each other – twinned species of *wanderlust* that lead him first toward Cora, then away from her (as when he and Madge Allen, trainer of wild circus cats, get away to Mexico for a time), and then, tragically, back to Cora again. His eros is excessive, risky, and a consistent challenge to the versions of "rooted" social life modeled by Cora and Nick's domestic arrangement at Twin Oaks, both a marriage and a business. In this way, Cain uses the threat of Frank's rootlessness in a fashion consistent with period understandings of the tramp's erotic impropriety, which, as Michael Trask has argued, consistently likened the vagabond's excessive desire to "the risks of dislocation and comingling that imperiled the imagined community of national culture."[3] As Trask explains, these transient bodies, and the kinds of class instability and contamination they indexed, helped the era's social scientists come to terms with the modern mobility of class relations themselves. This uncertainty was made painfully acute in the context of the Great Depression, which laid bare the catastrophic effects of a fluctuating capitalist world market.

But Frank is not the only figure of transient, modern personhood in the novel. Cora herself is a transplanted Iowan, winner of a high-school beauty contest that earns her an ill-fated trip to Hollywood. Her dream of stardom denied, she quickly resorts to working in a hash house and moonlighting as a prostitute. Cora's desire for domestic security amounts to a desperate, murderous agenda of upward mobility haunted by the constant risk of a backward slide into destitution. So she marries Nick Papadakis, "the Greek," a well-meaning, unsuspecting sap whose "greasiness" and "smell" disgust Cora, making "her feel she wasn't white."[4] These are the drifting anchors of The Postman's social and cultural world: a lustful vag, a desperate climber, and an immigrant who has swallowed the American Dream, hook, line, and sucker. Some of the more influential accounts of modernity have identified part of the dynamism of modern life in the movements of people – their dislocation, displacement, or migration from tradition or ancestral home. Anthony Giddens, an important sociologist of modernity, coined the term "disembedding" to refer to modernity's "'lifting out' of social relations from local contexts of interaction and their restructuring across indefinite spans of time-space."[5] This term suggests that, in the modern world, not only are people like Frank, Cora, and Nick literally on the move, displaced from locality, tradition, and origin. More profoundly, they are also subject to abstract, intangible, social networks and systems that seem distant from them, but that nonetheless powerfully determine the course of their lives more than their individual desires or actions.

For Giddens, the key agents of modern disembedding are the "expert systems" – the vast governmental and corporate bureaucracies peopled by professionals and experts like lawyers, doctors, and insurance agents. Such modern systems exist, in principle, to secure the conditions of modern social life by reducing risk and the cost of accidents. In the United States of the 1930s, the force of these systems intensified under F.D.R.'s New Deal, a series of aggressively interventionist regulatory regimes and benefits programs, such as social security, designed to assuage and reverse the effects of the Depression. As Sean McCann argues, the tradition of 1930s American hard-boiled crime fiction was particularly cynical about this version of the welfare state. At the same time, hard-boiled fiction and the state shared an understanding of the American citizen as neither a totally free agent nor a passive victim, but rather as a member "of various population groups whose interests were represented by a complex web of interlocking and competing national bureaucracies."[6] These knotted systems are most evident in the novel's extended subplot concerning the legal battle between the lawyers involved in Nick and Cora's case and the three insurance companies carrying policies on the Greek's life. Cain insists that Cora and Frank are victims not just of their sexual passion, but of precisely these competing systems of expertise and their challenges to individual agency. Ironically, the system of modern justice acquits Frank and Cora of the murder they actually committed, but executes Frank for the accidental death of Cora.

Postman offers a vision of local culture and individual agency as curiously devoid of particularity – dislocated and abstracted from the specificities of local context. For Cain, paradoxically, the cultural specificity of America is that there is no specifically real, authentic America – its distinct lack of uniqueness makes it unique. The Twin Oaks tavern is "nothing but a roadside sandwich joint, like a million others in

California."[7] In the novel's disembedded terrain, the concrete particularities of local places give way to a more abstract sense of space. So, when Frank presses Cora to ditch her husband and "blow," he can only appeal to "anywhere," "all over," or "anywhere we choose,"[8] just as Cora's vague desire to "be something" is matched by an equally indistinct wish "to go somewhere else."[9] The inauthenticity of place is doubled at the level of individual desire and agency. Cora realizes, late in the novel, that her and Frank's ideal of romantic love is doomed in their mass-produced environment: "We had all that love, and we just cracked up under it. It's a big airplane engine, that takes you through the sky, right up to the top of the mountain. But when you put it in a Ford, it just shakes it to pieces. That's what we are, Frank, a couple of Fords."[10]

In these terms, the novel's picture of individual freedom needs to be understood in the context of the hard-boiled novel's vexed populism – a form of politics organized around an appeal to the interests and values of common, ordinary people. Marc Vernet, for instance, has argued that the very modernity of hard-boiled individualism – incarnated in the figure of the detective, that iconic noir protagonist – emerged in the 1930s to mediate a "contradiction inherent in the economic and political system of the United States" that the Depression had made newly urgent: between the putative rights of the individual citizen and that citizen's sense of the pervasive power of broader networks – economic concentrations, expanding bureaucracies and other expert systems, and a newly interventionist state.[11] However, if hard-boiled populism is tied to a particular strand of American nationalism, its deep anxiety about the fate of democratic citizenship was shared by continental populisms of the interwar period. In Jean Renoir's La Bête humaine, the problem of the citizen's relationship to the abstracted systems of modernity – so pressing for Cain's "couple of Fords" – replays itself in the film's murderous love triangle between a railway man, his lover, and his "wife," Lison, who happens to be a train. In its anatomy of the world of the locomotive, one of modernity's most storied emblems, Renoir's noir is also an elegy for a prewar populism derailed by the seemingly unstoppable forces of global war.

Poetry and Politics in Interwar France: the Case of Jean Renoir

The first international adaptation of *Postman* was initially submitted to Jean Renoir, who would urge Visconti to adapt the film after Pierre Chenal had made his own French version (*Le Dernier tournant*) in 1939. As we'll see, Visconti's *Ossessione* reads Cain's noir novel not only through Renoir's stylistic influence and political sensibility, but more specifically through Renoir's film *La Bête humaine* (1938). In fact, Visconti was attracted to Cain's novel, in part, because of its narrative and tonal resemblance to *La Bête humaine*, another pessimistic story about adultery, murder, and compulsive behavior, and featuring the same amorous triangle of husband, wife, and lover on the move.[12]

At first blush, Renoir may seem an unlikely practitioner of a noir sensibility. The terms most often applied to his work are "humanist" and "realist," adjectives that seem ill suited for film noir's preoccupations with cruelty, irrational violence, and unconscious desire, or with its more familiar visual style of off-kilter compositions and unnatural, high-contrast lighting. And yet the terms "humanism" and "realism" have decidedly noir inflections. Noir humanism, as in *Postman*, offers a specific vision of human agency as increasingly governed by forces beyond reason or rational control, not only within the human (passion, madness, paranoia, trauma, and the like), but beyond and abstracted from human capacity in the very modernity of the modern world: industrialized, commodified, bureaucratized, and rationalized in a means–end logic so ruthless as to become, itself, irrational. Noir realism is equally multifaceted. It can be psychological, laying claim to a more accurate, because more subjective, version of modern life. It can be sociological, offering testimony to actual socio-historical conditions. Or it can be more properly aesthetic, influenced by certain kinds of realism associated with specific artists and aesthetic practices: the so-called "New Objectivity" (*Neue Sachlichkeit*) movement in Germany in the 1920s, or French surrealism of the 1920s and 1930s, or Italian neorealism, which begins to announce itself in *Ossessione*.

There is no realism, then, but only realisms, and global film noir is inflected by various forms of it.

The interwar period saw a growing preoccupation with the elusive reality of Parisian life in French film and photography, and a tremendous boom in French crime fiction – a vogue sparked by the success of British and American hard-boiled fiction (another realism). In this cultural environment, Renoir would make a series of films, starting with the trio of *La Chienne/The Bitch* (1931), *La Nuit du carrefour/Night at the Crossroads* (1932), and *Boudu sauvé des eaux/Boudu Saved from Drowning* (1932), whose pessimistic atmosphere of darkness, night, and rain one critic has wittily dubbed "genre noir."[13] As Alan Williams has it, despite Renoir's reputation as a "gentle, genial humanist," in most of his films of the 1930s "people are, quite simply, out to kill one another sooner or later."[14] *La Chienne*, in fact, was later remade in Fritz's Lang's now-canonical American noir *Scarlet Street* (1945). *Night at the Crossroads* was one of the first of many adaptations of Renoir's friend Georges Simenon's Maigret novels and shared the "realism" of their geographical and sociological specificity. And *Les Bas-fonds/The Lower Depths* (1936) fits squarely within the 1930s French tradition of what Ginette Vincendeau has called "sociological voyeurism," a tendency in prewar films inviting audiences to "slum" in the dark spaces of working-class Paris.[15] And Renoir's *Le crime de Monsieur Lange/The Crime of Mr. Lange* (1936) treated noir subjects – murder, criminality, and compulsive behavior – in a playful, exuberant tone, bending then-current French fascinations with criminality and American genre fiction into a fantasy of class solidarity.

With this in mind, we can begin to understand the various political registers of noir "realism" in the interwar period. *La Bête humaine's* political aesthetics are situated between the anti-fascist agenda of the Popular Front and the specific tradition of poetic realism, a stylistic signature of 1930s French national cinema often cited as a precursor to the American film noir.

The Popular Front, with which Renoir was associated, names a broad, anti-fascist political coalition of socialists, anarchists, communists, and various other members of the left. Between 1932 and 1934 – in the throes of a global economic depression, high unemployment, rising anti-semitism and xenophobia, and increasingly active proto-fascist and hypernationalist political subcultures – France experienced a succession of five short-lived parliamentary governments before the Popular Front finally achieved the legislative victory that established Leon Blum as prime minister in 1936. However, Blum's government proved equally fragile, falling from power early in 1938. When Renoir began shooting *La Bête humaine* in August of that year, Adolf Hitler had moved the German army swiftly through Austria and was poised to attack Czechoslovakia, a country France had pledged to defend.

In this fraught atmosphere, Renoir chose to shoot *La Bête humaine* in a brooding, atmospheric style critics would later identify as "poetic realism." The vexing term, much like "film noir" itself, was not originally an aesthetic doctrine, like surrealism, or a self-conscious generic marketing label, like "western" or "musical." Rather, as Dudley Andrew has argued, the term was primarily a "fabrication of the critical establishment, and it remains so today."[16] First used by a French reviewer to describe Pierre Chenal's *La Rue sans nom/Nameless Street* (1934), it was used in the 1940s to describe a diverse range of moody, often urban French dramas from the 1930s like *Les Quai des brumes/Port of Shadows* (1938), *Le Jour se lève/Day Break* (1939), *Hôtel du Nord* (1938), and *Pépé le Moko* (1937), a film we will discuss in more detail in Chapter 2. Such films are often set in proletariat, lower-middle-class, or criminal milieus, are steeped in romantic pessimism, and feature a highly atmospheric mise-en-scène. They tend to be "realist" in a sociological and aesthetic sense, taking "low," often working-class, characters as their subject matter and establishing them in carefully defined social environments. They are "poetic" in their tendency to imbue these environments with fantastic or lyrical dimensions, and in their romantic preoccupations with alienation and a melancholic displacement from a fullness of being.

Somewhere between the end of the Popular Front and the critical invention of "poetic realism," La Bête humaine appears, and is one of the first French films to be called a film noir.

As we'll see, just as film noir emerges as a spectator genre in post-war France to describe a new pessimism in American thrillers, so too does film noir circulate in French film culture in the years immediately before the war. Here, though, it names not the allure of American-style democracy, but the decay of the French nation on the eve of global war. As Charles O'Brien has demonstrated, the term "film noir" first appeared mainly in right-wing publications devoted to economics and politics rather than in the major film weeklies of the 1930s, and it was an "essentially affective response to a group of films that seemed to transgress the morality of the national culture."[17] These critics placed films like La Bête humaine and Port of Shadows within the tradition of French literary naturalists like Émile Zola. Naturalism, yet another realism, could in crude terms be understood as realism inflected with a post-Darwinian sense that biology is destiny; individuals are creatures of their environment or victims of hereditary flaws with little capacity for self-determination.

The Fatal Engines of La Bête humaine

An adaptation of the Zola novel of the same title, Renoir's La Bête humaine concerns the doomed affair between train engineer Jacques Lantier (Jean Gabin) and Séverine (Simone Simon), the young wife of Roubaud (Fernand Ledoux), a deputy stationmaster at Le Havre. In the opening prologue, which quotes directly from Zola's novel at its most deterministic, we learn that Lantier's blood has been poisoned by generations of alcoholism, which compels him to "commit acts beyond the control of his will." If sexual desire in the world of The Postman is subject to restless drifting, in La Bête humaine eroticism functions through fits and failures of an automatism that blurs the lines between humans and machines, will and reflex.

From the film's first, frenetic opening sequence on the rails to Lantier's last suicidal leap, the world of the train dominates La Bête *humaine.* On the one hand, the visual and aural omnipresence of the locomotive inflects the film's realism with a documentary quality, establishing the concreteness of its particular working-class milieu. The film's exhilarating railway sequences were shot on location in Le Havre, where the SNCF (Société Nationale des Chemins de fer Français) provided Renoir and his crew with a train and ten kilometers of track. On the other hand, the train is a particularly storied symbol of modernity and a powerful agent of modern disembedding. It embodies the speed, size, and raw power of industrial technology. It symbolizes the vast, networked world of commerce, exchange, and mass mobility. It models modern technologies' tendency to connect far-flung places, collapsing spatial distance with speed. And it depends upon a world of temporal efficiency and precision – of standardized, scheduled time.

Just as Cain used the Ford as a metaphor of Frank and Cora's mass-produced desire, Renoir employs the train to reflect on the fate of modern humanity, whose emotional core seems to be everywhere structured by the train's machinic rhythms. This blurring between human and mechanical orders is most apparent in Lantier's so-called "marriage" to his train, Lison, which underscores how the film's characters live their intimate lives through the times and spaces of the railway system. The train's intrusion into the space of intimate or private life – when humans, liberated from work, are supposedly free to be most *themselves* – is the hallmark of the film's naturalism. In this pessimistic understanding of human biology, which Renoir's film inherits from Zola's source novel, human nature has itself become somehow machinic, the social environment of modernity powerfully contaminating the vital processes of the body.

As a result, bodies are reduced to their baser instincts, reflexes, and habitual functioning, and cultural and natural orders become impossibly confused in the film. "Lison" the train, for example, can be "thirsty," just as we learn that the appetites of the human workers can be sated by the random violence of the train plunging through the countryside, killing the occasional partridge or cow. However, by this same naturalistic logic, Lantier, like Lison, is also prone to mechanical failure. His seizures of violent passion are caused, we learn in the prologue's voiceover, by his "poisoned" blood. But this "madness" is the human equivalent of Lison's overheated axle. In this sense, not only does Lantier move and see with Lison, forced to stop when she stalls, but he is also, as a function of degenerate biological heritage, given to fits and starts of energy, as well as abrupt failures of passion and will. We see this clearly in the haunting night-time scene in which Lantier, revved up by Séverine, fails to summon the desire to kill Roubaud, his stalled energy echoed in the mise-en-scène of stilled traincars. Indeed, the mutual attraction between Séverine and Lantier is based less on love or tenderness than on the building up and release of fluid desires and animal needs (Figure 1.1). So, when they meet on a rainy night to make love in an abandoned railyard shack, Renoir pans theatrically from the door discreetly closed against the consummation of their

FIGURE 1.1   Passion in a trainyard (*La Bête humaine*, 1938).

brimming passion to a water bucket overflowing its edges; when we fade to the calm surface of the water bucket the next morning, we know that their passion is stilled. Passion has its moments of violent intensity, but sustaining this energy requires constant fuel. The boiler needs stoking. In the absence of these stimuli, moments of intensity pass, returning the lovers to the pervasive torpor and misery of their lives, more drained and despondent than before. Such is the decadent temporality in *La Bête humaine*.

Time itself is another of the film's chief concerns, one it pursues through an initial contrast between the public time of historical and social progress – measurable, quantifiable, and advancing inexorably to the future – and the private time of the self, given to memories and feelings that can't be easily clocked. In the world of public time, the trains, emblems of modernity, must run on time, keeping the social world efficiently humming along. However, Renoir's leftist politics make clear that the temporal order kept by the large clocks so prominent in the train stations is, in effect, linked to a broader social hierarchy – a rigid class system whose excesses are embodied by Grandmorin and his gold pocketwatch. Notice how Grandmorin's watch becomes a charged metaphorical object in the film: it survives its owner's murder to be literally buried under the floor of Roubaud and Séverine's home, haunting their attempts to forget their actions, and later it dangles ominously from Roubaud's hands as he discovers Séverine's strangled corpse (Figure 1.2). Through Grandmorin's watch, which links the film's two murders, Renoir underscores the static violence of this system of social power, whose so-called progress consistently founders in repetitive action. After Grandmorin's murder, the social system he represents will affirm the brutal realities of class by wrongly sentencing the working-class Cabuche (Jean Renoir himself) to hang for Roubaud and Séverine's crime. Cabuche's impassioned self-defense makes clear that Grandmorin's relationship with Séverine was no one-time affair, but instead part of a broader history of sexual violence against his maids as routine and unstoppable as a train. Roubaud too, having killed Grandmorin, still honors the class

FIGURE 1.2 Time's up for Séverine (*La Bête humaine*, 1938).

system he represents: a good bourgeois, he can neither ditch the watch, because of its value, nor sell it, which would be improper. Secreted at home, Grandmorin's watch contaminates his marriage to Séverine, revealing it to be a sham of middle-class respectability, inherited (like his job) from his wife's lecherous godfather. In this sense, the watch, ticking away, points to the way so many of the film's characters will be seen mechanically going through the motions of their social lives. Roubaud will remain in a loveless marriage with Séverine, who will continue to pursue romantic relationships with other men, though she claims to have loved Lantier. And Lantier will return mechanically to the train after murdering Séverine since, as Pecqueux tells us, he "has never been late in all the time [they've] worked together."

If public, progressive time seems eerily unchanging in *La Bête humaine*, the private time of the self is also compromised in the film.

This decadent temporality of the self is apparent both in the sputtering passions of Lantier's blood and in Séverine's fatal eroticism. Lantier's corrupt genealogy finds a match in Séverine's non-reproductive sexuality, which Renoir uses to link the temporality of his lovers' desire to a kind of deadly biological stasis – the same redundancy that haunts the world of public time. In *La Bête humaine*, there is no real change from the stalled, public world of the train, no liberating moments of chance, contingency, or the hopeful opening to a different future. Transformative moments are always linked to death: Séverine, for example, explains that the moment of Grandmorin's murder on the train "was more intense than the rest of my life combined." To be a human beast is to live an animal's life of brutal contingency: Roubaud, Séverine explains, "almost got crushed by a train the other day; one minute you're alive and the next you're dead." And so, while death is posited as the film's only outside to its modern world of repetitive time, death really does nothing to change the course of the film's social world. Ironically, in fact, Lantier's final act of suicide, which comes after he's shown up on time for his final trip with Lison, is no challenge to the world of the train. Instead, Renoir's final sequence insists on the cruel efficiency with which the tracks are cleared of his body to make way for the next train. In the film's decadent worldview, Lantier's death is the last, best way of being on time. On his body's clock, he has even arrived ahead of schedule.

French Film Noir and the Decay of the Nation

Coming from the most quintessentially French of French directors, and starring an actor who, by 1938, was synonymous with authentic, working-class French masculinity, *La Bête humaine* was inevitably read as a commentary on French national culture. In these terms, the film's linked preoccupation with trains and time amounts to a devastating national anatomy in which the progressive, historical time of the French nation and the willful, desiring individuals who would be the agents of national destiny are alike suspended in a repetitive cycle of despair, decay, and irrational violence typical of the prewar French films noir. On the eve of war, the naturalist overdetermination of these films' doomed or suicidal protagonists by their environment was diagnosed as a sign of national sickness, of a diseased country that had lost its will, as well as its sense of moral purpose and hope.

But it was not just right-wing critics who saw in prewar films noir a national decadence. Famously, Jean Renoir himself called Marcel Carné's *Port of Shadows* (1938) a "fascist" film because the weak interiority of its aimless characters seemed "to justify the perception of need for an authoritarian political leader."[18] Later, Renoir's *La Bête humaine* would fall victim to similar criticism – that its suicidal working-class protagonist amounted to a betrayal of Renoir's leftist commitments. The shared assumption of such critiques by and of Renoir, consistent with the various socialist or leftist modes of realism in the 1930s, is that *proper* realism requires heroic working-class action, or at least some glimmer of optimism in the form of political or national futurity. Notice again the thoroughly ambiguous politics of film noir, even in its first incarnation: prewar films with drifting and despairing protagonists could be read as a leftist critique of a democracy in ruins (what Renoir later *claimed* he was saying), or a right-wing appeal to organize a decadent nation with more authoritarian leadership (the proto-fascist reading), or a betrayal of working-class solidarity (the communist reading).

Noir's political ambiguity also bears on noir's nationality and on the concept of the nation itself. The very idea of national "decadence" suggests an organic model of national culture with the nation as a living communal body that can be healthy or sick, that can be rejuvenated or atrophy and die. This rhetoric is, of course, essential to a range of nationalisms and fascisms sweeping the globe in the 1930s. But this vital body proves rather malleable in the prewar debates about film noir; its contours shift and are reimagined depending on the understanding of national "health" each critic brings to bear on the films. Such national drifting is especially evident in the trajectory of "films noir" that later became "poetic realism" and then, in America, films noir once again. Poetic realism, today the sad jewel in the crown of French "national cinema," was, as Vincendeau argues, always a fully "multinational affair, comprising practitioners from Germany, Russia, Italy, and the USA, alongside indigenous personnel."[19] The same was true of Hollywood, which had always aggressively recruited from abroad, luring foreign directors and stars to make films in Hollywood rather than distributing foreign films in America. During the war, Los Angeles became a refuge for directors, cinematographers, writers, actors, and set designers trained in various European centers – Moscow, Berlin, London, and Paris – who fled fascist, militaristic Europe for the sanctuary of America's democratic shores. French studios of the 1930s hosted an influx of the same German émigrés – including Robert Siodmak, Fritz Lang, Jacques Tourneur, Billy Wilder, and Curtis Bernhardt – who had fled Hitler in 1933, and later made some of the greatest American films noir with a sensibility informed by both Weimar cinema and poetic realism. Though there is no singular experience of exile that may apply to all those who fled, critics have been inclined to probe the connection between film noir, on the one hand, and, on the other, an exilic critique of modernity sharpened through first-hand encounters with unstable democracies and violent fascism – forces that fueled their transatlantic migration, first to France and then to the US.

For this reason, fascist historians of the French cinema referred to poetic realism as a "Judeo-German" aesthetic.[20] However, in the first book-length study of American film noir, *A Panorama of American Film Noir* (1955), French critics Raymond Borde and Etienne Chaumeton insisted on the distinction between French poetic realism and the "typically American" atmosphere of film noir: "There remained France, where the 'three greats' (Duvivier and, above all, Renoir and Carné) had created a certain noir realism. Did *Pépé le Moko*, *Quai des brumes*, and *La Bête humaine* announce American film noir? We think not."[21] The distinction, not surprisingly, turns on the question of realism: French films are not noirs because their "action is located in a well-defined social milieu," and what's more they lack the "oneiricism and strangeness," the "gratuitous violence," and the eroticism that, to the surrealist tastes of these critics, constitute the noirness of American film noir.[22]

This postwar embrace of American noir at the expense of the French tradition was less about making convincing distinctions between national cinemas that had always been international, but rather, as we'll see, part of a broader European reckoning with the postwar global geo-political and economic order, presided over by America. Our point is neither to illuminate thematic or formal continuities between French prewar poetic realism and American film noir (although many exist) nor to insist on their national specificity. Rather, we want to emphasize how film noir, both before and after World War II, raises questions about the status of national culture itself under the conditions of modernity. To clarify this point, let's follow *Postman* to Italy.

Cain in Italy: The Decade of Translations

Luchino Visconti's *Ossessione*, the Italian adaptation of *Postman*, was the fruit of the transnational literary and film culture of interwar Italy that persisted even under the repressive conditions of Mussolini's fascist state. Recall that it was Renoir who, on the eve of World War II, gave Visconti a French translation of Cain's noir thriller and suggested that he film it. Visconti's version of Cain is thus twice translated: an Italian film based on a French translation of a sensational American novel. More importantly, its noir sensibility is a double translation in a broader cultural, aesthetic, and political sense: it is a product of interwar Italy's complex reception of American culture, and it marks a transfer of political sensibility from the French Popular Front of the 1930s to the left-wing aesthetic resistance movement in the early 1940s of which Visconti was a part. This group of young film critics and aspiring directors, many of whom (including Visconti) would be imprisoned by the fascists before the war's end, clustered around the journal *Cinema*, promoting in its pages their collective dream of a new, modern realism that would deform the staid vision of Italian life propped up by the cultural arms of Mussolini's fascist state. In this context, *Ossessione*'s hybrid noir vision – its aesthetic synthesis of American fiction, French poetic realism, and Italian locations – became a sign of the *Cinema* group's so-called "emergency cosmopolitanism," which hoped "to reopen Italian film to foreign influences and to reestablish contacts with the world culture disrupted" by "fascist isolationism."[23]

We can better understand Visconti's take on Cain's novel in the context of the curious status of American culture in Italy in the 1930s and early 1940s. As Steven Ricci has recently argued, the cultural life of interwar, fascist Italy was defined by an important contradiction "between the heavy presence of American culture and the fascist drive for autarchy" – that is, the state's desire for economic self-sufficiency and cultural independence from foreign influence.[24] This ideal of cultural autonomy, however, had to contend with the reality that "traces of Americana traversed virtually every sector of the public sphere in Italy, even at the height of the campaign for autarchy."[25] In 1923, the year of Mussolini's March on Rome, which led to the foundation of the fascist state, MGM had opened its distribution offices in the city, and during most of the 1920s and 1930s Italian screens were dominated by foreign products, especially Hollywood's. Further, because Italian systems of cultural production were slow to modernize and had trouble keeping up with demand for books and films by Italy's growing urban population, they depended on foreign imports. Indeed, many Italian writers in the 1930s, discouraged from their own writing by the threat of censorship, relied on translation work to earn a living.

Thus, Italy's complex cultural climate of the 1930s would become known as "the decade of translations," catering to a new vogue among Italian readers and literary figures for American fiction (of Saroyan, Hemingway, Caldwell, Dreiser, Steinbeck, Pound, and Fitzgerald, chiefly). This Americanophilia fueled a literary movement, the "Americanisti," that "was anti-Fascist in politics and vernacular and 'Hemingwayesque' in style, and that looked to the example of America for its ideals and literary techniques."[26] The Americanisti were taken with its vernacular treatment of spoken language and dialect, with its sense of region and place, and of humans' proximate relationship to this environment, with its turbulent eroticism that flew in the face of fascist moral taboos, and with its protagonists – marginal men like Frank Chambers, social outcasts who offered a radical break from the fascist predilection for *übermenschen* and healthy middle-class family men. In other words, American culture offered Italian anti-fascists both a symbolic *elsewhere* – the lure of an *other* to fascist cultural life – and a way of reseeing the very *here-and-nowness* of Italian locality and Italian national character that had been suppressed by the fascist version of national life.

Luchino Visconti's Ossessione and Noir Cosmopolitanism

Hollywood films and American novels were not the only foreign influences on the "emergency cosmopolitanism" of *Ossessione*. Visconti's attempt to open Italian culture to transnational influence was also informed by his first-hand experience of the France of the Popular Front period, and the Parisian culture of the 1930s, where Visconti met Renoir. A cultured aristocrat and horse-trainer from Milan, young Visconti had the resources to travel widely in the 1930s, and made many extended trips to Paris, then a vital center of international modernism. Compared to the restrictive version of sexual normalcy promulgated in fascist Italy, Paris also enjoyed a liberated sexual culture, where Visconti's homosexuality was freed from the kinds of stigmas and repressions of his home country. Here also Visconti's friend, fashion designer Coco Chanel, introduced him to Jean Renoir. Visconti's relationship with Renoir was, first, a cinematic apprenticeship: Visconti served as an assistant director and costume designer on Renoir's *Partie de campagne/A Day in the Country* (1936), worked on *Les Bas-fonds/The Lower Depths*, and would later collaborate on the script for Renoir's Italian film *La Tosca* until its shooting was interrupted in 1939 when Italy declared war on the Allies and Renoir was forced to leave the country. But it was also an apprenticeship in the leftist politics of the Popular Front and in politically committed filmmaking. When he first met Renoir in Paris he was not a socialist, but a right-wing socialite, a self-described "kind of imbecile – not a Fascist, but unconsciously affected by Fascism, 'colored' by it." But "the people around Renoir were all Communists, card-carrying Communists," and in this company, and in the Popular Front environment of political optimism and vitality, Visconti underwent a profound political awakening that would culminate in *Ossessione*.[27]

Ossessione adapts Cain's *The Postman* in the service of an anti-fascist manifesto, one whose script was signed by Visconti and several other members of a clandestine anti-fascist group already under investigation by the Italian secret police when shooting began in 1942. When production began, in the middle of the war, Italy was fighting (and starting to lose) in the Mediterranean; shortly after the production ended, Allied forces would land in Sicily and begin moving inland on the peninsula. Importantly, this radical wartime film opens with a ninety-second traveling shot that pays homage to the initial railway sequence of Renoir's *La Bête humaine*, whose overpowering force seemed appropriate for a France moving toward war. However, Renoir's energetic placement of his viewer on a train rocketing down the tracks from Paris to Le Havre is changed to a point-of-view shot from the inside of a truck moving swiftly down a dusty road that twists and bends alongside the Po river. The shot confirms that we are in a specifically Italian place because, in this film, location is everything, even as it is peopled with dislocated characters frustrated with their places in life.

Near the city of Ferrara, the truck stops for gas at a roadside gas station and restaurant, the Italian equivalent of Cain's Twin Oaks tavern. The owner of the establishment, Bragana (Juan de Landa), discovers the vagabond Gino (Massimo Girotti) sleeping in the back of the truck. Stopping in the restaurant for a bite to eat, Gino meets Bragana's wife, Giovanna (Clara Calamai), and they are mutually overcome by desire. An adulterous triangle forms, much as in Cain's novel, and the lovers plot to escape together to an unnamed "somewhere." Like Cora, Giovanna is trapped in a loveless marriage to a boor, Bragana, whom she married to escape her former life as a prostitute. Like Frank, Gino lives on the road, taking work where he can find it and when he wants it. Bragana has the Greek's bulk but none of his charm. Stingy, vulgar, and mean, he embodies a grotesque parody of fascist family values, haranguing Giovanna for her failures to maintain his home, duck-hunting with the local priests, and extolling the virtues of military service.

Interestingly, *Ossessione*'s script, sticking fairly close to Cain, was approved by the fascist censors because the foreignness of its source novel meant that the film's noir amorality and criminal violence could be read, in fascist terms, as a sign of American decadence rather than as an indictment of fascist Italy. It is important to keep in mind that cinematic production of the fascist period in Italy tended to be split between films that openly propagandized fascism (a relatively small fraction of Italy's annual output during the 1930s) and a host of so-called "white telephone" films – generally sentimental comedies or romantic melodramas shot in studios and featuring well-heeled characters and elegant settings far removed from the darker realities of everyday Italian life. The Italian state's censorship policy "attempted to suppress all representations of Italian criminality" on the screen, which didn't mean that crime did not exist on Italian screens, but that "it did not exist within the regime's social borders."[28] So, for example, Hollywood films that depicted unseemly criminal subject matter were allowed as long as the crime and corruption clearly existed on foreign soil. Similarly, the rare Italian films actually set in America during the fascist period took a fascist view of America's moral decay, connecting this malaise to the evils and instability of the modern city – for Mussolini, the site of a potentially threatening working-class uprising.[29] In this climate, Cain's novel functioned as a kind of symbolic Trojan horse that allowed Visconti to smuggle onto the screen a savage critique of the venerable pillars of the fascist nation – morality, law, religion, and family – disguised as yet another image of Yankee corruption.

Unlike Cain's Cora, whose allegiance to the home is linked to upwardly mobile desires, Giovanna doesn't seem to know what she wants, beyond some form of economic security that will keep her from prostitution. And Visconti's Bragana neatly turns Cain's characterization on its head: if Nick "the Greek" was, for Cora, disqualified as a proper American patriarch because of his ethnic roots, Bragana, the film's most rooted character, is normative Italian masculinity in the sweaty flesh. Through Bragana, Visconti depicts the fascist household as ruled by intertwined forms of economic and patriarchal exploitation. From the start, Giovanna is represented as Bragana's property – to be defended anxiously against the lurking threat of social unrest embodied by wanderers like Gino and the "chicken thieves" Bragana names as a sign of mounting instability "these days." Visconti shows us that this exploitive domestic relation is corrupt, systemic, and inescapable: Giovanna's enslavement to Bragana is only doubled in her and Gino's murderous and mutually destructive "bond," which will, ironically, produce the pregnancy desired by Bragana. Yet this promise of a happy domestic future, like Bragana's life, is cut short. This explains why, even after the murder, Gino still feels trapped "keeping watch on a dead man's house."

Gino is therefore stuck between the pressures of location – not just the bourgeois home but the broader fascist social order it represents – and the pleasures of travel, of a modern and mobile social world. In *Ossessione*, this is a predicament of character as well as the sign of a broader tension between the film's cinematic investment in specific Italian locales and traditional social forms and its portrait of a modern society filled with dissociated or alienated characters who "dangle from the Fascist social fabric by a thread."[30] Visconti signaled his commitment to place in the film's original title, *Palude*, "marsh," which refers to the wetlands of the Po valley, the southern Italian setting of the film. In the same year in which *Ossessione* was made, Visconti wrote a brief essay for *Cinema* titled "Anthropomorphic Cinema," in which he explained that his primary goal as a filmmaker was "to tell the stories of living human beings, men living in the middle of things."[31] We see this Renoirian tendency to embed characters in the density of social life repeatedly in the film. For example, during the singing contest sequence, Visconti cuts back and forth between the newly reunited lovers in the midst of the audience and the individualized competing singers, isolated in close-up on the stage. Only once do the lovers get the tight close-ups that isolate their passion from the environment (Figure 1.3). Instead, Visconti generally frames them in a medium shot, where the lovers occupy the foreground of the image, the assembled audience crowds the middle ground, and the singing Bragana hovers over Gino's shoulder in the background.

This desire to anchor the film's realism in the depiction of ordinary people organically located in a concrete social environment would soon become a hallmark of postwar Italian neorealism and its humanist moral vision. Given Visconti's nascent neorealist impulses and his French apprenticeship, it makes sense that location in *Ossessione*

FIGURE 1.3 A rare close-up in *Ossessione* (1943).

would become an aesthetic solution – a symbolic mode of anti-fascism. Thematically, however, location is experienced by the film's characters as unfreedom, as that which binds them to a repressive fascist cultural order. While Visconti's compositions place the passions of Gino and Giovanni in the midst of others, and among quotidian social scenes, these environments themselves are not the solution to their problems – they *are* the problem. Instead, what is modern about *Ossessione* is the sheer force of the wayward desires of its central characters, and the gap between the freedom they imagine and the stultifying reality of life under fascism.

This freedom is best embodied in the character of "the Spaniard" (Elio Marcuzzo), Visconti's most interesting addition to Cain's novel. It is no coincidence that Gino meets the Spaniard, a traveling performer, on a train, since this character, who is from Trieste but earned his nickname because he used to work in Spain, joins together all the promises of movement: literal travel, liberty from the nation and its restrictive political and social realities, and homoerotic freedom. Indeed, through the Spaniard Visconti rewrites the very concept of "foreignness" in Cain's novel. For Cain's Cora, the ethnic foreignness of the Greek amounted to a dirty un-Americanness that sullied her dream of national belonging. But, for Gino and Visconti, the Spaniard promises dislocation from fascism's static national life. In this sense, the Spaniard challenges the fascist forms of social attachment, especially bourgeois notions of marriage, money, and property, with more restless, mobile forms of cosmopolitan attachment – of feeling beyond the nation.

His vaguely Spanish provenance gestures towards the recent Spanish Civil War (1936–1939), a conflict that anticipated the political fault lines of World War II and became an important rallying point for anti-fascists of various nations. The Spaniard's relationship to money, connected as it is to his general spirit of good will, is thus coded as a form of political solidarity that he seeks to teach Gino: "Two people," he notes vaguely, "can do a lot of things together." Or, again, "If you stay with me, I'll show you that the streets aren't just for making love." At the same time, the sexual innuendo of these lines, his lingering, longing gazes at a sleeping Gino, and his insistence that the promise of movement is incompatible with Giovanna's desires are all ways in which Visconti connects the promises of liberating political and sexual feeling. Visconti's critique of the restrictive heterosexuality of fascist life makes even more obvious than *Postman* the associations between the mobile life of the tramp, modern class instability, and erotic impropriety. Visually, Visconti thus juxtaposes the kinds of populated or claustrophobic environments in which Gino and Giovanna's destructive passions play out with the liberating exterior spaces associated with the Spaniard: the road, the rails, and the ports, where, in one telling composition, Gino and the Spaniard sit on an elevated pier, their backs toward a church, their faces toward the open sea.

The alluring promises of movement and travel, however, are betrayed by the film's bleak ending. In a sense, this is in keeping with the representation of travel in fascist entertainment cinema in general. As Steven Ricci has recently argued, while fascist films frequently used the representation of trains, buses, ships, and other modes of transportation to explore temporary social dislocation or unstable relationships between class strata, they generally dislodge their characters "only to return them to *where they belong*: that is, to a restabilized social order framed by an idealized family."[32] However, while *Ossessione* blocks Gino's movement away from the fascist national family, putting him back with Giovanna on the road to a happy domestic life, this return to social form ends in disaster. Such are Visconti's politics of revolutionary despair, leaving Gino adrift between the ruin of fascist social forms and the absence of any other means to satisfy his restless desires.

Accounts of the film's initial reception seem to confirm its radical image of national life. The censors, having demanded to see some of the film's rushes, requested cuts, but Visconti refused, presenting his edit at a special screening in Rome in May of 1943. As Visconti tells it, the intellectuals and critics in attendance loved the film, while the swells on hand were repulsed. According to another well-known version of screening, Vittorio Mussolini, son of Il Duce and editor-in-chief of

Cinema, stormed out of the room shouting, "This is not Italy!"[33] The film enjoyed a brief theatrical run in 1943, where its claim to fascist "reality" was savaged as foreign decadence (what else?), and in terms that recall the conservative reception of French films noir like *La Bête humaine*. In fact, a Bologna daily newspaper made the French connection explicit, taking the film to task for "imitating the French kind of realism that must not be transferred to Italy. The movie is a concoction of repulsive passions, humiliation, and decay. It is an offense to the Italian people, which it pretends to portray on a thoroughly imaginary and impossible level."[34] Not surprisingly, the film was also condemned by the Catholic Film Center, and some reports describe priests performing exorcisms on theaters that had screened it. In any case, Visconti's cut was quickly withdrawn from distribution, and had a very limited postwar distribution, not because of its politics, but for the more mundane fact that Visconti had violated Cain's copyright, and the rights to the novel, following Tay Garnett's Hollywood adaptation, were now owned by MGM.[35] No matter, since this international translation of Cain had already done its noir work, puncturing the fascist picture of organic national culture with another version of the local that many Italians refused to recognize as their own. Leftist and anti-fascist critics, on the other hand, celebrated the film as the "July 25th of the Italian cinema" – alluding to the day, in 1943, when Mussolini's government fell and the German occupation of Italy began.[36]

PART II: HOLLYWOOD NOIR AND THE POSTWAR CULTURE OF OCCUPATION

Postwar France and the "Invention" of American Film Noir

What today we refer to as American "film noir" was not initially an event of production. Hollywood studios marketed what we call noir as melodramas, gangster films, and thrillers. Rather unique to this genre, "film noir" was formulated at the level of film reception – specifically the French reception of American cinema after World War II. That is, as a genre, film noir was first identified not in the US, where these films were made, but in France, where the films were seen with different eyes. As we will see, noir became a genre of international currency because through it directors could at once enact their cinephilic attachments to Hollywood's internationalism while also critiquing the long-term effects of a world war and the new global era of the so-called "American age."

The story of noir's critical invention is a familiar one. Cut off from Hollywood during the war owing to the Nazi film ban, French critics were poised to perceive a shift in American cinema that began in the early 1940s, as signaled by a turn towards gritty realism, urban themes, moral ambiguity, on-location shooting, and a stark, high-contrast visual style that cut across conventional, industry-designated genres. This new tendency in Hollywood production recalled some elements of prewar French poetic realism and the cinema of the Popular Front as well as French noir fiction of the 1930s and the many translations of American hard-boiled fiction that circulated widely before the war. But these films also anticipated postwar skepticism, if not cynicism, towards world justice, consumer culture, domestic happiness, and democratic enfranchisement.

It was the ambiguous politics of noir (perhaps more than the visual style) that was especially relevant to French intellectuals who had endured the wartime Nazi occupation of their country. The Nazi ban on American books, films, and what the Nazis considered black jazz music not only kept US cultural forms officially out of circulation, but necessarily politicized these products as threats to the fascist regime. Jean-Paul Sartre anecdotally explains that, when the Germans prohibited all printing and reprinting of American authors, student activists created a black market for such fiction. At its most politically naive, "the reading of novels by Faulkner and Hemingway became for some a symbol of resistance. Stenographers believed they could demonstrate against the Germans by reading *Gone with the Wind* in the Metro."[37] But for Sartre and his leftist compatriots there really was something radical about the rebellious, "unconscious spontaneity" of Hemingway, Faulkner, Dos Passos, Cain, and especially Steinbeck that could be harnessed for French anti-fascism. Without reflection or intellection, these authors "described from the outside" characters mired in the cruelty of American capitalism and class inequality that often propelled them into social exile.

> What fascinated us all really . . . was the constant flow of men across a whole continent, the exodus of an entire village to the orchards of California, the hopeless wanderings of the hero in *Light in August*, and of the uprooted people who drifted along at the mercy of the storms in *The 42nd Parallel*, the dark murderous fury which sometimes swept through an entire city, the blind and criminal love in the novels of James Cain.[38]

The authors' emphasis on external action and their refusal of deep psychological explanations meant that readers had to reconstruct characters' thoughts based on descriptions of their conduct, "as in life."[39] This brutal, observational fiction (which many American literati had dismissed as outdated and low-brow) was, to Sartre's taste, the only mode of writing adequate to the unthinkable atrocities of his time, including the civil war in Spain, the concentration camps throughout Europe, the refugee crisis, and World War II, which had engulfed the globe. "Here a new literature presented its characters to us synthetically. It made them perform before our eyes acts which were complete in themselves, impossible to analyze, acts which it was necessary to grasp completely with all the obscure power of our souls."[40] For this reason, American novels became the foundation for what Sartre characterized as a much more theorized and deliberate existential literary technique in the work of Albert Camus, Simone de Beauvoir, and, of course, Sartre himself. "We have treated consciously and intellectually what was the fruit of a talented and unconscious spontaneity."[41] Just as the American novel inspired an anti-fascist aesthetic during the "decade of translations" in which Visconti's *Ossessione* emerged in Italy, so too in postwar France American fiction gained admirers for its regionalism and for its mode of proto-existentialist observation that could be harnessed for a more studied political literature.

For Sartre, moreover, the criticisms leveled against capitalism in 1930s American fiction were not interpreted as a wholesale rejection of the American system (as some anti-American propagandists hoped) so much as "a manifestation of liberty" that is only possible in a democracy where citizens may freely speak out against such injustices.[42] As we will see below, in the history of film noir's invention and critical afterlife, there is a curious affinity between representations of social brutality and perceptions of democratic vitality. Since many of the authors Sartre celebrated wrote the novels and short stories on which 1940s films noir were based (Faulkner, Cain, and Dashiell Hammett), it is little wonder that French film critics, conversant in existentialism, would be similarly attracted to noir's criminal irrationality, primitive violence, and ecstatic realism, especially as it dovetailed with a waning surrealist sensibility. As James Naremore explains, noir's sadistic gangsterism attracted the surrealists "in part because such pictures depicted violent, antisocial behavior, and in part because they bestowed an aura of the marvelous upon urban decor."[43] Noir's criminality and convoluted plot structure struck the surrealists as having the form of incoherent nightmares and thus might give expression to desublimated desires. Compared to the standard American fare, noir fascinated as an "outlaw genre, systematically reversing Hollywood's myths."[44]

Among the first French critics to coin "film noir," Nino Frank announced the death of the European detective formula in 1946 after seeing The Maltese Falcon (1941), Double Indemnity (1944), Laura (1944), and Murder, My Sweet (1944). In contrast to the over-rational and tired detective genre from France's prewar era, these films conveyed "a sense of 'lived experience'" and "enigmatic psychology."[45] The American noir hero was not the "thinking machine who cleans and fills his pipe," but a complicated character who operated outside of both the law and the criminal underworld.[46] Echoing Sartre, Frank praises noir's emphasis on "faces, behavior, words," rather than on action or even plot. "Misogynistic," "hard-hearted," and "fragmentary," the stories resemble the tone and style of contemporary American popular fiction that seemed to be responsive to the realities of the twentieth century.[47] Like the novel, the film plots turn less on the question of legal guilt and more on how characters process and respond to a more generalized state of criminal affairs, a state all too familiar to the survivors of war. "Today's spectator," he remarks, "is sensitive to nothing more than this impression of real life, of lived experience, and – why not? – of certain disagreeable realities that do in truth exist, whose repression never served any purpose; the struggle of life is no invention of our own time." So trenchant are these "films noir" that they may, in Frank's estimation, come to "outclass Paris once and for all."[48]

THE MALTESE FALCON AS EXISTENTIAL PASSIONPLAY

Though Frank does not offer a detailed reading of any of the films under review, we might briefly consider how a film like *The Maltese Falcon* conveys a sense of "lived experience" in its emphasis on behavior, faces, and words, and why such a film may be more adequate to the disagreeable realities of wartime life than previous Hollywood films. Starring Humphrey Bogart as private detective Sam Spade, *The Maltese Falcon* features characters who are so psychologically opaque to us that we can make sense of them as people only by scrutinizing their actions and looking for signs of sincerity in their speech and gestures, a process this film frustrates (and thus brings to the fore) at every turn.

In the opening scene, Brigid O'Shaughnessy (Mary Astor) visits Spade's office. She presents herself as Miss Wonderly and spins a yarn for Spade which results in his partner, Archer, being shot. Huston stages this initial exchange between Wonderly and Sam in a fairly conventional – master shot, shot, reverse shot – editing pattern. But as the camera cuts into closer views of Wonderly we can't help but notice that her eyes dart around the room beneath the tool-adorned hat that shades her face. We may guess that her hesitant speech is a product of nervousness, lying, genuine fear, or all three. Or maybe this is part of an elaborate seduction. We cut to a medium close-up of Sam, whose eyes are calmly fixed on hers, and his responses to her questions are both reassuring and impersonally professional. We cut to a wider shot when Archer enters the office and is immediately drawn to Wonderly's appealing figure. He stands behind her chair eyeing her approvingly and exchanges a conspiratorial glance with Sam, who has, so far, betrayed no signs of interiority. After showing Wonderly out, the two men pocket the two hundred-dollar bills she's left as payment. The only debriefing to which we are privy comes from Archer, who says, "Ah, she's sweet."

Confronting Brigid the next day after Archer's been shot, Spade explains that he and Archer were not duped by her initial act: "We didn't exactly believe your story . . . we believed your two hundred dollars." As this second scene between them unfolds and Brigid purports to talk on the level, Sam compliments her on even this demure performance when she pleads for his help. "You're good," he remarks. "It's chiefly your eyes, I think, and that throb you get in your voice when you say things like 'Be generous, Mr. Spade.'" Hearing this, Brigid once again changes her demeanor, revealing, we think, her true, worldly nature. But even this is only an act that Spade admires: "Now you *are* dangerous." In their third meeting, he once and for all calls the bluff on her "schoolgirl manner." Now Brigid has lost the innocent act, and she merely reveals in her anxious sputtering that she has something to hide. She desperately needs Spade's protection. In exchange, Spade demands her affections, which is perhaps what Brigid was counting on all along. Playacting has by now become a form a seduction. Where Brigid's many-layered performances would seem to be the province of a scheming femme fatale, she merely does more obviously what Spade manages throughout the film: namely to cause us to question the difference between being and appearing to be, between acting and authentically emoting.

Spade is himself no stranger to performance, even if that performance mostly manifests itself as inscrutability. As Spade himself says to the district attorney, "everyone has something to conceal." In the first scene with Brigid, he conveys no sense of his skepticism or sexual attraction. It seems he's mostly in it for the money. In their second meeting, he takes more money from Brigid as a retainer of sorts, but later agrees to work for Joel Cairo (Peter Lorre) and for Kasper Gutman (Sidney Greenstreet), who are competing with each other and with Brigid to locate the titular falcon around which all of this deception and death revolves. Profiting from this general culture of distrust, Spade seems as crooked and unprincipled as they come. With no access to his inner thoughts and conjectures, we may judge him only by actions that are always coolly calculating. When Spade does lose his temper – for example, with Brigid in their third meeting, or later with Gutman when Spade suddenly throws his cigar and smashes his glass in mock apoplexy – we realize these flare-ups are enacted to make people think he is more "wild" and "unpredictable" than he actually is. Even we, who are occasionally in on his performances as such, cannot know where Spade stands. In contrast to the depiction in the novel, in which Hammett describes characters' involuntary physiology – the blushes, tremors, blood-drained grimaces – that distinguishes real from false emotion, Huston's direction gives us only a series of performances. *The Maltese Falcon* teaches us that, in the realm of observable action in this film, as in life perhaps, there may not be a measurable difference between acting and being.

In the film's final scene, the falcon is discovered as a fake, and Spade sides with the law. He turns Gutman, Cairo, and Brigid over to the police, in part to save himself from arrest. Given his behavior in the rest of the film, Brigid laughs nervously, thinking this is another of his "wild and unpredictable" stunts. But, as the truth sinks in, Brigid sobs on the divan, hoping that her visible despair will change his mind. Then Spade offers his most dramatic and revealing speech, finally laying his cards and options on the table (Figure 1.4)

> When a man's partner is killed, he's supposed to do something about it. It
> doesn't make any difference what you thought of him. . . . [W]hen one of

FIGURE 1.4 Reading faces (*The Maltese Falcon*, 1941).

your organization gets killed, it's . . . bad business to let the killer get away with it, bad all around, bad for every detective everywhere. I've no earthly reason to think I can trust you, and if I do this and get away with it you'll have something on me that you can use whenever you want to. I couldn't be sure that you wouldn't put a hole in me someday. All of those are on one side. Maybe some of them are unimportant. I won't argue about that. But look at the number of them. And what have we got on the other side? All we've got is that maybe you love me and maybe I love you.

Separating the facts from his tentative feelings, Spade opts for the practical, self-preserving, and conveniently legal course of action. Sean McCann argues that the gift of Hammett's liberal cynicism is that Spade "must arrest [Brigid] and his own desire [for her] in order to be free."[49] That is, Spade's continued freedom comes at the cost of another's imprisonment and the suppression of his own passions.

"Little seems redemptive or consolatory about such a situation," in which one must choose between two forms of unfreedom. "Forced into an unhomely alienation," Spade is finally guided by his unfeeling, professional pragmatism.[50] On the other hand, the film version leaves open the possibility that he may never have loved Brigid. Suspecting all along that she had killed his partner, he was merely playing – and then refusing to play any longer – her sap.

Though the novel was written in the 1930s, during the era of New Deal liberalism, the film version played in France in 1946, and, in fact, was among the first American films to reach the liberated territories as the US Army advanced.[51] Against the culture of moral absolutism promoted by the Nazis and fascists, film noir presented a world of moral ambiguity in which the protagonist must, nevertheless, decisively act. The Nazi occupation and Vichy collaboration, likewise, had forced everyone into a position of collaboration or resistance. Tony Judt argues:

> [I]ntellectuals would find themselves discovering in the very act of political disobedience the freedom they would later defend. The dilemma between "being" and "doing," which had seemed so significant before the war, collapsed. To do was to be: no longer a universal consciousness vested in a singular self, the intellectual was bound within the organic community and there presented with apparently simple choices, all of which entailed action of one sort or another.[52]

For those who did not engage in collective politics, the war years in France were experienced "as a sequence of individual choices, exemplary and binding upon themselves, but above all a private experience, lived in public."[53] In these terms, film noir, and especially *The Maltese Falcon*, became a potential cipher for the experience of occupation (and we will consider this in more detail with Germany and Japan below). And it also exemplified certain strains of existentialist thought.[54]

Not all French critics agreed that noir was the best mode for postwar reckoning. A few months after Frank's essay was published,

Jean-Pierre Chartier wrote his far less enthusiastic response to Hollywood's "noir" turn in his review of *Murder, My Sweet*, *Double Indemnity*, and *The Lost Weekend*, films that set a new bar for "despairing pessimism" and "a disgust for humanity."[55] US censorship, far more prudish about the representation of sex than violence, is to blame for these films' failure to reveal the carnal desire motivating criminal behavior. "The result is that what these characters do seem controlled by an unshakable criminal destiny." Populated by unsavory types – "insatiable Messalines, brutal or senile husbands, young men willing to kill in order to win the favor of a femme fatale" – the films nonetheless accomplish a striking and horrifying psychological verisimilitude that implicates the viewer "in the chain of morally reprehensible events."[56] Of course, the title of the essay, "The Americans Are Making Dark Films Too," reminds us that the Americans were not the first to take a walk on the dark side. The poetic realist films of the 1930s, however, had "hints of revolt" and, to Chartier's sensibility, managed to instill in viewers hope, sympathy, and pity. "Nothing like that here," he writes of the American productions. Where Frank finds in film noir a cynical vitality upon which French auteurs might improve, one senses in Chartier's review that the "murky, dreamlike visual style" of noir (a style that, for him, recalls the surrealist avant-garde of the prewar period) augurs a new genre of "fatal, inner evil" that Paris might do well to repel.[57]

Together, these reviews sound the vexatious nature of Franco-American relations during this period of transition. But they also echo French reactions to their own realist cinema of the 1930s as being variously a leftist critique of capitalist culture or a signifier of national decay. The difference now was that noir was a "foreign" production trend emanating from a powerful country to which France was politically, financially, and even culturally indebted. As Mark Vernet argues, to the French, the United States was a liberator that offered France's war-weary population a cinematic vision of a better quality of life. At the same time, the US threatened to use its victorious status and preponderant economic power "to impose upon France values and a culture that [were] not its own."[58] Thus film noir was a particularly attractive critical object because it was available to the politics of both the left and the right. Vernet muses, "invented by French criticism, [noir] allows one to love the United States while criticizing it, or more exactly to criticize it in order to be able to love it."[59]

Hollywood, Americanization, and Market Empire

What were the values and culture being imposed on the French? What did "Americanization" mean to those living in Europe in the immediate postwar period? And how, in light of this cultural imposition, might noir emerge as a good object?

Questions of film culture were necessarily connected to the sustainability of national culture that, in the immediate postwar period especially, hung in the balance of massive trade deficits, dollar gaps, and the exigency of rebuilding a shattered European economy. These interconnections were particularly evident in the terms of the 1946 Blum–Byrnes Accord. The US government would forgive France's war debt and grant the country a low-interest loan of $650 million, provided that the French lift all barriers to foreign trade. The Americans hoped that a boost in the Gallic economy would enable the French to buy American goods and materials for reconstruction and thus keep the US economy from sinking back into the prewar depression and, just as important, prevent France from falling to communism. The French agreed to the terms of the accord with one exception: French film producers had to have some guarantee that their films would reach French audiences once the market was open to Hollywood. Prime minister Leon Blum forestalled this desperately needed transaction until some restrictions on Hollywood were in place, despite there being numerous industries decimated during the war that would have benefited from similar arrangements. The compromise reached was a quota stipulating that 30 percent of screen time in France would be reserved for French films.

France was by no means the only country trying to protect its national culture and economy by protecting its film industry from

Hollywood. The British Labour Party in 1947 imposed a 75 percent tariff on all American films imported to the UK and then, under pressure from the Hollywood firms and British exhibitors, conceded finally to a 30 percent screen quota.[60] And where such measures were either not in place or feebly enforced, such as in Italy, Hollywood dominated the market. Yet there, as in France, film aficionados who "had been attracted by the myth of America before the war," and who welcomed the liberators and their putatively anti-fascist culture, "displayed attitudes which oscillated between love and hate, attraction and repulsion" in the face of American film culture. They too were impressed that the Hollywood vision of the US was not always "sunny side up."[61]

These cultural protections were particularly fearful to US companies because Hollywood emerged from the war with studios intact and with a huge backlog of films that had yet to be distributed in Nazi-occupied Europe (but had already earned profits in domestic distribution). Hollywood greeted war's end as an opportunity to reestablish its international dominance, especially in the face of waning box-office profits at home. To aid them in this soon-to-be-global mission, both the US Department of State and the Department of Commerce negotiated with foreign governments to lift trade barriers including screen quotas, subsidies, and other measures designed to protect national cinemas in the face of Hollywood's global expansion. Underwriting the US government's support was the basic belief not only that American films could advertise American goods to foreign consumers, but that, in the postwar era, Hollywood could help spread the English language, American culture, capitalism, and democracy as the basis for a new, much more homogenized, internationalism (as opposed to the more urban cosmopolitanism of the prewar proto noir film movements). With the help of the State Department, the Hollywood companies were largely successful in their bid for foreign markets. By the mid-1950s, American films commanded at least half of the screening time in most countries in the world.[62]

Hollywood's strategies were part of a much more pervasive American policy to restructure the economies of Europe and Japan. As the leading creditor nation after the war with the most to gain by unfettered trade, the United States achieved its rise in global power by advancing what Victoria de Grazia calls "Market Empire," a capitalist-driven program that promoted consumer democracy as the alternative both to the planned economies of the Soviet Union and to the welfare state policy dominating 1930s and 1940s Europe and New Deal liberalism in the US.[63] By promoting efficient, pragmatic capitalist practices and granting states only limited jurisdiction over their economies, Market Empire promised to bring affluence to all through the rising tide of world trade. Touted as the peaceable alternative to Nazism, communism, and fascism, moreover, this form of empire supposedly laid the foundation for an enduring peace by eroding forms of economic nationalism and creating interdependent economies. On the ground, it presumably encouraged democratic citizenship through consumer culture. An individual's ability and freedom to choose from a range of films (or blenders, or cars) in a competitive market was good preparation for making political choices as well. Thus consumer and political savvy were mutually reinforcing. "In the best of possible worlds, consumer freedom was the most basic of all freedoms."[64]

Market Empire's most sterling example was the Economy Recovery Program or, as it was more commonly known, the Marshall Plan. Under the Marshall Plan, the US would provide governments with low-interest loans and grants in order to help Europe buy (from the US) needed materials without incurring further debt, and to help European industry modernize, thereby stimulating national economies and elevating European standards of living. As de Grazia argues, the Marshall Plan was less significant in terms of actual dollar amounts, and it should not be seen principally as a gesture of "enlightened benefaction." Rather, the capitalist ideology it encoded made it most important as a "bearer of new ways of thinking about producing affluence."[65] The implementation of the Marshall Plan required that European industry become more modern, lean, and efficient at the cost of subduing and disciplining labor, and postponing a rise in living standards for the entire population. De Grazia argues that "the cornucopias of populist tradition" in Europe were sacrificed on the altar of capitalist abundance.[66] Americanization then was less about turning European citizens into Americans than an ambitious program to transform America and the rest of the world into one global market in which consumer democracy became universal.

Europe and Japan would enjoy an economic boom or "miracle" in the 1950s thanks, in part, to American aid. In the immediate postwar years, however, most of these citizens existed on meager food rations amid the ruins of bombed-out cities. Further, many (especially those living in occupied Germany and Japan) subsisted at the margins of a free-market economy, forced instead to trade on the black market. Or, worse, they fell prey to the barter system where goods and services (often contraband and prostitution) were exchanged in dark alleys and subway stations, overseen by marketeering gangsters and subject to police raids. Meanwhile, in local theaters, moviegoers glimpsed images of American plenty and a better life, except, of course, in the world of film noir. In this genre associated with subterranean economies and stolen goods, luxury was a sign of corruption and it was clear that American capitalism – if not also its presumed democratic culture – had run amok.

In Japan and Germany, American films arrived on the heels of the US occupation army, whose presence announced the practical end of national sovereignty. Though regarded by some as liberators, the Americans were also conquerors who implemented ambitious plans to politically reeducate the defeated populations in part by reforming their film culture. To this end, more than two hundred Hollywood films, newsreels, and documentaries were shown in these territories to tutor audiences in democratic (American) ways of life. Under US military censorship, postwar Japanese and German films were carefully vetted so that only those that supported the broad democratic and cultural reforms – and that upheld the authority of the occupation – would reach local screens. And it was under these circumstances of foreign occupation that the Germans and Japanese became reacquainted with American film noir.

Germany: Occupation Noir and the Shadow of Weimar

From 1945 to 1949 Germany was partitioned into four zones, one for each of the Allied countries (the US, France, Britain, and the Soviet Union) to occupy, in which each power attempted to remake Germans in their own image, literally, by projecting films from their home country. If the cosmopolitanism of the prewar era had waned under fascism, the occupation became a form of imposed cosmopolitanism, especially in Berlin (a city itself divided, like the country, into four parts), where the film cultures of the occupiers and occupied mixed, clashed, and vied for political primacy. Most historians agree that Germans were cool if not outright hostile to Hollywood cinema and especially American film noir during the occupation. The reason is likely that, for the first year after the war, Germans living in the American zone saw only Hollywood films, which, to boot, were presented to them as superior models for their more "enlightened," democratic future.[67] Hollywood was thus not the cinema *opposed* to occupation; in Germany it was the cinema *of* occupation. Inclined to read Hollywood films as overt propaganda, German critics questioned the efficacy of using criminal, morally ambiguous films to reeducate a Nazi mass public. This sentiment was pointedly evident in reviews for Robert Siodmak's *Spiral Staircase* (1946), a film set in the Victorian era and featuring a proto-Nazi antagonist, Professor Warren, who is obsessed with social Darwinism and bent on killing all women who fail to live up to the highest physical standards. Lutz Koepnick argues that this film was part of Siodmak's ongoing "confrontation with Nazi Cinema and its Wagnerian ideologies of embodiment."[68] And Siodmak would have known this ideology well, since he, like many others working in Hollywood in the 1940s, was born and began his career in Germany. By punishing the murderer and saving the life of the last "mute" victim, *Staircase* exterminates the Nazi-like character. Further, the complex mechanisms of looking and objectification used to signify Warren's murderous gaze are turned against him when his stepmother, Mrs. Warren, picks up the rifle and sends him spiraling down the staircase. Mrs Warren is both the killer's killer and the final authority of the film's narrative. Thus, Siodmak "valorizes Mrs. Warren's magic humanism over the professor's fascistic cinema of incorporation and projective horror."[69]

For Koepnick, this film is a plea for humanism not because it emphasizes external action and "lived experience" – the elements of noir that interested the French critics. Rather, the film rejects Nazism and asserts a "magical" humanism when Mrs. Warren exterminates the anti-humanist. But for German audiences, he explains, the film was perceived as part of a larger program of "Hollywood imperialism and aesthetic banality" that was particularly unsuited to the crises of post-war reckoning. One German film critic wrote of this film: "Whoever as a victor of war waged in the name of ethical principles, assumes the responsibility of reeducating and spiritually reshaping Germany, should be able to recognize that murder films are not exactly an appropriate instrument to eradicate fascistic convictions."[70] In general, argues Koepnick, German critics, unlike their French counterparts, perceived nothing new or politically vital in noir. Such films merely "attested to the inauthenticity of American mass culture" and the deeply misguided notion of using Hollywood films for reeducation.[71]

And yet German audiences and critics genuinely embraced other American noirs. George Cukor's melodrama-noir Gaslight (1944) was voted the most popular film among Munich audiences in 1948.[72] Hitchcock's Suspicion received roundly positive reviews. And the film critic for the Rheinische Post praised the "perfect realism" of Call Northside 777 (1948), a procedural police drama starring Jimmy Stewart that was shot on location in Chicago's stockyards and working-class districts. In particular, the critic was impressed with Call Northside's affinity with Neue Sachlichkeit, or the New Objectivity cinema from the Weimar era, "street films" that were famously shot in vast studios where mini-cities (and their slums) were meticulously constructed.[73] The difference, however, was that the American objectivity was achieved not in studio sets but on location in Chicago, where director

Henry Hathaway borrowed techniques from newsreel cinematography, an approach as indebted to the hard-boiled plots from the 1919s as to Italian neorealism. In an odd reversal, a noir made by a German émigré director (*Spiral Staircase*) signifies Hollywood's decadent domination, but a police drama (*Call Northside*) directed by a California-born American signals Weimar's return with a difference.

Just as interesting is the fact that the first films produced in both the Soviet and the American zones of occupation owed something to an emerging and global noir aesthetic quite independent of the American noirs screened there (most of which came to Germany – and then only in the American and British zones – *after* these local films were produced). Because most of the German studios were either destroyed or turned into displaced persons' camps, filmmakers were forced to take their cameras to the streets and into the overwhelming rubble of the major cities. Faced with severe shortages in housing, food, and fuel, to say nothing of raw film stock and equipment, German directors created what critics at the time referred to as *Trümmerfilme* (rubble films), the first two examples of which were not simply films shot in the rubble. They engage the milieu of black markets and off-limits nightclubs, the problems of homelessness and displacement, and questions of guilt and accountability for the reign of Nazi terror that led to the miseries of postwar occupation. They did so using low-key lighting, on-location shooting, and complex flashback structures organized around narratives of detection and discovery. These films look back to earlier German culture but evince the anti-fascist influences of their occupiers.

For example, Wolfgang Staudte's *Die Mörder sind unter uns / The Murderers Are among Us* (1946), the first post-WWII German feature film that was produced in the Soviet zone of occupation, uses the rubble as both the historical setting for the story and a mise-en-scène expressive of the main character's tormented psychology – in the spirit of the Weimar classic *Das Cabinet des Dr. Caligari / The Cabinet of Dr. Caligari* (1919).[74] And, though the film was first conceived during the war under the Nazis, its anti-capitalist message echoes the ideology of the Soviet occupation authority. The plot revolves around Hans Mertens, a returning war veteran traumatized by the Nazi atrocities he witnessed while serving as a surgeon in the Wehrmacht. He arrives back to his war-ravaged Berlin apartment only to find that it is now occupied by a woman, Susanne (Hildegard Knef), who spent the war years in a concentration camp. Plagued by nightmares of his wartime service, Mertens becomes an unstable alcoholic, and Susanne, in turn, devotes herself to restoring Mertens to his profession while transforming their berubbled apartment into the semblance of an impoverished home. But Mertens becomes obsessed with revenge when he finds Brückner, his former commanding officer and the person who ordered the death of masses of civilians, comfortably ensconced in a profitable postwar industry. The very fact that Brückner thrives – belly full, well dressed, body, psyche, and bourgeois household intact – points to the failures of postwar justice and suggests that the capitalist system itself props up and hides the unrepentant Nazis in our midst.

Mertens's struggle with alcoholism, war guilt, and pervasive poverty is contrasted with Brückner's indulgences in rich foods, dance-hall girls, and drunken merry-making. One particularly damning scene begins with a close-up of a newspaper announcing to the world the realities of the gas chambers. The camera then pans up to reveal Brückner drinking coffee and stuffing his mouth with buttered bread oblivious to the newspaper's implicit accusation. Thus is the contrast: Mertens drinks to suppress the past and the present-day hardships; Brückner eats and drinks to revel in his postwar good fortune.

The noir elements are evident in the film's narrative structure and visual design. The film's complex temporality is motivated by the flashbacks that provide Mertens's wartime backstory and the source of his anguish. It is also a drama of revenge. Decked out in a trench coat and fedora with a gun concealed in his pocket, Mertens, in his last scene in the film, lurks on the periphery of Brückner's factory, planning to lure him to his death. According to Tim Bergfelder, the original script has Mertens shooting Brückner in the end. But the Soviet censors forbade any representation of vigilantism.[75] Thus the scenario's noir-like moral ambiguity gave way to unambiguous due process. Hearing Susanne's plea, Mertens turns Brückner over to the military police after he confronts him with his wartime crimes. Stylistically, the film conveys the harshness of postwar life in low-key lighting and shadows cast on and from the other-worldly landscape of the rubble. Canted angles convey Mertens's unsettled psyche and the objective strangeness of coming home to an erased city whose real location speaks for itself (Figure 1.5).

Though made completely apart from the Hollywood noirs that were just beginning to play on West German screens, *Murderers*, like *The Maltese Falcon*, espouses what Bergfelder calls an "ethical pragmatism," most evident in Staudte's treatment of Susanne and Mertens's relationship. They live together, unwed, and grow to love one another because, frankly, there is nowhere else to live and no one else left to love. The

FIGURE 1.5   Rubble noir (*The Murderers Are among Us*, 1946).

film presents the sober practicality of justice, life, and love in the ruins. As a Soviet production, and perhaps also as a noir, is it deeply skeptical of capitalism. In contrast to America's consuming, free-market ethos, capitalism in this film is a sign not of a coming democracy but of the remnants of Nazi decadence.

We should also emphasize, however, that while this film would seem to mirror the "democratic" film culture of the US and Weimar Germany it was first conceived during the Nazi period. Bergfelder reminds us that the Nazi cinema also had "noir elements." "The bleak pessimism and determinist inevitability that pervades many Nazi melodramas, complete with matching visual aesthetics, has, whether one likes it or not, much in common with both American noir and Hollywood's gothic melodramas of the 1940s."[76]This likeness between Nazi and Hollywood noir may explain not only the noir elements of *Murderers*, but also the popularity of *Gaslight* and the complicated under-lying reasons for the German critique of Siodmak's *Spiral Staircase*.

The first German film produced in the US zone likewise had an affinity with noir. Harald Braun's *Zwischen Gestern und Morgen/Between Yesterday and Tomorrow* (1947) is about a man who returns to Munich from his wartime exile only to be accused of having stolen jewels from a Jewish woman just before her death in the late 1930s. Told as a series of flashbacks, the film leads us through the Nazi period, at which time our hero meets the Jewish actress, who has left the hovel where she hides from the Nazis and has checked into a grand hotel to experience Weimar luxury one last time. Her capture by the Nazis, who roam the hotel dressed like 1940s American gumshoes, is imminent. In the present day, our hero, Michael (played by Nazi-era star Viktor de Kowa), searches for the jewels in the rubble of the hotel lobby in order to clear his name. There he encounters Kat, a bright-eyed hotel waitress (also played by Knef), who, having found them earlier, now retrieves the jewels from the black market where her brother is about to trade them for desperately needed food and clothing. Exonerated in the end of any misdeeds, Michael, like Mertens before him, finds solace and hope in the loving arms of a woman played by Hildegard Knef.[77]

American directors were likewise drawn to the noir elements of Germany's rubble. *Berlin Express* (1948), directed by French-born Jacques Tourneur and co-written by Curt Siodmak (Robert Siodmak's brother) and Harold Medford, follows a contingent of Allied personnel through the American zone to Berlin, where one in the group, a German professor in exile, will attempt to negotiate for the reunification of the country. In Berlin, however, he is kidnapped and his Allied group must fan out across the rubble to find him before the remaining Nazis (who seem to benefit from the chaos of occupation) see that he is killed. With all external scenes shot on location in Berlin – much of it at night – *Berlin Express* pivots on the fragile relations among the French, British, American, and Soviet occupiers, who are as suspicious of each other's designs on Germany as they are of the German people themselves. But it is Billy Wilder's cynical and controversial satire-noir *A Foreign Affair* (1948), shot (and later banned) in occupied Berlin, and the British film *The Third Man* (1949), directed by Carol Reed and shot in occupied Vienna, that connect a certain lawless frontierism in the occupied territory equally to the lingering effects of Nazism and to the presence of American soldiers whose moral, democratic rectitude is undercut by their participation in shady deals and black marketeering.

Wilder, an Austrian Jew who worked as a journalist and crime reporter before beginning his film career first in Germany and then in France, came to Hollywood in 1935. He first rose to prominence as an unorthodox and even controversial director when his *Double Indemnity* premiered in 1944. Shortly thereafter, Wilder returned to Germany as a member of the US Occupation Army Film Unit. After his relatively short stay, Wilder flew to Hollywood with an idea for a film that would not be for German reeducation, but about the culture of occupation. Wary and weary of didacticism and government propaganda, Wilder returned to Berlin to make *A Foreign Affair*, a satire whose noir elements looked back to *Double Indemnity* and anticipated Wilder's dark, satiric look at Hollywood and at POW camps in his films to follow.

A Foreign Affair situates Captain John Pringle (John Lund), an American denazification officer serving in Berlin, in a love triangle between his Nazi siren, Erika von Schülow (played by the legendary Marlene Dietrich), and the squeaky-clean Republican congresswoman Phoebe Frost (Jean Arthur), who visits from Iowa to investigate the "moral malaria" afflicting US occupation troops. Frost's suspicions are confirmed when she stumbles into the world of black markets and off-limits nightclubs all propped up by a fraternizing economy in which US soldiers trade their rations in exchange for amorous relations with the local Fräuleins. Erika is herself part of this economy, pledging allegiance to whomever can provide food and nylons. "I have a new Führer now – you," she says to her American lover. "Heil, Johnny." To protect Erika from Frost's investigative zeal, Pringle decides to seduce the congresswoman, but in the process learns that Erika is harboring a most-wanted Nazi criminal. With this revelation, the film takes a decidedly dark turn as Pringle and the other soldiers attempt to use Erika as bait to lure the Nazi out of hiding. But it is around the question of Erika's Nazism that the film's noir ambivalence turns. Erika's decadence is reflected in her sadomasochistic sexual repartee with Johnny, her love of champagne, cigarettes, and nylons, and her association with the Lorelei cabaret. All of these habits and tastes mark her as a holdover from an unAmericanized Germany. In fact, Frost finds proof of Erika's Nazism in German newsreels that show her at a Wagner opera where, adorned in a sequined gown, she intimately jokes with the Führer himself! On the other hand, Erika as played by Marlene Dietrich channels a long history of femmes fatales, including Dietrich's own storied role as Lola Lola in Joseph von Sternberg's 1930 German film Der blaue Engel/Blue Angel. To this extent she is part of the decadent Weimar culture Nazism railed against. Moreover, German and US audiences knew Dietrich as a stalwart American patriot whose United Services Organization (USO) shows and star image made her into a safe object of "democratic sex."[78] Perhaps Wilder's most wily and controversial decision was to depict the frosty congresswoman – with her blonde hair braided on top of her head, her scrubbed, unadorned face, and her empty political rhetoric – as a kind of ideal Nazi woman played by an American actress, in contrast to Dietrich's unquestionable (and German) allure.[79] Andrea Slane explains that, while Pringle chooses Phoebe over Erika because of the latter's unreconstructed Nazism, the film must strain to make Phoebe a plausible romantic figure while not propping up Nazism's desexualized aesthetics of beauty as having something in common with American femininity. Thus, Slane concludes of the film's many layers of history and political signification: "Dietrich's performance, which on one level is meant to emblematize 'Nazi' allure, also quite explicitly quotes the actress's anti-Nazi activism."[80] The film's representation of American democracy – imposed in Germany in the form of baseball games, amorous affairs, denazification camps, and congressional triumphalism – calls into question the moral absolutism associated with postwar America.

Occupied Japan and Kasutori *noir*

In American-occupied Japan, too, the culture, politics, and urban experience of occupation were registered darkly in Japanese films made under American censorship. The American occupation presence in Japan combined with the physical and emotional tolls of total, ultra-nationalist war, complete surrender, and postwar economic chaos and poverty gave way to what was popularly referred to as the "*kyodatsu* condition," or the collective experience of psychic exhaustion and despair.[81] At the same time, these circumstances produced a vibrant and multifaceted culture of defeat. Historian John W. Dower isolates three especially compelling and overlapping subcultures that emerged during the occupation that were "mesmerizing symbols of the collapse of the old order and the emergence of a new spirit of iconoclasm and self-reliance."[82] These subcultures, flourishing at the periphery of traditional and so-called upstanding institutions, seemed cut to the measure of film noir. They included: 1) the milieu of the *pan-pan* prostitutes who serviced the occupation soldiers and were thus cynically associated with "the newest and most democratic" features of postwar Japan; 2) the culture of "pragmatic materialism" in the uniquely Japanese black market, known for its "hardened hearts and harsh dealing"; and 3) the resurgence of the *kasutori* culture (named after a potent rotgut associated with Japanese pulp fiction) and a renewed celebration of decadent authenticity and sexual liberation.[83] Indeed, the very titles of some of the pulp magazines published during the occupation – *G-men, Neoliberal, Pinup, Blood and Diamonds* – connect political liberalism to crime and promiscuity in hard-boiled terms.[84] As Dower explains, these cultures of material and erotic exchange "came to exemplify not merely the confusion and despair of the *kyodatsu* condition, but also the vital, visceral, even carnal transcending of it."[85]

Perhaps the greatest advocate for the *kasutori* worldview was novelist Ango Sakaguchi. In his famous 1946 essay "Discourse on Decadence," he argued that the deterioration of the Japanese state and the military, social, and economic fall of its people were the basis for a new postwar order. "Japan was defeated and the *samurai* ethic has perished," he declared, "but humanity has been born from the womb of decadence's truth."[86] Reduced to basic biological needs and carnal desires, the Japanese had finally fallen as a political community. But this was not cause for despair. Rather, Sakaguchi argued, "We have only returned to being human."[87] As Dower concludes of Sakaguchi's critique, he "was affirming something that moral philosophers and other intellectuals were also wrestling with: that only a society based on a genuine *shutaisei* – a true 'subjectivity' or 'autonomy' at the individual level – could hope to resist the indoctrinating power of the state."[88] As some critics have noted, the postwar crisis of *shutaisei* in Japan had affinities with French existentialism and the larger question of individual responsibility and free will.[89] In fact the war crimes tribunals in Japan (as in Germany) pressed the issue of how individuals could and should be held accountable for their actions even when those actions were carried out under military orders within an imperial regime.

On one hand, the destruction of war and the culture of occupation were connected to a decadence that marked a break with and a rejection of the traditional, military culture of Japan's long history. On the other, Sari Kawana shows us that the pulp fiction of *kasutori* culture represented a revival of interwar Japanese detective novels, some of which were translated and adapted from such familiar writers as Hammett, Edgar Allan Poe, Arthur Conan Doyle, and Franco-Belgian detective writer Georges Simenon.[90] Responding to the unique challenges of industrial modernization, Japanese detective fiction writers of the 1920s and 1930s self-consciously participated in an already cosmopolitan culture of modernity (and even decadence) that could, nonetheless, speak to the particularities of interwar Japan.[91] During the war, however, hard-boiled detective fiction went underground or into self-imposed exile because its decadent elements ran counter to the spirit of Japan's wartime organic nationalism, a trend that we also witnessed in Mussolini's Italy.[92] Thus, when the American films noir came to Japanese theaters during the occupation, they were not necessarily part of a different national culture so much as a reminder of a shared, translational idiom of urban experience and liberalism.

Under American-imposed censorship, Japanese directors, like their German counterparts, were expected to make films that upheld the broad reeducation program of American-style democratization in the service of creating a postwar liberal state. Directors were mandated to avoid themes that could counteract this goal. Because the Americans believed that Japan's militarism was rooted in its long feudal history and, in particular, the authoritarianism implicit in the samurai's loyalty to (and brutality in the service of) warrior lords, directors were encouraged to take up contemporary themes and plots or to pointedly undercut samurai ethics.[93] Despite US censorship, most directors felt they had more freedom during the occupation than under wartime Japanese law.[94] Given the rise of a newly energized decadent subculture and the mandates of film production under a US-oriented ideology, it is unsurprising that the first postwar Japanese noirs were produced during the occupation – at a time when the exigencies of day-to-day life and the pressures of Americanization promised to deliver forms of liberation but also raised fears of cultural erasure.

From Cesspools and Slums to Far-Fetched Amusements: Akira Kurosawa, Sam Fuller, and Carol Reed

These reeducation directives are instantiated in two films made by Akira Kurosawa during the occupation: *Yoidore tenshi/Drunken Angel* (1948), a film that subtly critiques the feudalism of the samurai code through a condemnation of contemporary Japanese yakuza (gangster) culture; and *Nora Inu/Stray Dog* (1949), which features a detective who must hunt down a small-time gangster in order to retrieve a stolen gun. Kurosawa's own initiation into film culture, a model of cosmopolitan education, provides further evidence of cinema's internationalism. Growing up in Tokyo in the 1910s and 1920s, he watched films by Charlie Chaplin, John Ford, Fritz Lang, Jean Renoir, and Sergei Eisenstein, along with Japanese auteurs including Kenji Mizoguchi, Yasurjiro Ozu, and Sadao Yamanaka.[95] Though Kurosawa had directed six feature films before 1948, he considered *Drunken Angel*, made under US military censorship, to be his first true directorial achievement. "In this picture I finally discovered myself. It was my picture."[96]

Drunken Angel's strong affinity with noir is reflected in its focus on Japan's yakuza culture. Though the yakuza gangs took root in the ubiquitous black markets of the immediate postwar period, they came to prominence in the 1930s when the emperor instituted food rations in preparation for war. Like the bootleggers and gangsters during the prohibition era in the US, the yakuza were usurious entrepreneurs in an era of scarcity. Kurosawa does not romanticize this underworld culture of protection rackets, smuggling, and decadence, but instead exposes it for its corruption and what he takes to be its outdated moral codes of loyalty to an immoral yakuza boss. But of course one could trace these yakuza codes back to the samurai culture of Japan's feudal past.

The story pits the young, tubercular yakuza Matsunaga (Toshiro Mifune), whose every move, comments Kurosawa, "reeked of flesh and blood," against the alcoholic doctor Sanada (Takashi Shimura), the "drunken angel" bent on curing the youth of both his gangsterly ways and his deathly affliction. Halfway through the film (and his treatment) Matsunaga is pulled back into the world of gangster hierarchies and self-destructive behavior when his gang boss Okada (Reisaburo Yamamoto) returns from prison and reestablishes his dominance over Tokyo's underworld. These yakuza young and old are not soldiers or former prisoners of war; they are merely the drifting thugs who have always prospered in Japan's hard times.

Shot on an elaborate studio set, Drunken Angel is spatially organized around a polluted sump that separates the rubbled slums from the thriving black market and American jazz clubs with their flashing English neon signs. As in the German rubble films that used the backdrop of ruined cities to symbolize the inner turmoil of distressed characters, the sump at Drunken Angel's center is likewise both a dump and a repository of recent Japanese history, and it serves as a symbol of Matsunaga's illness and moral decay. Moreover, as Stephen Prince notes, "if the sump is the source of the disease, it is linked to another disease, pernicious foreign influence and the loss of Japanese culture during and after the American occupation."[97] Though Americans are never seen in this film (likely owing to US military censorship), their "pernicious influence" is most pronounced in the scene where Matsunaga visits a jazz club with the evil Okada. Disregarding Dr. Sanada's orders, Matsunaga drinks, smokes, dances, and, soon after, nearly dies. But the film takes a bizarre turn in this scene when the music begins, the lights dim, and the ecstatic performer Shizuko Kasagi takes to the stage with her brass band to sing "The Jungle Boogie." Matsunaga, dappled by the reflections of the mirror ball, stumbles onto the dance floor with a girl and breaks into a frenzied jitterbug (Figure 1.6). At one point, cued by the song's "jungle" lyrics, he is inspired to ape a giant ape in his improvised dance moves. The scene trades on film noir's own racial unconscious by linking African exoticism to both American culture and a regressive human animality. As Prince argues, this scene comments "on the Americanization of Japan" and how the "disturbance of indigenous culture is killing

Matsunaga as much as the tuberculosis."[98] However, it is also a kind of homage to (and perhaps critique of) American film noir and the Hollywood musicals that were dominating Japanese screens at this point in time. If Hollywood narratives construct American criminals by associating them with foreign characters and locales, then these "foreigners" can play that game too. For Donald Richie, however, this scene is not about anti-Americanism (because the so-called "Westernization" of Japan began decades before the occupation). Rather, Matsunaga's downward spiral represents the film's existential lesson. "Though I don't think Kurosawa ever used or even heard the word [existentialism]," this scene culminates in the logic that "we don't have any personality" or core subjectivity beyond the choices we make.[99] The narrative then becomes a lesson about the failure of Matsunaga's self-determination in the face of an outmoded gang culture and despairing postwar order. By the end of the film, Matsunaga,

FIGURE 1.6 "The Jungle Boogie" (*Drunken Angel*, 1948).

already on the brink of death, expires after losing a surreally staged fight to Okada; the stunning sequence begins in an uncanny mirrored composition that recalls the famous hall-of-mirrors sequence from Orson Welles's *The Lady from Shanghai*, released the same year (Figures 1.7 and 1.8). In showing us Matsunaga's tubercular decline as connected to other forms of bodily indulgence, Kurosawa challenges the *kasutori* celebration of decadence. Almost didactically, he promotes instead a sober examination of individual will and existential freedom.

Drunken Angel taps into a noir sensibility through its representation of gang culture and the milieu of the seedy, urban, postwar underworld. Kurosawa's *Stray Dog* takes us fully into the international noir mode. Made just one year later, this film reunites *Drunken Angel*'s key actors in a police drama featuring Mifune as rookie detective Murakami, who must search Tokyo's black markets, grindhouses, and

FIGURE 1.7   Kurosawa's room of mirrors (*Drunken Angel*, 1948).

FIGURE 1.8 Welles's hall of mirrors (*The Lady from Shanghai*, 1948).

amusement parks in search of a gun stolen from his own pocket on the
city bus by a desperate ex-soldier named Yasu. Murakami's mentor,
Detective Sato (played by Shimura), tutors him in police procedure as
they hunt for the gun and take down the big yakuza boss, Honda,
played by *Drunken Angel*'s crime boss Reisaburo Yamamoto. This story
was inspired by the dramatic rise in crime abetted by shortages in food
and gainful employment in Japan, and was set in Tokyo's soon-to-be-
disbanded black market. But Kurosawa based much of the police procedure on the detective novel formula perfected by Franco-Belgian
writer Georges Simenon, whose novels were widely translated in the
1930s and adapted for the screen by several notable directors, including Jean Renoir in 1932. Rather than recreate this world in studio
sets as he had done in *Drunken Angel*, Kurosawa was reportedly
inspired to shoot on location after seeing in local theaters Jules
Dassin's American procedural noir *Naked City* (1948)[100] (itself inspired

by the documentary style of Italian neorealist films then playing in the US).[101] *Stray Dog* is a rather amazing document of a hidden and now lost Tokyo where the most desperate citizens are forced into criminal activity in order to survive. In this respect, *Stray Dog*'s themes and locations also resemble the German rubble noirs discussed above, even though it is unlikely that Kurosawa had seen these films. These influences and connections speak to the international currency of film noir (and the fiction on which it is based) as well as to the culture of occupation and liberation that gives noir a historical transnational relevance.

Prince explains that the theme that really drives *Stray Dog* is connected both to the unique circumstances of occupied Japan and to the more universal (at least in the late 1940s) question of individual responsibility in the face of moral chaos at war's end.[102] Murakami and Yusa embody postwar Japan's most troubled demographic: the returning defeated solider. Both soldiers, we learn, return from war to a city destroyed, an economy in ruins, and crime rampant, and both have their army-issue knapsacks stolen on the train ride home. Murakami responds to these events by joining the police force; Yusa enlists with the local yakuza. Victims of the same circumstances, they are differentiated by the choices they've made. But Yusa is not an evil character, especially from Murakami's perspective. The detective sees this criminal as a fellow victim of war tortured by overwhelming despair. Indeed, Kurosawa rejects the tidy binaries of good and evil, taking his cues for Yusa's character not from Simenon but from Dostoyevsky's portraits of criminality and alienation in such novels as *Crime and Punishment* and *Notes from the Underground*.[103]

At the same time, this film, like *The Murderers Are among Us*, is also quite critical of an emergent capitalist culture and its sway over weak people. It is not until the last half-hour of this two-hour film that we learn the reason why Yusa pinched Murakami's gun: so that he could steal a white sequined cocktail dress from a shop window for his girlfriend Hurami (Keiko Awaji), who now works as a dancer at a low-end cabaret. Murakami confronts Hurami in the dingy tenement flat she shares with her mother. With the incriminating dress laid out on the floor in front of her, Hurami admits to her conspiracy with Yasu (Figure 1.9). But she faults not her own appetite for expensive fashion nor Yusa's criminal means, but the culture at large. "I saw it in a shop window when we were taking a walk," she explains as she fondles the dress and averts her eyes from the camera:

> I said I wished I could have a dress that pretty just once. He [Yasu] stared at me with the saddest expression. A week later he brought it to me back-stage. . . . That's right, he committed a crime for me. But I would have stolen it myself if I'd had the guts. They deserve it for flaunting these things. We have to do worse than steal if we want things like this. It's the world's fault. A world where people steal a vet's knapsack.

While we know that a life of crime is not the only outcome for a soldier so wronged upon his homecoming (Murakami again reminds

FIGURE 1.9 Hurami's incriminating dress (*Stray Dog*, 1949).

us that he was in the same position as Yasu), Kurosawa seems to grant Hurami this point – that an emerging capitalist system creates insane desires beyond most people's means. But the power of these objects only really becomes clear a few moments later. At Murakami's request, Hurami tries on the dress. The storm that has been pending outside finally gives way to lightning, and Hurami, now dressed, finds this stolen object utterly electrifying. She twirls herself into a mad fury, declaring, "This is wonderful, so wonderful! Like a beautiful dream!" Her mother, aghast, strips the dress off, slaps her daughter down, and throws the glittering mess into the rain.

Hurami is a petulant girl to be sure. Yet she has grown up entirely in the austerity of war. She is perhaps a sign of what these new capitalist goods and consumer culture will do to Japan's youth, especially if the new market system comes too fast. Kurosawa's critique of class inequality and the eroded values under capitalism is thus implicitly a critique of the long-term consequences of Japan's war and the short-term effect of the American system. His critique will be even more forceful in his later, magnificent noir *Tengoku to jigoku / High and Low* (1963), made at the height of Japan's postwar prosperity and, significantly, based on Evan Hunter's 1959 hard-boiled American novel *King's Ransom* (written under Hunter's pseudonym Ed McBain). The point here is that, if capitalism is the bedrock of democratic liberalism and the peaceable antidote to militarist regimes, it is also what fuels criminal desire born of material inequality, as American crime novelists know all too well.

We find an interesting answer to Kurosawa's occupied Japan in Sam Fuller's noir *House of Bamboo* (1955), credited as the first Hollywood feature to be shot on location in Japan. According to James Ursini and Alain Silver, Fuller set out to make a film noir (a term that by the 1950s had critical currency) but he wanted to make it in color and CinemaScope in place of the black-and-white cinematography typically associated with these films. And, in a twist befitting our book's thesis, he wanted to make a noir in what he considered to be a "Japanese style," influenced, as he was, by the films of Kurosawa, Ozu, and Mizoguchi.[104] As in many of the noirs discussed above, Tokyo, bustling with people, is not just the backdrop to this drama; it functions as another character in the film, especially when Fuller uses long takes and crane shots to place his actors fully in the scene of everyday life and, with his Deluxe film stock, local color (Figure 1.10). But this film marks a radical departure from the Japanese films that inspired it in its representation of Americans and their culture. If Americans are absent in Kurosawa's film except through the signs (quite literally) of jazz clubs, dance halls, and a culture of commerce, Fuller's Tokyo is crawling with brutal, insensitive Americans who are the explicit source of postwar corruption and gangsterism, a source that only other Americans undercover can eradicate.

Actor Robert Ryan (known for his previous noir roles) plays the gang leader Sandy who, with his band of ex-US soldiers, has established his own black market economy in Tokyo. Eddie (Robert Stack) is an undercover US solider who arrives in Tokyo and infiltrates the gang. In the process, Eddie develops a romantic bond with Mariko (Shirley Yamaguchi), the Japanese wife of one of Sandy's fallen men. And Sandy, it seems, falls hard for Eddie, who in short order becomes his right-hand man. Taking his viewers to such diverse locales as Tokyo's many pachinko parlors, Buddhist shrines, and the boat houses and waterfront markets on the Sumida river, Fuller gives us glimpses of a complex culture over which Americans ride roughshod. A great

FIGURE 1.10   Local color and ugly American (*House of Bamboo*, 1955).

example comes in the final scene, in which Eddie works with the local police to hunt down Sandy at a rooftop amusement park perched high above the city and that features a bizarre gyrating globe of the world. With hundreds of locals inhabiting this real location – including scores of excited Japanese children – these American good guys and bad brandish their guns in their own deadly game of hide-and-seek, oblivious to the family scenes they disrupt. The Japanese authorities manage to evacuate the amusement park, but prove otherwise ineffectual, just as Eddie and Sandy begin to exchange fire. Sandy, now completely mad with rage, begins shooting directly into the Japanese crowd far below. In a series of stunning wide shots, Fuller frames his actors against the colorful Tokyo skyline until Sandy and Eddie have their final showdown on the revolving globe: two Americans, two guns, and the world spinning between them. Only Eddie alights (Figure 1.11).

This scene is not only a spectacular end to this struggle; it is, knowingly or not, a homage to the great occupation noir, Carol Reed's *The Third Man* (1949). Our main character, American pulp fiction writer Holly Martins (Joseph Cotten), finally learns that his best friend, Harry Lime (Orson Welles), has been running a penicillin racket in occupied Austria resulting in hundreds of painful deaths. After Martins has chased Lime all around this partitioned city, the two men finally

FIGURE 1.11   Global showdown (*House of Bamboo*, 1955).

meet in a Ferris wheel. At the top they look down on the sparsely populated amusement park and the rubbled city all around. Confronted with his crime, Lirne directs our attention to the tiny people below (Figure 1.12):

> Look down there. Tell me. Would you really feel any pity if one of those dots stopped moving forever? If I offered you twenty thousand [British] pounds for every dot that stopped, would you really, old man, tell me to keep my money? Or would you calculate how many dots you could afford to spend? . . . Free of income tax, old man . . . the only way you can save money nowadays.

By the end of the film, the British and American forces finally kill Lime and presumably end this medical nightmare. But it is clear that the ground in occupied Austria, Japan, and Germany is fertile for shady

FIGURE 1.12 Fascist amusements in *The Third Man* (1949).

deals and noir fantasies. In the world of American film noir, the occupation is itself a giant protection racket. Of course, the very fact that this critique could be leveled at all in these films is also a sign of noir's connection to freedom and an emerging global democracy. We might say, as Sartre did, that noir's mode of criticism is also "a manifestation of liberty."

PART III: THE TIMES OF FILM NOIR

Out of Mexico's Past

Consider the following scene of national border crossing in Warner Brothers' noir classic *Out of the Past* (Tourneur, 1947). The setting is Acapulco, Mexico, and the scene is embedded in the middle of a lengthy, subjective flashback – a hallmark of noir narration. Our narrator is Jeff Bailey (Robert Mitchum), a former private detective who, in the film's present, has moved to the small town of Bridgeport, California to escape his shady past and settle down with his girlfriend Ann (Virginia Huston). An impossibly earnest good girl, Ann listens with concern as her boyfriend reveals the story of his other, noir life as Jeff Markham – specifically, of his involvement with the murderous bad girl Kathie Moffat (Jane Greer), girlfriend of his former employer, racketeer Whit Sterling (Kirk Douglas). After discovering Markham's hiding place in Bridgeport and his new identity as the respectable owner of a local gas station, Whit has come calling for Jeff, the dead hand of the past ripping Jeff from his present domestic idyll with Ann. As he drives, Jeff tells Ann how he and Kathie first met, and fell in love, south of the border. Hired by Whit to find Kathie, who had shot Whit and fled with $40,000 of his money, Jeff tracked Kathie to sun-drenched Acapulco. There, time seemed to stop, and Jeff drowsed through his days waiting for Kathie to appear. Ann's introduction to Kathie is the viewers' own, similarly filtered through Jeff's wistful voiceover:

> Near the plaza was a little café called La Mar Azul, next to a movie house.
> I sat there in the afternoons and drank beer. I used to sit there half asleep
> with the beer and the darkness, only the music from the movie next door
> kept jarring me awake. And then I saw her, coming out of the sun. And I
> knew why Whit didn't care about that forty grand.

The scene's powerful romanticism depends not just on Jeff's nostalgic memory of this first encounter, but on the specific Mexican staging. In this film, "Mexico" connotes for Jeff a past fullness of desire and
feeling that probably never existed in the first place. Aurally, Jeff's
approach to La Mar Azul is cued by the jaunty strains of local, and
seemingly diegetic, "Mexican" music. Visually, Tourneur frames Jeff's
entrance to the café by the "Cine Pico" behind him, by the picturesque
peasant woman he passes on the sidewalk outside, hawking street
food, and by the inevitable tout lounging in the doorway (Figure
1.13). Momentarily, José Rodriguez, this "most excellent guide," will
interrupt the lovers' first meeting to cycle through his wares before
disappearing when Jeff buys a cheap pair of earrings. The salad days of
Jeff and Kathie's short-lived romance will play out against the backdrop of such familiar Hollywood signifiers of "Mexicanness" – not
historical Mexico itself so much as an imaginary national space of
romantic longing for the film's alienated protagonists. Kathie herself
makes this clear when, at the end of her first meeting with Jeff, she
suggests, "If it gets too lonely there's a little cantina down the street
called Pablo's. It's nice and quiet. A man there plays American music for
a dollar. You can sip bourbon and shut your eyes. It's like a little place
on 56th Street. I sometimes go there." Like Jeff, half asleep in the darkness of La Mar Azul when Kathie appears, materializing as if from a
dream, so is displaced Kathie dreaming of her American home in the
sleepy silence of a Mexican bar. The symbolic space of Mexico allows
the lovers to imagine briefly that their alienation is overcome and their
desires fulfilled in a sunnier, more sentimental climate.

But this lost plenitude is a kind of fantasy, a fact confirmed by
Kathie's eventual betrayal of Jeff and by *Out of the Past*'s self-conscious

FIGURE 1.13   "Cine Pico" (*Out of the Past*, 1947).

reference in this scene to the movies themselves. Set under the neon
sign of the "Cine Pico," the lovers' ill-fated first meeting in Mexico is
not something just out of the past, but also out of the movies.
Hollywood film noir's fondness for Latin American locales was first
evident in the Rita Hayworth star-vehicle *Gilda* (1946), a film in
which Hayworth's alluring, fatal sexuality is virtually synonymous
with the "exotic" Buenos Aires nightclub where she sings and dances.
As we'll see, the terms of *Gilda*'s threatening otherness could be easily
reversed in different contexts of reception: in Italy and Spain, *Gilda*
would signify not the romantic danger of points southward but rather
Hollywood's postwar dominance and the spread of a decadent
American democracy. In Hollywood, the trend for Latin American
locales continued through the 1940s and 1950s in films like *Notorious*
(1946), *Border Incident* (1949), *Where Danger Lives* (1950), *His Kind of
Woman* (1951), and *Touch of Evil* (1958). As James Naremore explains,

there were ample political and economic reasons for Hollywood noir's many trips south of the US border: "Hollywood's support for the Roosevelt government's 'Good Neighbor' policy; the postwar topicality of stories about Nazi refugees in Argentina; the RKO-Rockefeller interests in Western Hemisphere oil fields; the general importance of Latin America as an export market, and so on."[105] Further, this Latin American staging, Naremore continues, deployed a familiar symbolic shorthand, in which the Latin world "is nearly always associated with a frustrated desire for romance and freedom; again and again, it holds out the elusive, ironic promise of a warmth and color that will countervail the dark mise-en-scéne and the taut, restricted coolness of the average noir protagonist."[106] In the case of *Out of the Past*, unreal "Mexico" is positioned in relation to two other space-times in the film: the chaotic and murderous world of urban modernity, represented by San Francisco, whose dangers are embodied in Kathie's sex appeal; and the more "natural" world of the American small town, which seems simpler and safer, but is also more restrictive, pious and, well, *boring*, and is incarnated by fresh-scrubbed Ann.

Torn between these spaces and the women that represent them, Jeff experiences an acutely modern psychic disjuncture – a crisis of time common to many noir protagonists. The dangers of urban modernity are never fully past for him, but keep forcing themselves into the present, while the promise of small-town domestic security (also gendered female) is never fully present. Instead, as in many postwar American films, the lure of folksy homeliness is haunted by a traumatic past and may, like Mexico, itself be another vanished ideal.[107] Mexico, in *Out of the Past* and in other Hollywood films noir, is a kind of existential balm to time's wound because it is positioned as *outside* of time: dreamy, sleepy, or otherwise fantastic rather than the site of lived, historical experience. Mexico's time is that of neither the modern city nor the small-town, rural existence that, developmentally speaking, preceded it and only barely manages to keep the menace of the city at bay, as the film's opening montage makes clear. Rather,

Mexico is consigned to a much more distant, primitive premodernity – a fantastic space of timelessness.

On the one hand, then, the film's narrative movement challenges a notion of temporal progression, since Jeff is blocked from moving easily from past, to present, to future. On the other, *Out of the Past* assumes a familiar developmental model for understanding modern temporality that has dominated accounts of modernity. While global film noir responds to the broader social-historical condition of modernity, modernization itself doesn't happen across nations at the same time. Nor does it pose identical threats to more traditional forms of cultural and political life or spawn the same anxious visions of the future. Instead, scholars today tend to understand global modernization as a complex process of uneven development, in which nations and societies modernize at different speeds and intensities, and under different political pressures. In the process, these nations suffer varying degrees of trauma as traditional systems of social life, economic production, and political organization are overthrown or transformed to make way for modern ones. In general, scholarly debates about the global spread of modernity depend upon a developmental timeline. On it, mature industrial powers like the United States, Great Britain, and France are positioned as fully "advanced" or "modern," having joined capitalist modernization to stable, liberal-democratic politics. Slightly behind them are "late-developing" nations like Italy, Germany, and Japan, countries that underwent very rapid, state-sponsored economic modernization in the first half of the twentieth century, often without the mediating force of liberal democracy, and hosted fascist political regimes. Bringing up the rear are the sadly "underdeveloped" nation-states from Europe's former imperial periphery in Asia, Africa, and Latin America. Such nations, like Mexico, have slowly emerged out of the past and into economic independence after centuries of colonial exploitation.

This developmental model is flawed for several reasons. most obviously, it assumes that "normal" social development happens along the timeline of the West. Measured by this single temporal yardstick, some nations are fully modern, while others are "latecomers" whose hasty modernization led to the political aberrations of fascism and socialism rather than proper liberal democracy. Still others, often formerly colonized nations without the economic means to "catch up," are consigned to the sphere of timelessness, left, like La Mar Azul, out of the world's inevitable march to modernity. Additionally, this model flattens time within nations, refusing to see the unevenness of development within societies and nations themselves, in which modern and traditional modes of social and economic organization exist in complex, hybrid combinations. Whereas liberal-democratic proponents of this developmental model posit the happy global evolution toward an ideal order in which citizens of all modern nations share economic prosperity, individual rights, and democratic freedoms, critics of this model – especially Marxist critics – hold that capitalistic modernization inevitably works to *produce such unevenness* between and within societies, which becomes apparent in disparities in wealth and class antagonism. If the promise of the liberal view of modernization is a future in which uneven development is overcome, the Marxist riposte is that perpetual unevenness is "simply the truth of capitalist development."[108]

As we've argued, film noir is particularly attuned to this dark truth, emerging in response to the world-wide trauma of the Great Depression, when the promises of stable capitalist development rang especially hollow. Similarly, the culture of political occupation that proved so hospitable to films noir also involved a radical resetting of modernity's clock for the citizens of World War II's newly berubbled nations. Starting over in "year zero," the defeated Germans and Japanese – late arrivals to economic modernity in the first place – would rapidly re-modernize their industries under the aegis of the United States' Marshall Plan, which joined consumer and political freedoms with uneven results. This time, however, European economic modernization would be joined forcibly to the path of liberal democracy, and set to America's watch. For these reasons, in the postwar period that is film noir's heyday, the distance from or proximity to American-style modernity became a matter of pressing political, economic, cultural concern across the globe. And this was true not just for the devastated industrial nations of the Axis powers, forced to become modern again in a new "American age," but also for "late-developing" or "underdeveloped" countries on the margins of the war's theater – nations like Mexico, Spain, and India. It should therefore come as little surprise that these countries have films noir too.

Films noir from Mexico, Spain, Italy, India, Iran, and Hong Kong use the noir idiom to offer local reflections on the uneven development of modernity as a global force in the twentieth century. Such historical differences force us to reconsider how critics have categorized the times of film noir itself – how and why we divide the aesthetic phenomenon of film noir into specific periods (e.g., "classical" or "historical" noir vs. "neo"-noir) with clear points of origin or ending. Given the sheer range of films that have linked a noir sensibility to a form of historical or aesthetic "modernity," what, if anything, makes "neo-noir" particularly new? In many ways, noir has always been both new and old, never entirely progressive or reactionary. The many times of film noir thus present a challenge to the postwar geo-political order in which "modernity" came to be associated solely with the progressive time of American capitalism and its twinned promises of free markets and political democracy.

If *Out of the Past*'s "Cine Pico" were an actual theatre in Acapulco rather than a romantic fiction of a Hollywood studio, what movies might have played there? It could very well have been an American film noir like *Laura* or *Double Indemnity*. But, in 1947, Jeff was also more likely than ever before to have seen a Mexican genre flick – a *comedia ranchera* (ranch or rural comedy), a family melodrama, a revolutionary epic, or, given what we know of Jeff's thing for urban bad girls, a *cabaretera* (cabaret/brothel) musical, a genre with decidedly noir elements. This is so because Mexico's national cinema, like the nation itself, was in the throes of intense, state-sponsored industrial development in the late 1940s. Since the early 1920s, the Mexican film industry, like much of the world, had been forced to contend with the global dominance of Hollywood, which had conquered foreign markets in the wake of World War I and established itself as the industrial vanguard of cinema. In the immediate aftermath of the Mexican Revolution (1910–1920), which overthrew the last in a series of repressive dictatorships that had governed Mexico since its independence from Europe in 1867, Mexico was the leading Latin American consumer of Hollywood's product. However, sparked by Hollywood's brief decline in Latin American markets following the coming of sound, the Mexican industry grew rapidly in the 1930s. Its first state-sponsored film studio was created in 1935, and in 1936 it had its first bona fide international smash – Fernando de Fuentes's *comedia ranchera Allá en el Rancho Grande/Over at the Big Ranch*. By 1947, then, Mexican cinema was at the height of its so-called "Golden Age," an era that saw a precipitous rise in film production aided, in no small part, by the founding in 1942 of the Banco Cinematográfico, a bank devoted solely to funding national film production and by distribution, and by Mexico's advantageous geo-political position during World War II. Critics disagree about when exactly the Golden Age began and ended, but they concur on its fruits: the emergence of a bankable star system and the consolidation of a genre-based national cinema consisting of state-sponsored features that successfully competed with Hollywood fare in Latin American markets.

Most importantly for our purposes, Mexico's flourishing cinema of the 1940s and early 1950s was enabled by, and negotiated, a period of explosive modernization spearheaded by the economic policies of President Miguel Alemán (1946–1952). An energetic cheerleader for "modern" development, Alemán repealed the agrarian subsidies of his predecessor, and chose to fund instead a sweeping program of urbanization that expanded infrastructure and manufacturing, but also exacerbated disparities in wealth between the commercial and lower classes. Aided by the US and other capitalist countries, the pro-business, pro-industrial development policies of so-called *alemanismo* led to one of the most important and traumatic demographic shifts in modern Mexican history – the mass migration of uneducated rural peasants from the countryside to Mexico's swelling cities. A prime example of modernity's processes of disembedding, this massive demographic upheaval also entailed a broader ideological transformation as the kinds of traditionally "Mexican" values and social roles often championed in post-revolutionary popular culture were challenged by the new urban realities of a postwar economy, a climate that also proved germane to the phenomenon of film noir in Italy and Spain, as we'll see. While genres like the *comedia ranchera* tended to be anti-modern, reinforcing traditional values under the pressure of modernization, other genres, especially the *cabaretera* film and the *cine de arrabal* (slum film), spoke directly to the "new restlessness" of urban Mexican society and its potential threat to traditional social values.[109] The *cabaretera* musicals – city films set in cabarets, nightclubs, or brothels – featured scrappy, ill-fated young women forced by circumstance into careers combing singing, dancing, and prostitution. Another form of urban melodrama, the *cine de arrabal* film, consisted of heartwarming, largely sentimental tales about the noble poverty and neighborhood values of Mexico's disenfranchised ghetto dwellers.

The *cabaretera* and *arrabal*'s shared generic investment in the dilemmas of a rapidly modernizing nation begins to suggest how Mexico's national cinema in the late 1940s had become "classical" and "modern" at once. How do we account for this paradoxical temporality? Like classical Hollywood, Golden Age Mexican cinema had evolved into a stable, genre-based mode of production united by a series of familiar stylistic norms, norms that hewed close to Hollywood's perfected continuity system. At the same time, as Miriam Hansen argues, the American classical system that Mexico appropriated and adapted was perceived, not just in Mexico but in "modernizing capitals all over the world," as "the incarnation of *the modern*."[110] Hollywood genre cinema was understood as modern, Hansen continues, because its industrial mode of production was perceived as a symptom of Western technological and cultural modernity. More importantly, though, Hollywood was modern because it provided, both at home and abroad, "the single most inclusive cultural horizon in which the traumatic effects of modernity were reflected, rejected or disavowed, transmuted or negotiated."[111] By circulating genres that appealed to spectators on a bodily level (adventure serials, melodramas, detective films, slapstick comedies), Hollywood schooled its global audiences in the dynamics of modernity on a sensory, affective level. Slapstick comedies, for example, allowed audiences to engage playfully with the threats of modern mechanization to the human body, or to experiment with new modes of sexuality, gender, or intimacy. By taking up, in various generic forms, the sensory experience of modernization as its content, Hollywood cinema functioned as a form of "vernacular modernism" that helped to establish its global dominance and international appeal.[112]

Hansen's influential thesis invites us to consider how film noir itself might operate, in Mexico and in a range of unevenly developing nations, as a kind of vernacular modernism that evolved "in relationship to American – and other foreign – models while drawing on and transforming" local aesthetic traditions.[113] In the case of Mexico, we can see how a noir sensibility might operate as a vernacular modernism by briefly considering two films of the Golden Age, both released in 1950: Alberto Gout's *cabaretera* classic *Aventurera* and Luis Buñuel's *Los Olvidados / The Young and the Damned*, a decidedly noir twist on the *arrabalera* genre. While taking up some of the same modern problems and dynamics, the films refashion the emotional appeal of melodrama – a genre with a long Mexican tradition – to produce strikingly modernist engagements with Mexican modernity and midcentury national culture.

The plotting of Gout's *Aventurera* is quick, complex, and filled with bizarre twists of fate whose very excesses are central to the film's melodramatic effect. The film's protagonist is Elena (Ninón Sevilla), a perky, impulsive teenager from a seemingly proper bourgeois family. Elena's stable home life is thrown into disarray early in the film when her mother's affair with the family lawyer leads to her father's suicide. Blaming her mother for her father's death, Elena leaves home, seeking employment in a cold, modern city, where she eventually finds work as a prostitute and performer at the cabaret of Dona Rosaura (Andrea Palma). Elena escapes to another city and another cabaret. There, she meets and becomes engaged to Mario (Ruben Rojo), a handsome lawyer and a scion of one of Guadalajara's most prominent families. However, in the film's central twist, Elena meets her future mother-in-law, who turns out to be none other than Dona Rosaura herself – a high-society matriarch who moonlights as a Ciudad Juarez madam. During the rest of the film, Elena exacts her revenge on Dona Rosaura by marrying Mario, seducing his younger brother, threatening to expose Rosaura's "other" life, and generally making a spectacle of herself and a mockery of Rosaura's propriety. In the film's final noir sequence, Rosaura's cruel henchman Rengo (Miguel Inclán) kills Lucio (Tito Junco), Elena's evil ex-boyfriend, with a well-thrown knife (Figure 1.14), and looks on

FIGURE 1.14 Henchman *ex machina* (*Aventurera*, 1950).

with sentimental approval as Elena and Mario kiss on a shadowy street.

The many pleasures of *Aventurera* come from its dizzying reversals of fortune, and from the abrupt oscillations between moral virtue and villainy – all of which have been a staple of theatrical melodrama since the nineteenth century. In Mexico, melodrama emerged with the coming of sound as the dominant cinematic form, and was typified by the kind of generic hybridity we see in *Aventurera*'s delirious hash of family melodrama, musical, and film noir.[114] However, as Ana López explains, Mexican melodrama's characteristic hybridity and excess must also be understood as formal, industrial defense against the colonization of Latin American markets by Hollywood genre films. Mexican cinema was imitating Hollywood genres, to be sure, but also mixing and reappropriating them, inflecting them with local and national idioms. Melodrama's very excess and exaggeration – its tendency to accrue and blend alien forms and styles – became, "in the Mexican case, a way of cinematically working through the problematic of an undeveloped national cinema."[115] At the same time, melodrama's typically exaggerated distinctions between good and evil have generally been understood as a conservative aesthetic response to a world in which "the traditional imperatives of truth and ethics have been violently thrown into question."[116] Here, then, we can begin to sense the national appeal of melodramatic moral certitude in Mexico's post-revolutionary period of rapid modernization and its many challenges to traditional Mexican life and its domestic anchor – the patriarchal family.

Aventurera, however, offers no such certitudes. Its noir subversiveness comes from the way its very emotional and narrative excess blurs clear moral and social distinctions. Instead, Elena's exuberant movement through Mexican society points to a world of restless, unsettled desires and unfixed social categories and conventions. As in much Mexican melodrama, *Aventurera* renders the conflict between traditional, patriarchal social life and modern decadence in a spatial opposition between the private space of the home, prone to patriarchal repression, and the public world of urban modernity, epitomized by the hedonistic pleasures of the cabaret-brothel. However, *Aventurera*'s central irony – that the loving, long-suffering mother is also the shrewd brothel businesswoman – collapses the distinction between respectable domestic life and a modern, public world that trades in sex for money. Begging Elena not to shatter her sweet, liberal son Mario's fantasy of his mom, Rosaura explains: "I'm a mother who's sacrificed everything for her son. . . . My business dealings have not been clean, but at least I've fulfilled my obligations as a mother." Such moments, like the sheer ridiculousness of the plotting, render conventional assumptions about familial behavior absurd, showing that their pressure in fact produces Rosaura's perverse double life. Gout's clever casting of Andrea Palma only compounds the absurdity of Rosaura's sham dignity, despite Mario's characterization of his mother as an "old-fashioned" woman who "rarely travels," only going occasionally to the US on business. Palma, a cosmopolitan actress who worked in Hollywood in the 1930s, was famous from her breakthrough role as a tragic prostitute in *La mujer del puerto/Woman of the Port* (1933), one of a host of Mexican films that used the fallen woman as an emblem of modernity and a challenge to the vanished moral order of Porfirio Díaz, Mexico's pre-revolutionary dictator. In other words, *Aventurera*'s audiences knew that this "good" mother was always already bad, corrupted by foreign influences.

Elena's revenge, then, is to prove how the traditional Mexican family is perverse at heart. We also see this truth in her own mother's sexual infidelity, in the absence of fathers in the film, or in Rosaura's bored son Ricardo's preference for Elena's havoc and fit-throwing over the comforts of class purity: "She may not be of our class," Ricardo observes, "but she's a lot more fun!" Also enjoying such extravagance, French film critic and future New Wave director François Truffaut wrote of Sevilla's performance in 1954, "From now on we must take note of Ninón Sevilla. . . . From her inflamed look to her fiery mouth everything is heightened in Ninón (her forehead, her lashes, her nose, her upper lip, her throat, her voice). . . . Like so many missed arrows, [she is an] oblique challenge to bourgeois, Catholic, and other moralities."[117] So much of the film's energy, Truffaut noticed, hinges on Sevilla's delightful performance as Elena, whose explosive tantrums and irreverent caprices make the film such fun. And much of this fun is that it is, like Elena's "oblique" desire, beyond good and evil. In this sense, *Aventurera*'s melodrama can be said to become acutely noir, and noir, which we've tended to discuss in its bleaker registers, can itself become the stuff of subversive enjoyment. As James Naremore has argued, Hollywood film noir is itself both "a type of commercial melodrama" prone to clear, conservative distinctions between good and evil, and "a type of modernism," characterized by modern moral and ethical ambiguities. If, as we've suggested, *Aventurera* is a work of vernacular modernism, and vernacular modernism plays chiefly on the senses, we can see this most obviously in the way the film's own dizzying extremes of emotion are set to the irregular, whimsical beat of Elena's desire, which eschews conventional morality, or stands it on its head, or sets it along what, in the film's final sequence, she calls her own "road to perversion."

The film is at once *about* the excesses of desire and feeling unbound from traditional social norms in the character of Elena and itself *enacts* this emotional play in its intoxicating shifts in plot, style, and tone. In this sense, we might begin to observe parallels between Sevilla's extravagant dance numbers in *Aventurera*, in which she dons and doffs a variety of exotic costumes (Egyptian, Martiniquan, etc.), and the film's own performance of Hollywood genre conventions, among them the more familiar visual style of film noir. Elena's brief stint as Lucio's wheel man during the jewel heist, when the plotting and visual style shift into a noir mode, is as much a kind of ethnic drag as her outrageous Chiquita Banana outfit. Sevilla herself was not Mexican, but a Cuban who became famous for her own exotic "foreignness," and specifically as a dancer of rumberas – musical numbers incorporating a mixture of Afro-Caribbean rhythms. Films like *Aventurera* made Sevilla synonymous with a kind of worldly, decadent eroticism unmoored from local, national, or traditional rhythms

FIGURE 1.15   Sevilla's cosmopolitan style (*Aventurera*, 1950).

(Figure 1.15). On another level, of course, the same could be said for *Aventurera*'s own hybrid visual style, in which the familiar trappings of Hollywood film noir becomes another foreign sign of worldliness within a rapidly modernizing national cinema. Already in *Aventurera*, film noir operates as a cosmopolitan signifier of style.

Made by an established avant-garde director, Luis Buñuel's *Los Olividados* (1950) earns its credentials as a noir work of vernacular modernism rather more directly than *Aventurera*, although it too is preoccupied with Mexican modernization, generically hybrid, and critical of melodramatic codes. In the interwar period, Buñuel was at the center of international modernism in Paris, and directly associated with the French surrealist group. There, working with fellow Spaniard Salvador Dalí, Buñuel made the two first unimpeachable masterpieces of cinematic surrealism, *Un chien andalou*/*An Andalusian Dog* (1929) and *L'Âge d'or*/*The Golden Age* (1930). In the 1940s and 1950s, however,

Buñuel was a political exile from General Francisco Franco's fascist Spain. Under these circumstances, this radical artist became a commercially and critically successful director in the Mexican film industry, producing a series of subversive films that married modernist experimentation with popular appeal. Buñuel's noir efforts in the Mexican industry include not just *Los Olvidados* but also *Él* (1952), an anatomy of male paranoia and violence that masquerades as a woman's melodrama, and *La Vida Criminal de Archibaldo de la Cruz/The Criminal Life of Archibaldo de la Cruz* (1955), a witty study of a decadent, homicidal aristocrat who manages the childhood trauma of the Mexican revolution through a series of fetishes, including, famously, a mannequin of one of his potential victims.

Buñuel's exilic status within the Mexican industry fueled a complex noir vision equally critical of the modernity of *alemanismo* and the traditional nationalist myths of patriarchal Mexico. As with the German exiles often associated with film noir, some of whose American work was inflected with the visual style of continental avant-gardes (e.g., German expressionism), Buñuel's noir aesthetic was informed by his thorough familiarity with both Mexican and Hollywood commercial genre cinema and his surrealist fascination with the subversive power of unconscious desire – a force hostile not just to generic codes but to social conventions writ large. Recall that it was just this kind of irrational break with Hollywood's melodramatic business as usual that postwar French critics, some historically connected to surrealism, saw in the "oneiric, strange, erotic, ambivalent, and cruel" qualities of those American movies it labeled "film noir."[118] Hollywood film noir, then, was for French critics like Borde and Chaumeton a kind of unintentional surrealism operating in popular culture. But surrealism was also a willful activity and, as Buñuel's case testifies, the more schooled the surrealist in popular generic codes – and their forms of emotional manipulation – the more fantastic and shocking his formal disruptions of them.

Generally regarded as the first great film of Buñuel's "Mexican phase," *Los Olvidados* is set in the squalid, impoverished slums of postwar Mexico City. An unruly mix of cinematic codes from a variety of national and international contexts, Los Olvidados's stylistic hybridity is a product of broader transnational dynamics – here, those afforded to Buñuel by virtue of his own exile and his work as a journeyman in the film industry's networks of international distribution. As Marsha Kinder argues, between his first French surrealist films and his postwar Mexican period Buñuel mastered the conventions of the sound film, "particularly within the flexible international genre of melodrama."[119] This tutelage began during Buñuel's first trip to Hollywood in 1930, and continued throughout the 1930s and mid-1940s, when he worked first dubbing American films for Paramount in Paris and Warner Brothers in Madrid, and later as a documentary editor at the Museum of Modern Art in New York, producing dubbed and reedited versions of Hollywood features for the Mexican market. Thus, when Buñuel set out to make Los Olvidados as a "documentary" about the horrid conditions of Mexico City's ghettos, he did so with a thorough familiarity not only with the codes of documentary and Hollywood melodrama (which necessarily included what the French had just invented as Hollywood "film noir"), but also with the more specific forms of Mexican melodrama like the cine de arrabal, as well as the conventions of Italian neorealism. Neorealism's wild international success in the immediate postwar years directly influenced the arrabalera, and helped spark the vogue for Mexican films about juvenile delinquency. In fact, Buñuel's producer came to him with the idea for Los Olvidados inspired by the authenticity of Vittorio De Sica's neorealist Seiuscià/Shoeshine (1946), and emboldened by the financial success of Ismael Rodríguez's Nosotros los Pobres/ We the Poor (1948), an arrabalera box-office smash influenced by both Italian neorealism and American film noir.[120] In 1950, melodramatic films about poor but lovable urchins were hot properties around the world. This disgusted Buñuel, who described Los Olvidados's unusual documentary quality as an attempt "to expose the condition of the poor in real terms, because I loathe films that make the poor romantic and sweet."[121]

The intensely ironic and ambivalent qualities of this noir "documentary" emerge in the film's preface, which begins with the written claim, superimposed on the still image of a darkened, but clearly fictional, slum, that "the film is based on true facts. No character is fictional." The vexed appeal to authenticity is followed by a brief montage of iconic (canned) images of Western cosmopolitan cities (the Manhattan skyline, the Eiffel Tower, London's Big Ben, and the sprawling plazas of Mexico City). The sequence is accompanied by the following voiceover:

> The great modern cities of the world – London, Paris, New York – hide, behind their wealth, poverty-stricken homes, where poorly fed children, deprived of health or school, are doomed to criminality. Society tries to find a cure. Success for its efforts remains very limited. The future is not bound to the present. The day will come when children's rights are respected, so that they can be useful to society. Mexico [City], a large modern city, is no exception to this universal rule. The film shows real life. It is not optimistic. The solution to this problem is left to the forces of progress.

The curious opening does several things at once: it codes its tale of disadvantaged youth as a documentary, it situates Mexico within a global community of modern cities that share Mexico's problem, and it cynically appeals to the logic of modern progress upon which urban development depends. Notice how the voiceover feigns sympathy with abstract "society": it acknowledges that the problem of great disparities in wealth is endemic to the growth of modern cities the world over, and, while eschewing optimism, insists that "the day will come" when the so-called "forces of progress" will solve the problem they themselves have created. In sum, the voiceover pitches a distant, happier future for Mexico City's children, a future "not bound to the present." And yet the logic seems shaky at best. If modern progress breeds poverty and crime as well as wealth, why would more progress eventually eliminate these ills? Might acknowledging poverty as a "universal rule" of modern life actually breed social complacency, a satisfaction in society's good intentions, despite its limited success? And what of the call to honor children's rights "so that they can be useful to society"? Does society's granting of human rights to its citizens require compensation in the form of social utility? Are children resources to be used efficiently and not wasted? Undercutting his "documentary" voiceover with irony and ambivalence, Buñuel's film mocks the cheerleaders of modern progress from the jump.

The film's brutal plot underscores its prefatory cynicism about Mexico's better future. While the underdeveloped slums of Mexico City are the film's real protagonist, Los Olvidados focuses its image of urban wretchedness through the human example of Pedro (Alfonso Mejía). A moon-faced twelve-year-old boy, Pedro subsists meagerly on his single mother's occasional love and food, and on a life of petty crime in a hard-scrabbled gang of adolescent toughs led by Jaibo (Roberto Cobo), older, wiser, and clearly sociopathic. When the film opens, Jaibo assumes his place as the leader of the gang after a yearlong stint in prison, proving his dominance by brutally killing Julian, a former member of the gang whose snitching Jaibo blames for his jailtime. While less far gone than Jaibo, Pedro is no angel either. And, as he is a witness and partial accomplice to Julian's murder, Pedro's efforts to be a good boy are stymied by irrational forces beyond his control, incarnated in the actions of the malevolent Jaibo, whose most stinging betrayal is the seduction of Pedro's mother (Estela Inda). Ultimately, the good feelings of society's "progressive forces" prove impotent in this film, and the liberal reform of wayward Pedro ends in disaster: Pedro is murdered by Jaibo, his corpse unceremoniously dumped in a trash heap, and Jaibo is shot and killed by the police.

The trappings of progress glimpsed in the film conceal the truth of waste and loss. This, the cruelest irony of Los Olvidados, plays out in its central juxtaposition between the telltale signs of Alemán's efforts at modern development and the arrested development of Pedro and Mexico City's other forgotten children, whose daily lives are defined by irrationality, fear, violence, non-productivity, and waste – precisely the forces modernity hopes to eliminate. The signs of alemanismo are everywhere in the film, perhaps most obviously in the character of "Los Ojitos," the indigenous peasant boy, dumped by his father in the marketplace. Standing in for the broader disembedding of Mexico's rural poor from the countryside to its urban centers in the 1940s, "Los Ojitos" also points to the subsistence of the premodern within Mexican "modernity." Underfed, he drinks milk directly from the udders of a cow. Superstitious, he carries a talismanic dead-man's tooth as protection against the evils of the city. Bereft of family, his labor is quickly exploited by another relic of an earlier time, Don Carmelo, a blind beggar and street performer who performs folk cures with dead pigeons and is consumed by nostalgia for the dictatorship of Porfirio Díaz.

Amidst a city in the throes of modernization, Los Ojitos and Don Carmelo are holdovers of other times and other modes of social organization – "in my general's day," Don Carmelo notes, "grown-ups were respected" and "criminals were shot." And yet Buñuel clearly has no truck with Don Carmelo's appeals to past forms of patriarchal authoritarian behavior to cure present ills. So, while we learn that Pedro and Jaibo never knew their fathers, and that Julian's dad is a drunk, Buñuel refuses to lay the blame for Mexico's wayward young on deadbeat dads, unloving moms, or bleeding-heart liberal politicians. The film seems as dissatisfied with Don Carmelo's reactionary calls for a return to the simpler times of brute dictatorial violence as he is with the liberal pieties of the farm-school superintendent that, "deprived of affection, children look for it anywhere," or that Pedro, like all people, just needs snacks and sweetness: "Give him food. People are better after they've eaten." Clearly unloved, Jaibo isn't looking for nurturing, but sex, violence, and the thrill of his daily struggle for survival. For Jaibo, the sentimental cliché of the orphaned boy pining for the maternal milk of human kindness is a convenient line to bed Pedro's mom. Similarly, although the school superintendent's gifts to Pedro of food and trust do seem briefly to make him better, they also put him back on the street to be victimized and killed by Jaibo. The arrested development of these children is a temporal dilemma common to noir protagonists – to be trapped between a vanished past and an equally impossible future. Thus is the hopeful fiction of liberal voiceover betrayed by the brutal facts of daily life that seems anything but "modern."

Stuck in the irrational present of the film, there is mostly inhuman cruelty and animal violence. The most stunning contrast between the promise of future development and the brutal realities of the present appears in the famous staging of Julian's murder. Seeking revenge, Jaibo gets Pedro to lure Julian from his productive day job as a construction worker. Feigning an injured arm, Jaibo confronts Julian, and accuses him of ratting him out, a charge Julian denies before attempting to walk away. When Julian's back is turned, Jaibo removes a large rock from his sling, smashes it against Julian's head, and then beats him savagely with a tree branch. The brutality is shocking, but stranger still is Buñuel's surreal staging of the killing against the backdrop of a ghostly high-rise building, the architectural promise of Mexico's modern future, and a gigantic weeping willow (Figure 1.16). The mise-en-scène shocks in quintessentially surrealist fashion, maximizing incongruity within the image by juxtaposing indifferent culture and emotional nature, urban futurity and the end of life, human progress and the regressive qualities of violence. The emotional payoff of such contradictions is our sense of the irrational incoherence of "reality" itself. In this scene, and in the more obviously fantastic sequences in the film (Pedro's dream, or Jaibo's dying vision), Buñuel stakes out his ideological opposition to neorealism. The problem with the "neorealist tendency," Buñuel later explained, was that its "reality is partial, official, above all reasonable; but poetry, mystery, are absolutely lacking in it. If it were possible for me, I would make films which, apart from entertaining the audience, would convey to them the absolute certainty that they DO NOT LIVE IN THE BEST OF ALL POSSIBLE WORLDS."[122]

The scene's affective uncertainty also exemplifies the way its violence disrupts our emotional responses to the film's events. *Los Olvidados*'s refusal to sentimentalize youth, so obvious in this cruel

FIGURE 1.16 Arrested development (*Los Olvidados*, 1950).

scene, is also clear in the way such violence is in fact pervasive in the film. Isolated from the rest of the film, we might easily read this scene as an indictment of Jaibo's evil nature. But, in fact, all of the film's characters are prone to brutality: even sweet, orphaned "Ojitos" momentarily contemplates braining Don Carmelo with a rock, an uncanny echo of Jaibo's act. Such irruptions challenge our tendency to sympathize with these characters, as does Buñuel's consistent equation between the conditions of slum dwellers and the lives of animals. Rather than noble or dignified, poverty in Los Olvidados is base and dehumanizing. In this sense, the sensory dimension of Los Olvidados's vernacular modernism lies in its refusal of the conventions of melodramatic feeling. Unlike Hollywood melodrama, the film doesn't allow our sentiments to settle into clear moral binaries of good and evil. If the Mexican *arrabalera* offered viewers noble, happy, and often singing poor folks, Los Olvidados's protagonists are much more likely to erupt in violence than song. And, whereas neorealism's famous humanism would cultivate spectators' sympathy with the simple being of people – and reality itself – as they freely exist, Buñuel's noir modernism opts for strategic dehumanization and explores the pervasive unreality of "modern" Mexican life. By using irony and disorientation to block melodrama's more familiar emotional paths, and by refusing an ending that would either warm our liberal hearts by making the reality of the poor our own, or cathartically purge our feelings of sadness, the stalled, uncertain emotions of Los Olvidados suit its parable of non-development. And so, while stylistically and generically hybrid, the film achieves what, just five years later, Borde and Chaumeton would describe as film noir's "consistency of an emotional sort; namely, the state of tension created in the spectators by the disappearance of their psychological bearings."[123]

From Neorealism Nero *to Antonioni's Noir Modernism*

Vittorio De Sica's canonical neorealist feature Ladri di biciclette/The Bicycle Thief (1948) has the main character, Ricci (Lamberto Maggiorani), learning how to hang posters on street kiosks in impoverished postwar Rome, a job he desperately needs to feed his family. Ricci watches his coworker's technique: over a poster for Italy's national water polo team, the man pastes an image of Rita Hayworth's voluptuous body in a huge ad promoting the American noir Gilda. Marsha Kinder argues that this reference to American cinema sets up a contrast between the neorealist commitment to "document and analyze" the plight of Italy's working class during this period of national crises and "Hollywood's lucrative escape into the pleasurable excesses of spectacle, melodrama, and stardom."[124] Yet Gilda is not just any Hollywood movie, but a film noir about the corrupting forces of wealth and corporate greed, even as it features the ever-alluring Rita Hayworth in one of her most controversial roles. Were we to peel another layer off this kiosk we might find an image of Visconti's Ossessione, which, based on the Cain novel, had only limited play under fascist rule. Thus, another reading of this *Bicycle Thief* scene presents itself. Perhaps this is not a wholesale critique of Hollywood, so much as an unwitting announcement that film noir, which in an important sense emerged with neorealism in *Ossessione*, has come back to Italy with the defeat of Mussolini.

As neorealism coalesced into a distinct movement involving on-location shooting, non-professional actors, and a left-leaning sociological observation of working-class life, Italian neorealism *nero* (black neorealism) turned on a darker visual style and melodramatic plotting. Alberto Lattuada's *Il bandito/The Bandit* (1946) and *Senza pietá/Without Pity* (1948), as well as Giorgio Ferroni's *Tombolo, paradiso nero/Black Paradise* (1947), dramatized in the noir fashion the crises of displaced persons, returning soldiers, and black markets in Italy's cities.[125] By the 1950s, however, many of the conditions in Italy that fueled the plots of neorealist films and their *nero* cousins gave way to a new era of prosperity and cultural conservatism. The 1948 victory of the Christian Democrats effectively marginalized the Communist Party, and the rapid modernization and urbanization of Italy, thanks in large measure to American Marshall Plan aid, brought about the post-war "economic miracle." As with the accelerated development of Mexico under *alemanismo*, in postwar Italy agricultural workers migrated en masse to industrialized centers, and big cities like Milan and Rome were host to a rising entrepreneurial class with its newly acquired bourgeois culture.[126] This period of capitalist transformation was cinematically marked as the transition from political neorealism (and its left-leaning hopeful humanism) to Italy's forthrightly modernist cinema, so announced by Michelangelo Antonioni's twist on noir, *Cronaca di un amore/Story of a Love Affair* (1950). This film looks forward to the auteur cinema of Federico Fellini, Roberto Rossellini, and Pier Paolo Pasolini, as much as it looks back and pays homage to Visconti's *Ossessione*, not least because these two films feature Massimo Girotti as the romantic, plotting anti-hero whose character in *Story of a Love Affair* is associated with the port town of Ferrara, Antonioni's home town, and the very same city to which Gino flees in Visconti's grim rendition. Thus, as one critic observes, film noir in Italy should be understood as "the gate through which filmmakers could evolve from one narrative and stylistic convention into another. Just like Visconti, who used his film noir to leave classical narrative for neorealism, by making his film noir Antonioni radically steps out of the neorealist universe toward modernism."[127] The hybridity of Antonioni's noir, moreover, which rejects neorealism's humanism while also complicating melodramatic simplicity, recalls strategies adopted by Buñuel in *Los Olividados*, though, as we will see, to rather different ends.

Where *Ossessione* takes us into the milieu of the Po valley underclass, *Story of a Love Affair* enmeshes us in the world of Milan's postwar, elite, industrial class. Paola, played by Lucia Bosé, first appears on the screen as she exits the city's premiere opera house, La Scala. Adorned in a luminous white-fur wrap, she greets her husband, Enrico Fontana, a wealthy textile manufacturer. Across the street, Paola spies her former lover from her school days, Guido (Girotti), a down-on-his-luck automobile salesman, who has come to Milan to warn Paola that they may be under investigation regarding the death of Guido's fiancée more than seven years ago (during World War II). As we learn in the film's first scene, Paola is under investigation, but not by the police: Paola's jealous husband, who has discovered photos of his wife from her youth, has hired a private detective to learn the details of her mysterious past. Where other noirs use the drama of detection to uncover a crime or bring an adulterous affair to light, this investigation actually produces the very conditions for such crimes. Suspecting they are under surveillance, the lovers secretly reunite in an affair that, in turn, will provide the husband with the evidence of betrayal that he seeks. Bound by a shared moral guilt for the fiancée's accidental death, the pair now begins to plot Fontana's murder. Like the duped noir husbands who came before him, Fontana dies at the end of the film leaving his wife with his fortune and her lover. But in Antonioni's unique modernist plotting, the lovers do not actually kill the man. Driving erratically owing to his rage at his wife's affair, Fontana crashes fatally just a mile from where Guido hides in wait. The instrumental logic of investigation leads not to answers or justice, but to devastation and dead ends. Unlike the lovers in *Gilda* who merrily escape together, or the doomed lovers in *Ossessione* who are separated by the woman's tragic death, Guido and Paola part ways at the end for reasons – guilt? fatigue? mutual disenchantment? – we can only ponder. In this film there is "only one single psychic structure: forms of moral and psychological emptiness," manifest not only in the characters' inexplicable actions, but also in the empty locations – the dark, rain-slicked urban streets, bleak river parks, and lost highways – that they inhabit.[128]

It is Antonioni's attention to Italy's postwar commodity culture that in the context of uneven development merits special attention. The Marshall Plan, recall, was envisioned as the economic mechanism that would bring to Europe prosperity and modern industry, but also, in the spirit of Market Empire, a democratic, just, and liberal public sphere. Antonioni's Milan, however, evinces signs only of empty wealth and evacuated subjectivity. Paola, for example, has clearly married Fontana during the war in order to break free of her modest upbringing – even now, the market will do nothing for her otherwise. Thanks to her husband's income, she lives not in provincial Ferrara but in cosmopolitan Milan in a luxurious house. It becomes clear after Guido comes back into her life, however, that Paola is unhappily married but addicted to the lifestyle her husband provides. Indeed, while Paola herself mindlessly buys dresses and bids on cars, in one exchange with Fontana she herself is the commodity. In Paola's boudoir, she preens in the mirror while Fontana, sitting in an armchair behind her, relays this joke:

Fontana: Luciani made me a business proposal.
Paola: Let's hear it.
Fontana: It involves you. He said, I'll buy your wife for 300 million lire.
Paola: Only 300? You know what an Eastern prince would have said?
Fontana: What?
Paola: You can have my wife for free . . . then I'll kill you.

Fontana: Maybe he would, but a Milanese industrialist, for free? He'd say, "Give me the money, you can have her . . . then I'll kill you." He avenges the insult, earns the money, and gets rid of his wife.

Even before Paola has put a price on her husband's head, he has virtually turned her disappearance into profit, a deal befitting the industrial savvy of the postwar era.

Elsewhere in the film, the sounds of industry and mechanical urbanity overwhelm the soundtrack and serve as reminders of our main characters' immoral desires.[129] Guido's fiancée, we learn, died by falling down an elevator shaft. And, though Guido and Paola did not push her, they wanted her dead and stood by doing nothing to help after she fell. In the present day, the lovers wind their way up the circular stairs of a multi-story building in the middle of which a loud and busy elevator occasionally obscures the characters from view. Here Paola and Guido begin to discuss Fontana's death, which will be realized with a genuinely accidental automobile crash (Figure 1.17). Cars and elevators, ubiquitous in economically flush Milan, carry out the malign wishes of the middle class who fetishize these instruments of literal and symbolic class mobility.

Untimely Death and Spanish Noir under Franco

If in postwar Italy Hollywood was generally associated with the empty culture of economic miracles, in fascist Spain it represented "an alternative 'imaginary' in opposition to dominant cultural practices" imposed by General Francisco Franco. Franco's dictatorship of Spain and censorship of its national film industry spanned from 1935 to 1975.[130] Film noir, in particular, with its dangerous independent women, its specious morality, and salacious appeal was anathema to Franco's Falangist, Catholic, and repressive rule. When *Gilda* premiered in 1947, members of Franco's party painted over the film's poster with black ink (an unwitting homage to *Bicycle Thief*, perhaps), and influential Catholic priests claimed that anyone who saw the film would be

FIGURE 1.17　Plotting accidental murder (*Story of a Love Affair*, 1950).

condemned to eternal damnation. Thus, as Kathleen M. Vernon explains of *Gilda*, the title alone "came to serve as a kind of short-hand reference to the political and psychic repression and material deprivation of the most stringent years of the dictatorship, the 40s decade of the *años de hambre* (years of hunger)."[131] Excluded from Marshall Plan funds owing to American disdain of Franco's regime, Spain struggled to recover from its brutal civil war. Though he denounced American culture, Franco continued to vie for American aid, which was finally granted in 1951 once Spain agreed to host American military bases.

One film to capture the paradox of Spanish–US relations is Luis García Berlanga's satire *Bienvenido, Mr. Marshall/Welcome, Mr. Marshall* (1952) in which residents of a small Castilian village refashion their town as an Andalusian tourist fantasy of Spain in anticipation of an American diplomatic visit. If the Americans like what they see, reason the villagers, they will dole out the dollars and relieve the town's economic woes. As the mayor presides over the town's transformation and the scripting of its inhabitants – all cast to the measure of Hollywood's vision of Spain – four of the townspeople dream about the American visit in sequences that explicitly reference Hollywood genres. In one, the town's arch-Francoist, the priest, is fanatically anti-American and especially disgusted by US cultural diversity. Yet he cannot help but dream in the style of an American noir. His slumber delivers him into the chiaroscuro world of American G-men and Kafkaesque courtrooms where his disparaging remarks about the US are played back to him, and a sadistic judge finds him guilty of un-American activities as charged. If noir is what Spanish dreams are made of, it is also, like a dream, an "indirect expression of thoughts censored by the conscious mind – or by a repressive government."[132]

Because there was not as robust a tradition of Spanish detective writing or the proto noir film culture that we find in Japan, France, and Italy, noir signified as a renegade, foreign, even democratic, genre that could be produced in Franco's censorial Spain only under cover, as it were, of satire or, as we discuss below, melodrama.[133] Marsha Kinder explains that melodrama, like noir, can work to naturalize "the dominant ideology by displacing political issues into the personal plane of the family, as in the case of most popular Hollywood genres and of the popular cinema made under Fascist regimes." Or it "can function subversively – either through excess and contradictions that are part of the genre itself or through radical innovations."[134] The forthrightly Spanish noirs (cine negro español) such as *Apartado de correos 1001/Post Office Box 1001* (1950) and *Brigada criminal/Criminal Brigade* (1950) "served as one of the most effective forms of political critique for both the Left and the Right." Noirs were tolerated by the Franco regime "because these films so blatantly imitated American and French action genres . . . and thereby appeared to minimize Spanish specificity."[135] These films also attested to the loathsome culture of French and American democracy to which Spanish fascism was opposed. Film noir in any form was evidence of American decadence.

Juan Antonio Bardem's *Muerte de un ciclista/Death of a Cyclist* (1955) plays melodramatic conventions both ways. It exposes the stylistic machinations of Hollywood melodrama while also borrowing the techniques and politics of neorealism and Italian noir, especially Visconti's *Ossessione* and Antonioni's *Story of a Love Affair*. In fact, starring *Story*'s Lucia Bosé as the adulterous, fatal wife of a wealthy industrialist, *Death of a Cyclist*, like *Story*, is a meditation on 1950s class consciousness in Franco's Spain and the corrupting effects of bourgeois opulence. Like *Ossessione*, *Cyclist* is also a study in the effects of guilt and the fated consequences of immoral desire.

We encounter the titular cyclist in the film's first scene. Adulterous lovers María José (Bosé) and Juan (Alberto Closas) drive along a deserted country road back to Madrid when they fatally hit a cyclist. Worried that their affair will be discovered if they bring the dying man to a hospital, the couple, at María José's insistence, leaves the poor man for dead. Though no one sees them on the highway, she begins to suspect that her secret is endangered when Rafa (Carlos Casarvilla), an art critic and parasite of Madrid's benighted upper class, threatens her with blackmail. But it is Juan, a veteran of Franco's army and a university professor (thanks to his family connection), who is overcome by guilt. As Juan sinks deeper into remorse, the film's visual style becomes decidedly noir: rain-slicked city streets, high-contrast lighting, and deep-focus compositions using wide-angle lenses all make Madrid expressive of Juan's waning moral comfort (Figure 1.18).[136] Like Antonioni and Visconti's films noir, *Cyclist* is more interested in the psychological effects of guilt than in the process of detection or the plotting of future crimes. Indeed, all of the violence in this film is accidental, impulsive, and carried out in the name of a moribund social order that María José, for once, is loath to jeopardize. When Juan decides to confess to the police – an act, he believes, that will begin to atone for his wrongful past – María José mows him down in the car at the exact location where the pair hit the cyclist just days before. This is also the site of a civil war battle in which Juan fought. In this way, Bardem connects the violence of the civil war to both the treachery of domestic melodrama and fascist history. María José herself then

FIGURE 1.18   Juan's professorial guilt (*Death of a Cyclist*, 1955).

succumbs to an accidental death. Speeding home to her husband and
material comfort that night, leaving Juan to die, she swerves to avoid a
cyclist and crashes. María José's punishment, befitting her guilt, is
surely a reference to *Ossessione*'s car-crashing end (which itself is based
on Cain's equally violent assassination of Cora).

Cyclist's critique of Madrid's elite class – all of whom prosper
thanks to nepotism, selfishness, and having been on the "right" side of
the civil war – is constructed in opposition to that of Madrid's working poor. As numerous critics have pointed out, it is in scenes of
class contrast that Bardem establishes the stylistic tension between
Hollywood's melodramatic glamour and neorealist observation.
María José and her husband, Miguel, attend a fashionable wedding.
The couple is framed in flattering, well-lit close-ups and followed in
smooth tracking shots as they mingle with the other guests. We then
cut to one of the working-class slums just outside of the city where

Juan attempts to locate the family of the dead cyclist. In neorealist style, he is framed in long shot against the crumbling facades of tenement flats teeming with shabby life. This more objective style renders the working class "without emotion or glamour, thereby offering a poignant contrast with the glossy melodrama of the rich."[137]

Another indictment of Franco's rule and American aid comes in the film's climactic scene. Miguel is wooing American investors and throws a party to which Madrid's champagne set is invited, including María José, Juan, and Rafa. It is here that Rafa will try to sell Miguel the secret of his wife's affair. This domestic business transaction finds its parallel in the American guests who, we are led to believe, give money to Miguel's company after being seduced by the flamenco dancers, the evening's entertainment. Just as the townspeople in *Welcome, Mr. Marshall* mount what is, in effect, a mode of ethnic drag for their would-be investors, the flamenco dancers, who perform against a painted backdrop of a rural Spain, create a vision of Andalusia – folksy, timeless, and alluring – that conforms to Franco's national program as well as American fantasies of Spanish premodernity. Ironically, this self-fashioned ethnic drag romanticizes underdevelopment in the attempt to fund further modernization (Figure 1.19). When the dance begins, the scene is jarringly edited. In low-key lighting, the dancers, musicians, Americans, and our main characters are variously framed in long shot and extreme close-ups, and in straight and canted angles. The rhythm of the music and the frenzy of the dance capture the Americans' fascination and reflect the mounting tension among the two lovers, the industrialist, and the blackmailing art critic. If the American deal comes through, these dollars will not support the imaginary Andalusian Spain on the dance floor. It will instead prop up the modern but morally retrograde culture of Madrid's fascist industrial class. This sly critique of Franco's rule (and the Americans who supported it) combined with the appropriation of an international noir style made Bardem the darling of the 1955 Cannes film festival when *Death of a Cyclist* premiered abroad. Arriving back in Madrid, however, his outspoken critique of mainstream Spanish cinema (and his

FIGURE 1.19   Ethnic drag for American investors (*Death of a Cyclist*, 1955).

implicit critique of Franco) led to Bardem's two-week-long imprisonment without charge.[138]

Both *Story of a Love Affair* and *Death of a Cyclist* were produced in Europe's southern, once imperial, countries that experienced industrial modernity belatedly compared to their central and northern European neighbors. And both films use the conventions of international noir to radically upset any narrative that modernization, urban culture, and market capitalism are necessarily the forces of progress or the democratic alternatives to fascism. Post World War II-era affluence – represented by cars, clothes, and luxury lifestyles – incarcerates Paola and María José in loveless marriages. Seeking a more authentic emotional future, both women are psychologically propelled back into a violent romantic past (coincident in both films with fascism and war), a past that traumatically returns in the present day in the form of unconsciously willed "accidental" deaths. Thus, just as Jeff, in *Out of the*

Past, finds himself caught between a dark, eruptive past and a precarious future, so too are the characters in these films trapped in a tumultuous temporality.

Postcolonial Noir: The Dark Streets of Bombay

From the belated modernity of Mediterranean Europe, we now move to the coastal city of 1950s Bombay, host to India's proliferate, popular Hindi film industry, more recently known as Bollywood. We focus our attention on C.I.D., a Hindi-language crime film from 1956 that was made concurrently with Hollywood's first wave of noir and the era of French criticism that coined the term. But C.I.D., made not even ten years after India's independence from British colonial rule, engages Bombay's urban modernity through the recent history of postcolonial independence, the pressures of new-found democracy, and the sweeping reforms India was then experiencing under the first prime minister, Jawaharlal Nehru.

Nehru sought to create an independent nation-state in the wake of colonialism (and the violent clashes over the partition of British India into predominately Hindu India and Muslim Pakistan) by rapidly modernizing India's economy and industry, and transforming its provincially religious, caste-based culture into a liberal, secular, and science-based society, tempered through a long tradition of Indian spiritualism and philosophy.[139] Though a model of modern culture and industry, Western capitalism and the acquisitiveness of its citizens were, for Nehru, the engines of colonialist brutality. In 1946, he wrote that, despite "all its great and manifold achievements," the modern West "does not appear to have been a conspicuous success or to have solved the basic problems of life," even for those who had benefited most from its exploits.[140] In step with film noir's own obsession with inauthentic feeling and empty experience, Nehru included himself among those who had been leached of vitality when he observed of Western subjects: "We eat ersatz foods produced with the help of ersatz fertilizers: we indulge ersatz emotions and our human relations seldom go beyond the superficial plane."[141] As Gyan Prakash explains, India's postwar modernization was a form of socialist populism that "had to articulate its aspirations as a critique of Western modernity and as a desire to institutionalize a culturally specific community."[142] Or, differently inflected, the new Indian nation was "a space for the critique of Western modernity while internalizing the program of modernization."[143]

Hindi directors were likewise influenced by Western cinema (especially Hollywood) and were conversant with global movements in film production, but committed to the idea of a national cinema. In 1952, for example, India was host to the First International Film Festival, which "rather dramatically" introduced Indian filmmakers to Italian neorealism and the postwar work of Akira Kurosawa.[144] Nehru himself applauded neorealism's leftist social critique, and the influence of both Italian and Japanese cinema on midcentury Hindi films was evident in the move towards on-location shooting, naturalist mise-en-scène, and, for some directors, the neorealist penchant for sociological observation in the name of progressive change.[145] But the signature of the Hindi popular film, regardless of genre, was (and still is) the often-exuberant music and dance numbers, the narrative's epic length, and the sheer range of tonal and emotional registers within one film (and sometimes within a single scene). These uniquely Hindi film traits, all rooted in India's rich musical past and in its hybrid, colonial theatrical traditions, meant that, however much directors adapted techniques and styles from abroad, "the local product was so thoroughly indigenized that it could hold its own against slick American entertainment." Indeed, for film critic Maithili Rao it is the Hindi film's "knack for quick assimilation and creative adaptation" that made this cinema "the perfect vehicle for forging new and instant mythologies for a colonized people emerging into Independence."[146] Insofar as Hindi cinema commanded audiences in South, Central, and Southeast Asia, Africa, the Caribbean and the Middle East (as well as the Indian communities in Britain, Canada, and the US), the Hindi film offers another example of a reflexive cinema as formulated by Miriam Hansen to describe Hollywood's global appeal.[147] Hansen, remember, argues that Hollywood films take as their primary subject the experience of modernization itself. Thus American cinema achieved a "global vernacular status" because it "provided an aesthetic horizon for the experience of industrial mass society" that resonated with audiences all over the world.[148] Post-independence Hindi cinema provided a similar function for recently decolonized audiences because it took as its implicit subject the culture and experience of newly established independence. That is, Hindi films certainly participated in the vernacular modernism of Hollywood, not least because they adapted Hollywood genres, but they could also provide the myths of independence for Indian filmgoers and to audiences around the world entering into the twinned shocks of belated sovereignty and urban modernity.

Though the Hindi crime film goes back to the early 1940s, C.I.D. is an especially interesting example of film noir, as it subtly upholds the ethos of Nehru's national platform while also dramatizing the ills of an urban modernity that occur too fast and too unevenly to be lawfully adjudicated. C.I.D. (the acronym for Crime Investigation Division – a hold-over from British rule) opens when a valiant newspaper editor is murdered because he plans to publish the unsavory truth about his wealthy assassin. Onto the scene comes Inspector Shekhar (played by Hindi heartthrob Dev Anand), who, in the process of tracking the hitman and the socially prominent criminal for whom he works, becomes himself a framed suspect. A trial wrongly finds Shekhar guilty of murder, but before being sentenced he manages to flee so that he may bring the real criminal mastermind to justice. This Shekhar manages while being seduced by the alluring femme fatale Kamini (Waheeda Rehman, in her debut role) and the modern, but thoroughly innocent, Rekha (Shakila), whom he openly embraces at the film's happy end. Similarly to Ann in *Out of the Past*, Rekha is associated with the pastoral countryside where she and Shekhar court one another along a timeless lakefront shore far from Bombay's urban noise. Kamini, like Kathie, is connected to the city, where she reluctantly helps to plot Shekhar's downfall.

Striking too are the quasi-neorealist scenes shot on location in Bombay's busy city streets, its oceanfront promenade, and modern subway system. In one such scene, the petty thief Master (played by comic actor Johnny Walker) sings a song about the city as he walks and rides down a grand boulevard. In broad daylight, he picks the pockets of the men he encounters and serenades passers-by. This scene directs our attention to the world that exists outside of this particular fiction, and the lyrics to this perky tune are telling:

> O gentle heart, life is an uphill struggle
> Be alert, be street wise, this is Bombay, my love
> There are buildings and trams and motor cars and mills
> There is everything to be had except a heart's thrills
> There's not a trace of humanity in this bustling city

Yet, as we find by the end of the film, the fictional Bombay does indeed have heart, since it is the subway that enables Shekhar to escape the thugs, and he is able to prove his innocence when Kamini, with whom he flees, agrees to testify against her co-conspirator.

With its arresting black-and-white cinematography, low-key lighting and night scenes, with its representation of Bombay's cosmopolitan modernity, and its stock hard-boiled characters, C.I.D. is also clearly indebted to Hollywood noir. As Cory Creekmur explains, C.I.D.'s first scene, in which the evil capitalist phones in the hit on the editor, is uncannily similar to the opening phone montage sequence of Fritz Lang's *The Big Heat* (1953) (Figure 1.20).[149] And yet, with its six musical numbers, its numerous comedy sequences, and its redemption of the femme fatale, C.I.D. is an emphatically Hindi film. And many of its noir plot elements have particular relevance for Nehru's liberal reforms.

Creekmur notes that the film stresses divisions of class over caste and in this way reflects Nehru's own Marxist leanings. For example, the working-class thugs are contrasted to their "respectable" wealthy employer who uses them to carry out his dirty work and regards them

FIGURE 1.20 Phoning in the hit (*C.I.D.*, 1956).

as nothing more than disposable labor. Thus the individual with the highest social ranking and greatest wealth turns out to be the least moral or deserving. Moreover, C.I.D.'s emphasis on the procedure of detection and the necessity of amassing evidence that will stand in a court of law shows viewers that even those who work for the law, such as Inspector Shekhar, are still subject to the law. Though he is framed for the murder of a suspect in custody, Shekhar's trial highlights the rights of prisoners and the importance of evidence. Shekhar's word and reputation alone cannot dispute hard facts anymore than Rekha's strong belief in his innocence. When Shekhar, having secured the testimony he needs to clear his name, turns himself in, he is expected to serve time for jumping bail. Though these legal procedures are the bread and butter of film noir, in this film they model in important ways systems of liberal justice in which equality under the law – irrespective of class, social position, or criminal history – reigns supreme. Yet, in showing how evidence can be produced and falsified, C.I.D. reveals the potential gap between due process, on one hand, and justice due innocent victims, on the other. This new modern culture produces both the heroic Shekhar and the prominent criminal men who can manipulate the press, plant false evidence, and lure the underclass into an immoral life. This system works only for those who know how to navigate its complexities. Given C.I.D.'s historical proximity to British rule, the film's critique of modern justice points back to colonial "justice" and the modernity associated with Western imperial power. The court's fetishization of empirical evidence as the basis for all truth is proved false, albeit through better, untainted evidence. But Rekha's heart got it right all along. So the lyrics of Master's song, "Be alert, be street wise, this is Bombay," are one of the noir mythologies C.I.D. offers its newly (or soon-to-be) independent viewers who are straddling colonial and postcolonial modernities, and who are wary of internalizing the very culture of empire they seek to overturn.

Perilous Developments? Iranian Noir and the Islamic State

Not unlike modernization in India, modernization in Iran was historically associated with Western imperialism and the authoritarian monarchy of Mohammad Reza Shah Pahlavi (the Shah of Iran), who, thanks to the Western Allies' intervention, ruled the country from 1941 until the Islamic revolution in 1979. Eager to bring Iran into an emerging global economy and to exploit its vast oil reserves in close concert with British and US corporations, the shah implemented a program of industrial modernization while, after a brief promising interlude, suppressing democratic and other liberal freedoms. Ali Gheissari and Vali Nasr explain that, during the first two decades of his rule, Pahlavi could implement these policies (which benefited a small segment of the Iranian population) and maintain his power only by stifling parliamentary democracy. "As such, democracy and development came to be viewed as mutually exclusive goals."[150] In 1963, the

shah initiated the "White Revolution," a series of reforms implemented from above with the hopes of quelling radical revolutionary
movements from below and proving to the Western powers that Iran's
monarchy was thoroughly modern and politically enlightened. The
shah stepped up the country's economic transformation from its
largely agricultural base to an economy oriented toward oil excava-
tion, and petrochemical and pharmaceutical production.[151] He also
implemented sweeping land reforms. These changes enriched the
country and were accompanied by the enfranchisement of women
and investment in higher education. For a variety of reasons, however,
the White Revolution did not usher in the modern monarchic utopia
envisioned by the shah. Rather it created an economy characterized by
"uneven development, rapid urbanization, and income inequality."[152]
By the early 1970s, the shah's culture of modernity produced "social
dislocation, cultural alienation, and new political demands that the
state was both unable and unwilling to deliver."[153] Thus reforms carried out by the shah to secure his power paved the way for his ousting.

According to film critic Hamid Reza Sadr, it was during the late
1960s and early 1970s, in the post-White Revolution era, that "Iran
discovered film noir."[154] Director Masud Kimiai first explored the
urban experience in his groundbreaking noir *Gheisar* (1969). The story
pivots on the titular protagonist, who avenges his sister's rape just
before he himself is shot by the otherwise ineffectual police. Like
other noirs we've discussed, *Gheisar* was striking for its use of on-location shooting in Tehran and its cagey juxtaposition of "gritty realism"
and "ironic lyricism."[155] Gheisar is also reminiscent of the protagonists from French poetic realism and American noir. Left behind by
Iran's modernization (Gheisar lives "amidst the historical ruins in
southern Tehran"), he represents the vitality of a singular but threatened "moral existence [that has become] an anachronism" in the era
of unequal plenty.[156] The commercial and critical success of this noir
made it a model for Kimiai's subsequent films featuring "embittered
anti-heroes" in plots that comment on the new state of economic
affairs. These films include *Motori / Reza, the Motorcyclist* (1970), *Dash Akol*

(1971), *Khak/The Soil*, (1974), *Baluch* (1972), and the rather infamous noir *Ghavaznha/Deers* (1975).[157]

The last in this list of Kimiai's noirs, *Deers*, merits brief attention. In it, two friends, one a drug addict and the other a political terrorist on the run, try to elude capture by taking refuge in one of Tehran's many ghettos, where each man tries, unsuccessfully, to rehabilitate the other. In the end they are caught, but the censored version of the film replaces their bloody shoot-out with the cops with a sanctimonious speech about moral action. "The best film of the decade and certainly one of the most politically controversial," *Deers*, writes Sadr, addressed with a clear eye the mounting pressures facing Iranians in the late 1970s: "political conflicts, armed struggle, police brutality, class divisions and drug addiction." Its use of Tehran locales such as the "populist theaters" and "crowded poorhouses," moreover, represented a society "on the verge of explosion."[158]

And how prophetic. During one screening of *Deers* in 1978, three young men linked to clerical dissidents set fire to the Rex Theater in Abdan, Iran, killing over three hundred spectators and igniting the Islamic revolution.[159] Soon cinemas and banks, beacons of the shah's Western orientation, were going up in flames all over the country. One year later, the shah's monarchy gave way to the Islamic republic under Ayatollah Khomeini. Hamid Naficy explains that, because cinema signified as a "Western import," religious leaders condemned it as an instrument of corruption, immorality, and decadence.[160] Indeed, the infective power of cinema was evident in the fact that the anti-shah rebels burned down a theater while it played a film noir about an anti-shah rebel. For Khomelni, only Islamization could redeem cinema for the Muslim state, where it could be used to combat Westernized Pahlavi culture and return Iran to its more authentic, traditional, and local roots.

In phrasing that so wonderfully encapsulates noir's own ambivalence to urban modernization, Ali Mirsepassi summarizes the place and concerns of Islam in its confrontation with an externally imposed industrial modernity in Iran:

Modernity and the West have been viewed [in Iran] both as an undesirable "other" and, if Iran is to have a viable future, as an inescapable fate. At the same time, Islam has been viewed as the authentic cultural identity of Iran, the imagined traditional community of the disappearing past. The Islamic discourse of authenticity embodies both aspiration for change and the Iranian encounter with modernity.[161]

While this particular discourse is unique to Iran, Mirsepassi argues that the tension between an unrecoverable authenticity and an inexorable, universalizing modernity aptly characterizes the culture wars of Weimar Germany (where, recall, German and Hollywood noir has roots). In fact, we've shown how this tension operated both in interwar debates about vanishing boundaries of "authentic" national culture and in postwar discourse about capitalist culture and Americanization. Across the globe, film noir's longing for locality and authenticity is, itself, another universal and trans-historical response to modernization and globalization, however much it is rooted in a specific set of circumstances.

It is perhaps then not so surprising that film noir returns to the Islamic state in 1991 with Rakhshan Banietemad's Nargess, her "groundbreaking film noir" about people marginalized by both Islamic culture and urban poverty.[162] Banietemad had been making socially conscious work in the spirit of social realism since 1984, but she came into the international limelight when Nargess won first prize at the Fajr Film Festival in 1991. Banietemad was the first woman in Iran to win this award.

In many respects, Nargess sets up a classic noir love triangle familiar to us from the plot of Out of the Past. Adel (Abolfazl Poorarab) is a petty thief who, as the film opens, is being pursued by the cops through the dark streets of Tehran with Afagh (Farimah Farjami), his older lover and partner in crime. Afagh cannot maintain Adel's pace, so he ditches her and takes refuge in a decrepit city hospital where he meets Nargess (Atefeh Razavi), a young, beautiful girl who is helping her destitute father through another bout of sickness. To hide from the police, Adel helps the father, but in the process he falls for Nargess and begins to imagine a proper married life and a new, upstanding, moral existence. Poor and relatively sheltered, Nargess (like Ann in *Out of the Past*) represents the best hope for Adel's future. She is traditional in her beliefs and wants desperately to reform Adel once she learns of his past. Afagh, old and desperate to keep Adel by her side, represents a criminal life from which he cannot escape. At the end of the film, Adel is penniless and unable to find employment and so is lured by Afagh into one last heist. Though they manage to pull it off, Nargess is enraged by Adel's lapse. In a final confrontation on one of Tehran's busy highways, Afagh realizes that Adel is lost to her forever. Holding a bag filled with stolen money, she steps in front of an oncoming truck. She is last represented splayed on the ground, with tomans (the Iranian currency) littering the wet pavement around her limp body. Indeed, the final image of Afagh is uncannily similar to our last image of Kathie (Figures 1.21 and 1.22). As with Jeff in *Out of the Past*, Adel's shady history and impossible happy future are embodied in two women.

FIGURE 1.21 *Nargess* (1991).

FIGURE 1.22   *Out of the Past* (1947).

Unlike Kathie, however, Afagh is not a cunning seductress, but a sympathetic victim of poverty and patriarchal violence under a perverse and outdated Islamic order. As Afagh explains, she was forced to marry a fifty-year-old man when she was nine and bore her first child at thirteen. After brutalizing her, her husband cast her into the streets, where she subsisted through petty crime and odd jobs. Years later she met Adel, who was likewise thrown out of his house by his abusive stepfather. So, while Adel longs for a traditional marriage and family life as the antidote to his criminal past, Banietemad suggests that family life is exactly what produces the conditions of injustice in the first place (importantly, however, given the year of *Nargess*'s release, these brutalities would have presumably taken place in the pre-revolutionary era under the shah).

More biting, however, is Banietemad's attention to the cycles of poverty and class inequality in present-day Tehran. Everywhere she turns her camera – from the crumbling and understaffed hospital, to Nargess's impoverished family courtyard, to the teeming prison where Adel is detained, to the hovel where he lives – Banietemad finds a modern city in ruins and disrepair. Adel is forced back into a life of crime, not because the temptation to steal is so great, but because legitimate jobs are so few. And Nargess's family give their daughter to Adel because they themselves can barely afford to feed her. Thus, one may surmise that the larger problem for these characters is not that modernization has come too fast; in these dark corners, it is achingly too slow. The only glimpses of opulence and happy marriage we spy come toward the end of the film, when Adel and Afagh break into a wealthy home. Here, in addition to cash and fancy knickknacks, Adel finds wedding photographs and family portraits perched on a table. Upstanding family life is not reserved for the faithful or the poor, but for the rich who can afford to live well and rightly. The traditional ideal, it seems, can only be achieved by the prosperous, modern few.

In this respect, Banietemad indicts both the Islamic revolution and economic modernization for failing to alleviate the suffering of Iran's many dispossessed citizens. Belying the revolution's promise for change, in this film there are no new beginnings or fresh starts. Thus, like so many noir protagonists, Adel finds himself suspended in a temporal no-man's-land: the longed-for traditional life is both an irrecoverable fiction of the past and for Adel – unemployed and down and out – an unattainable future. But Banietemad also slyly suggests that modernization is not opposed to Islamic traditional values, for only in a truly modern and prosperous Iran could all citizens enjoy equal access to an authentic, upstanding existence. Modern economic progress and development do not themselves erode the moral order; they may in fact be necessary to realizing the revolution's highest ideals.

California Dreaming in Chungking Express

Appearing in national cinemas from around the globe, films noir at once critique modernization (as Americanization) and articulate more local conditions of being, or resisting being, "modern." But, even as they do so, they themselves compete as products within global cinematic markets dominated by Hollywood. Films noir are commodities, after all. As such, noir's critique of the economic engines of global modernity is always ambivalent. This ambivalence only deepened in the last few decades of the twentieth century, when the threat of Americanization to national culture was supplanted by the even more baffling reality of full-blown globalization: a new, inescapable media environment in which a homogenizing Western consumer culture operates transnationally, and with blithe disregard of local traditions and values. Critics often discuss this later phase of noir's cultural internationalism alongside the broader condition of so-called postmodernism, an art of parody and repetition that turns the rich reserves of national cultures into a stylistic hodge-podge devoid of history and critical force. Such attempts to distinguish classical Hollywood film noir from postmodern "neo-noir" paint a rather despairing picture of contemporary noir's globalized "mediascape." But, as we've demonstrated above, global film noir since the 1930s has always been self-aware, intertextual, and hybrid in terms of both genre and media. And its international itineraries have consistently made noir "new" in a variety of local contexts. When noir is considered as an international phenomenon, the distinction between edgy, "authentic" noir and decadent, commodified neo-noir ceases to explain very much.

In fact, as the stylish Hong Kong film *Chung Hing sam lam/Chungking Express* (Wong Kar-wai, 1994) shows, contemporary noir often pursues the question of cultural "authenticity" with considerable subtlety, and with a clear historical compass. Contemporary Hong Kong, home to some 8 million people, is a special administrative region of China, and a center of global trade and finance. However, in 1994 Hong Kong was still a British colony, as it had been since the nineteenth century. As a result of its colonial status, Hong Kong modernized more rapidly than mainland China, and became a major trading hub of Western capitalism; it also hosted an influx of refugees from the mainland following the communist takeover of China in 1949. In the early 1990s, Hong

Kong was, by the Western yardstick, considerably more adapted to the times and speeds of capitalist modernity than communist China. A port city developing in this cultural crucible between West and East, Hong Kong is thus a rather unique cultural space, and an interesting place to conclude our discussion of film noir's uneven development.

As cultural theorist Ackbar Abbas explains, one of the effects of British colonialism in Hong Kong was a pervasive "import mentality" – the sense that "culture, like everything else," was "that which came from elsewhere: from Chinese tradition . . . or from the West."[163] However, during the 1980s and 1990s, after the Sino-British Joint Declaration set a date on which Hong Kong would be returned to Chinese control (July 1, 1997), Hong Kong experienced a new kind of localism – a desire to define a specific cultural identity neither British nor Chinese, but specific to Hong Kong. In the process, Abbas argues, emerged a "culture of disappearance" in Hong Kong, the curious condition in which what is most specific about Hong Kong's local culture comes into view only as it is on the verge of disappearing.

The early 1980s also witnessed the emergence of a revitalized Hong Kong cinema, spearheaded by a new generation of cosmopolitan Hong Kong filmmakers "educated in film schools abroad and with no direct ties to either China or Taiwan," who "turned to filmmaking after a period of apprenticeship in local television."[164] For Abbas, the films of Hong Kong New Wave directors like Tsui Hark, Patrick Tam, Ana Hui, and *Chungking Express*'s Wong Kar-wai, however unique and stylistically innovative, are also products of this culture of disappearance: they betray the uncanny feeling that dominated Hong Kong's cultural output in the years before the handover to China – namely, "that what is new and unique about the [cultural] situation is always already gone and we are left holding a handful of clichés, or a cluster of memories of what has never been."[165] In this context, films like Wong's *Chungking Express* play with the generic hallmarks of noir as part of a broader investigation about what, if anything, is "authentic" about Hong Kong's postcolonial urban culture of relentless movement, dislocation, and transition.

Like many Hong Kong movies, *Chungking Express* is a work of "cultural androgyny," an alluring confection of various genres and cultural idioms.[166] Wong's own familiarity with noir conventions comes not just through his exposure to Hollywood genre cinema and his acknowledged debts to the modernist European art cinema of Antonioni and Godard (who were themselves, we've begun to see, interested in American noir), but also through his literariness. Wong's wide reading in world literature includes the formally experimental work of Alain Robbe-Grillet and Gabriel García Marquez, as well as the American noir fiction of Raymond Chandler, the noir vision of exiled Argentine novelist Manuel Puig, whose fiction consistently returns to the dark plots of 1940s Hollywood melodrama, and the contemporary Japanese novelist Harumi Murakami, who, like Wong, playfully reworks hard-boiled conventions.[167] In other words, Wong's cinema is informed by a cosmopolitan sensibility in world literature that had already hybridized noir.

Chungking Express's hybridity is built into its fragmented form, of which only the first part is overtly noir. This section concerns the chance romantic encounter between an undercover Hong Kong cop, Number 223 (Takeshi Kaneshiro), recently dumped by his girlfriend May, and a mysterious femme fatale in a blonde wig (Brigitte Lin), who organizes a drug-smuggling operation with the help of a group of South Asian immigrants-turned-heroin "mules." Drowning his sorrows in a bar, Number 223 vows, in a noir voiceover, to fall in love with the next women to enter – the deadly blonde, who is later forced to kill her Anglo employer when her smuggling scheme is botched. However, Number 223 and the blonde do pass a lonely night "together" in a hotel, where they eat room service before the blonde falls asleep and the cop spends the night watching old movies on TV. The second part ditches the noir crime plot for a quirky romantic comedy, but it retains the typically noir feelings of urban melancholy and alienation. The second plot involves another cop, Number 633 (Tony Leung), who is also jilted by his lover, a flight attendant, before falling for the puckish Faye (Faye Wong), who works as a countergirl at the Midnight Express fast-food joint and dreams of moving to California. When Number 633 recovers from his break-up, he finally takes the advice of the Midnight Express's manager to "get another girl," and decides to ask Faye to a date at the California restaurant. When he shows up, he discovers that Faye has left for the real California, promising to return in a year. "We were in different Californias," Number 633 muses in voiceover. When the characters are reunited, both have changed: Faye is now a flight attendant, and Number 633 is the new owner of the Midnight Express, ready to reopen the business. The film ends as Number 633 presents the impromptu "boarding pass" Faye had given him as a goodbye letter, and offers to go wherever she wants to take him.

Chungking Express's disjointed form is thus a fitting enactment of Hong Kong's dislocated and fluid cultural space. On the one hand, Wong carefully chooses to stage his interconnected plots in recognizable Hong Kong locales. The crime plot is set in the Chungking Mansions, a combination of shops and flophouses for Hong Kong's immigrant population, while Wong stages the missed encounters of the comedy plot across Victoria harbor in the fast-foot joint and in Number 633's apartment, whose windows open onto the Mid-Levels escalators, a buzzing hive of pedestrian traffic in the heart of Central Hong Kong. On the other hand, these authentic locales, shot in very different parts of the city, are never put in any clear spatial relationship for the non-Hong Kong viewer. Instead, we notice their shared frenetic movement and energy. They become of a piece with Wong's consistent mise-en-scène of dislocation and indistinction – the transitional spaces of the hotel, airport, fast-food restaurant, or bar, where one can consume chef salads, Del Monte canned pineapples, or popular music, as Wong's sad, serial loners are wont to do. As critics have pointed out, the film's doubled plot is knitted together by a series of uncanny echoes and repetitions (e.g., the two cops, the two flight attendants, two women named May, two blonde wigs, the two Californias, the repeated temporal motifs of deadlines, clocks, and expiration dates). With such doublings, substitutions, and serial displacements, the anchors of authenticity itself are set adrift in Wong's vision of Hong Kong. Or perhaps we should say that *Chungking Express*, speedy and light, takes the whole notion of authenticity for a ride, since Wong's is a decidedly exhilarating take on a locality changing rapidly in the flows of global culture.

The price of a dislocated (and dislocating) world is, for Wong, felt most pressingly on the level of human intimacy and feeling. In *Chungking Express*, Wong's bravura visual style updates noir's penchant for expressionism by finding increasingly dazzling forms for tenuous intimacies and alienated feelings: soap cries, towels weep, and cans of pineapple keep time for expired love. In two signature shots, isolated characters are frozen in the stilled center of the frame as the world whirls in hurried movement around them. In other compositions, characters share the same frame, but seem to exist in separate times and spaces, in different Californias. The romance of displacement is perhaps best exemplified in the charming way Faye flirts with Number 633 by redecorating his apartment when he's not there. Given the keys to Number 633's flat by his now ex-girlfriend, Faye systematically repopulates his intimate space with new objects – a toothbrush, a fresh bar of soap, a clean shirt, new music in the CD player. This strange act of domestic haunting is made even odder by the fact that lovelorn Number 633, in the throes of romantic loss, doesn't notice the changes (Figure 1.23). In effect, Faye is helping Number 633 manage change, not by denying it, but by embracing it, by making more of it. The episode seems to double the effect of the film's own disorienting formal break into its second plot and a new time and speed, even as it offers an allegory about the status of Hong Kong's cultural environment in the early 1990s, itself on the verge of a new postcolonial identity whose future is uncertain. Change happens.

As we've discussed previously, the crisis of the dislocated present – of being left to chance between a vanished past and an unknown future – is a form of time common to films noir and central to their modernity. However, *Chungking Express* offers a rather more optimistic take on temporal dislocation than that felt by, say, Jeff Markham in *Out*

FIGURE 1.23   The romance of displacement (*Chungking Express*, 1994).

of the Past. The cultural dislocation of Wong's protagonists, while a function of the forces of global modernity, is also a site of possibility, fantasy, and reinvention. Consider the characters' relationship to popular
music and its infectious repetitions in Wong's telling soundtrack,
which combines famous American pop songs like Dinah Washington's
"What a Difference a Day Makes" (surely a loaded title in pre-
handover Hong Kong) and hybridized global music like reggae (a
genre with a politicized history of anticolonial resistance), as well as
Canto-pop versions of songs like the Cranberries' "Dreams." Faye's
anthem, "California Dreamin'," by the Mamas and the Papas, codes
her as a fantasist, and links her to the film's other dreamers of mass culture: Number 233's girlfriend, who thinks he looks like a famous
Japanese pop star; the blonde smuggler's boss, who makes his girlfriend perform a kind of ethnic drag in her blonde wig; the South
Asian boy in the Midnight Express, who stops work to lip-synch with
a carrot as a mike. What's more, Wong's cast is stocked with pop stars:
Takeshi Kaneshiro actually *is* a famous Japanese singer, Faye Wong is a
Cantonese pop chanteuse (it's *her* version of the Cranberries' song that
concludes the film), and Brigitte Lin is a major star of Hong Kong

cinema. In these ways, Chungking Express's soundtrack and casting exemplify the film's own relationship to global popular culture. In 1994, film noir is as much the stuff of global culture as the Cranberries, and like them gets playfully rerouted in Chungking Express for success in the global marketplace.

Recall that Out of the Past's Kathie, displaced in a "Mexican" cantina, listens to American music and dreams of overcoming her loneliness, returning home. Faye's "California Dreamin'," by contrast, seems to indulge in the capacity for creative refashioning endemic to a global media environment of constant recycling, repetition, and hybridization across national cultures and cinemas. In this world, can any culture ever be finally "local"? Chungking Express's optimism about the instability of national culture is thus Hong Kong's answer to the despairing rootlessness of James M. Cain, another California dreamer with whom this chapter's journey began.

NOTES

1 See, for example, James Naremore's chapter "Modernism and Blood Melodrama" in More than Night: Film Noir in its Contexts (Berkeley: University of California Press, 2007); Paula Rabinowitz's Black and White Noir: America's Pulp Modernism (New York: Columbia University Press, 2002); and Sean McCann, Gumshoe America: Hard-Boiled Crime Fiction and the Rise of New Deal Liberalism (Durham, NC: Duke University Press, 2000).
2 McCann, Gumshoe America, p. 23.
3 Michael Trask, Cruising Modernism (Ithaca, NY: Cornell University Press, 2004), p. 13.
4 James M. Cain, The Postman Always Rings Twice (New York: Vintage Crime, 1992), pp. 15, 7. Hereafter references abbreviated in the text.
5 Anthony Giddens, The Consequences of Modernity (Stanford, CA: Stanford University Press, 1990), p. 21.
6 McCann, Gumshoe America, p. 34.
7 Cain, The Postman Always Rings Twice, p. 3.
8 Ibid., p. 15.
9 Ibid., p. 90.
10 Ibid., p. 86.

11 Marc Vernet, "Film Noir on the Edge of Doom," in *Shades of Noir: A Reader*, ed. Joan Copjec (London: Verso, 1993), p. 20.

12 Mira Liehm, *Passion and Defiance: Film in Italy from 1942 to the Present* (Berkeley: University of California Press, 1984), p. 57.

13 Leo Braudy, *Jean Renoir: The World of His Films* (New York: Doubleday, 1972), p. 50.

14 Alan Williams, *Republic of Images: A History of French Filmmaking* (Cambridge, MA: Harvard University Press, 1992), p. 227.

15 See Ginette Vincendeau's "Noir Is also a French Word: The French Antecedents of Film Noir," in *The Movie Book of Film Noir*, ed. Ian Cameron (London: Studio Vista Books, 1994), pp. 49–58.

16 Dudley Andrew, *Mists of Regret: Culture and Sensibility in Classic French Film* (Princeton, NJ: Princeton University Press, 1995), p. 14.

17 Charles O'Brien, "Film Noir in France: Before the Liberation," in "European Precursors of Film Noir," *Iris* 21 (Spring 1996), ed. Janice Morgan and Dudley Andrew, p. 8.

18 Ibid., p. 13.

19 Vincendeau, "Noir Is also a French Word," p. 50.

20 Ibid., p. 52.

21 Raymond Borde and Etienne Chaumeton, *A Panorama of American Film Noir, 1941–1953*, trans. Paul Hammond, intro. James Naremore (San Francisco: City Lights Books, 2002), p. 23.

22 Ibid., p. 23.

23 Liehm, *Passion and Defiance*, p. 57.

24 Steven Ricci, *Cinema and Fascism: Italian Film and Society, 1922–1943* (Berkeley: University of California Press, 2008), p. 131.

25 Ibid., p. 129.

26 Donald Heiney, *America in Modern Italian Literature* (New Brunswick, NJ: Rutgers University Press, 1994), p. 71.

27 Gaia Servadio, *Luchino Visconti: A Biography* (London: Weidenfeld & Nicolson, 1982), p. 59.

28 Ricci, *Cinema and Fascism*, pp. 145, 141.

29 Ibid., p. 141.

30 William Van Watson, "Luchino Visconti's (Homosexual) Ossessione," in *Reviewing Fascism: Italian Cinema, 1922–1943*, ed. Jacqueline Reich and Piero Garofolo (Bloomington: Indiana University Press, 2002), pp. 172–193, p. 176.

31 Luchino Visconti, "Anthropomorphic Cinema," in *The Fabulous Thirties: Italian*

Cinema, 1929–1944, ed. Incontri Internazionali d'Arte Roma (Rome: Electa International, 1979), p. 54.

32 Ricci, *Cinema and Fascism*, pp. 16, 104–124.
33 Henry Bacon, *Visconti: Explorations of Beauty and Decay* (Cambridge, UK: Cambridge University Press, 1998), p. 16.
34 Liehm, *Passion and Defiance*, pp. 57–58.
35 Geoffrey Nowell-Smith, *Luchino Visconti*, 3rd edn. (London: BFI, 2003), p. 16.
36 Liehm, *Passion and Defiance*, p. 58.
37 Jean-Paul Sartre, "American Novelists in French Eyes," *Atlantic Monthly* 178 (1945), pp. 114–120, p. 115.
38 Ibid., p. 114.
39 Ibid., p. 119.
40 Ibid., p. 119.
41 Ibid., p. 120.
42 Ibid., p. 115.
43 Naremore, *More than Night*, p. 18.
44 Ibid., p. 19.
45 Nino Frank, "The Crime Adventure Story: A New Kind of Detective Film," in *Perspectives on Film Noir*, ed. R. Barton Palmer (New York: G. K. Hall & Co., 1996), pp. 21–24, p. 22.
46 Ibid., p. 22.
47 Ibid., p. 23.
48 Ibid., p. 23.
49 McCann, *Gumshoe America*, p. 90.
50 Ibid., p. 90.
51 Dana Adams Schmidt, "Our Movies Leave Germans Hostile," *New York Times*, July 23, 1946, p. 33.
52 Tony Judt, *Past Imperfect: French Intellectuals, 1944–1956* (Berkeley: University of California Press, 1992), p. 32.
53 Ibid., p. 34
54 See ibid., pp. 75–98; Naremore, *More than Night*, pp. 22–23.
55 Jean-Pierre Chartier, "The Americans Are Making Dark Films Too," in *Perspectives on Film Noir*, ed. R. Barton Palmer (New York: G. K. Hall & Co., 1996), pp. 25–27, p. 26.
56 Ibid., p. 27.
57 Ibid., p. 27.
58 Vernet, "*Film Noir* on the Edge of Doom," p. 5.

59 Ibid., p. 6.

60 Ian Jarvie, Hollywood's Overseas Campaign: The North Atlantic Movie Trade, 1920–1950 (Cambridge, UK: Cambridge University Press, 1994), pp. 213–246.

61 G. P. Brunetta, "The Long March of American Cinema," in Hollywood in Europe: Experiences of a Cultural Hegemony, ed. David W. Ellwood and Rob Kroes (Amsterdam: VU University Press, 1994), pp. 148–149.

62 David Bordwell and Kristin Thompson, Film History: An Introduction (New York: McGraw-Hill, 2002), p. 354.

63 Victoria de Grazia, Irresistible Empire: America's Advance through Twentieth-Century Europe (Cambridge, MA: Harvard University Press, 2005), p. 5.

64 Ibid., p. 343.

65 Ibid., p. 338.

66 Ibid., p. 338.

67 Jennifer Fay, Theaters of Occupation: Hollywood and the Reeducation of Postwar Germany (Minneapolis: University of Minnesota Press, 2008), pp. 39–44.

68 Lutz Koepnick, The Dark Mirror: German Cinema between Hitler and Hollywood (Berkeley: University of California Press, 2002), p. 184.

69 Ibid., p. 190.

70 Quoted in ibid., p. 194.

71 Ibid., p. 195.

72 Anna J. Merritt and Richard L. Merritt, eds., Public Opinion in Occupied Germany: The OMGUS Surveys, 1945–1949 (Champaign: University of Illinois Press, 1970), pp. 256–257.

73 "Neue Sachlichkeit im Film," Rheinische Post (Düsseldorf), December 10, 1950. Kenwort 777 press clippings, Archive, Deutsches Filmmuseum, Frankfurt am Main, Germany.

74 Tim Bergfelder, "German Cinema and Film Noir," in European Film Noir, ed. Andrew Spicer (Manchester: Manchester University Press, 1997), pp. 138–163, p. 144.

75 Ibid., p. 146.

76 Ibid., p. 144.

77 For more on this film in connection to American noirs, see Jennifer Fay, "Rubble Noir," in William Rasch and Wilfried Wilms, eds., German Postwar Film: Life and Love in the Ruins (New York: Palgrave Macmillan, 2008), pp. 125–140.

78 Andrea Slane, A Not So Foreign Affair: Fascism, Sexuality, and the Cultural Rhetoric of Democracy (Durham, NC: Duke University Press, 2001), p. 217.

79 Ibid., p. 237.

80 Ibid., p. 240.

81 John W. Dower, Embracing Defeat: Japan in the Wake of World War II (New York: W. W. Norton & Co., 1998), pp. 88–89.

82 Ibid., p. 122.

83 Ibid., pp. 133–148.

84 Ibid., p. 149.

85 Ibid., p. 123.

86 Ango Sakaguchi, "Discourse on Decadence" (1946), trans. Seiji M. Lippit, Review of Japanese Culture and Society 1:1 (October 1986), p. 5.

87 Ibid., p. 5.

88 Dower, Embracing Defeat, p. 157.

89 See H. Gene Blocker and Christopher K. Starling, Japanese Philosophy (Albany: State University of New York Press, 2001), pp. 156–157; Rikki Kerston, Democracy in Postwar Japan: Maruyama Masao and the Search for Autonomy (London: Routledge, 1996), p. 95.

90 Sari Kawana, Murder Most Modern: Detective Fiction and Japanese Culture (Minneapolis: University of Minnesota Press, 2008).

91 Ibid., pp. 22–24.

92 Ibid., pp. 152–155.

93 For an elaboration on US censorship in occupied Japan, see Kyoko Hirano, Mr. Smith Goes to Tokyo: The Japanese Cinema under the American Occupation (Washington, DC: Smithsonian Institution, 1992), pp. 47–104.

94 Ibid., p. 99.

95 James Goodwin, ed., Perspectives on Akira Kurosawa (New York: G. K. Hall, 1994), pp. 3–4.

96 Bert Cadullo, ed., Akira Kurosawa: Interviews (Jackson: University of Mississippi Press, 2008), p. 8.

97 Stephen Prince, The Warrior's Camera: The Cinema of Akira Kurosawa (Princeton, NJ: Princeton University Press, 1999), p. 85.

98 Ibid., p. 85.

99 Donald Richie, Drunken Angel DVD commentary released by Criterion in the Eclipse Series box set Post-war Kurosawa.

100 During the occupation, the US military government in Japan approved for release the following noirs: Casablanca, Now Voyager, Shadow of a Doubt, Suspicion, Gaslight, Laura, Lady in the Lake, The Lost Weekend, Dark Victory, The Dark Mirror, The Naked City, Spiral Staircase, Call Northside 777, Treasure of the Sierra Madre, Suspicion, Gilda, Secret beyond the Door, Notorious, Casbah, Act of Violence, The Night Has a Thousand Eyes. We thank Hiroshi Kitamura for sending us this list that he compiled

while researching his forthcoming *Globalizing Entertainment: Hollywood and the Cultural Reconstruction of Defeated Japan* (Ithaca, NY: Cornell University Press).

101 Gary Morris, "Stray Man: Kurosawa's Stray Dog on DVD," *Bright Lights* Film Journal 45 (August 2004), http://www.brightlightsfilm.com/45/ stray.htm. On the influence of neorealism on *Naked City* see Rebecca Prime, "Cloaked in Compromise: Jules Dassin's 'Naked' City," in Frank Krutnik, Steve Neal, Brian Neve, and Peter Stanfield, eds., *Un-American Hollywood: Politics and Film in the Blacklist Era* (New Brunswick, NJ: Rutgers University Press, 2007), pp. 145–146.

102 Prince, *The Warrior's Camera*, p. 94.

103 Ibid., pp. 89–96. See also Prince, Stray Dog DVD commentary released by Criterion.

104 James Ursini and Alain Silver, DVD commentary on *House of Bamboo*, 20th Century Fox.

105 Naremore, *More than Night*, p. 229.

106 Ibid., p. 230.

107 On the status of the stable American home as a common ideological fantasy or "vast act of imagination" in 1940s American film, see Dana Polan's *Power and Paranoia: History, Narrative, and the American Cinema* (New York: Columbia University Press, 1986), p. 253. See also Vivian Sobchack's influential reading of the transient spaces of film noir as examples of "the wartime and postwar period's myth of home and its loss," in "Lounge Time: Postwar Crises and the Chronotope of Film Noir," in *Refiguring American Film Genres: History and Theory*, ed. Nick Browne (Berkeley: University of California Press, 1998), p. 146.

108 Harry Harootunian, *Overcome by Modernity: History, Culture, and Community in Interwar Japan* (Princeton, NJ: Princeton University Press, 2000), p. xv.

109 Carl J. Mora, *Mexican Cinema: Reflections of a Society, 1896–1988* (Berkeley: University of California Press, 1982), p. 84.

110 Miriam Hansen, "The Mass Production of the Senses: Classical Cinema as Vernacular Modernism," *Modernism/Modernity* (1999), pp. 64, 65.

111 Ibid., p. 69.

112 Ibid., p. 65.

113 Miriam Hansen, "Fallen Women, Rising Stars, New Horizons: Shanghai Silent Film as Vernacular Modernism," *Film Quarterly* 54:1 (2000), pp. 10–22, p. 13.

114 For a nice overview of the diverse cinematic influences of melodramatic tradition in Mexico, including the Hollywood film noir, see Gustavo García, "Melodrama: The Passion Machine," in *Mexican Cinema*, ed. Paulo Antonio Paranagua (London: BFI, 1995), pp. 153–163. As García notes, "The

apprenticeship and mastery of the emotional machine of melodrama progressed from the irrational imitation of the silent period to incorporation of diverse influences, ranging from the fascist melodrama to Hollywood's film noir by way of Jean Renoir and René Clair" (p. 158).

115 Ana M. López, "Celluloid Tears: Melodrama in the 'Old' Mexican Cinema," *Iris* 13 (1991), pp. 29–51, p. 34.

116 Peter Brooks, quoted in López, "Celluloid Tears," p. 34.

117 François Truffaut, quoted in López, "Celluloid Tears," p. 43.

118 Borde and Chaumeton, *A Panorama of American Film Noir*, p. 2.

119 Marsha Kinder, *Blood Cinema: The Reconstruction of National Identity in Spain* (Berkeley: University of California Press, 1993), p. 294.

120 On the mutual aesthetic influence of noir and neorealism on Rodríguez and other directors of the Golden Age, see Eduardo de la Vega Alfaro, "Origins, Development, and Crisis of the Sound Cinema, 1929–1969," in *Mexican Cinema*, ed. Paulo Antonio Paranagua (London: BFI, 1995), pp. 79–93.

121 Buñuel, quoted in Mark Polizzotti, *Los Olividados* (London: BFI, 2006), p. 33.

122 Buñuel, quoted in Kinder, *Blood Cinema*, p. 32. Buñuel discusses his opposition to neorealism more fully in "Cinema, an Instrument of Poetry," in *The Shadow and its Shadow: Surrealist Writings on Cinema*, ed. Paul Hammond (San Francisco: City Lights Books, 2000), pp. 112–116.

123 Borde and Chaumeton, *A Panorama of American Film Noir*, p. 13.

124 Kinder, *Blood Cinema*, p. 18; see also Marguerite R. Waller, "Decolonizing the Screen: From *Ladri di biciclette* to *Ladri di saponette*," in Beverly Allen and Mary Russo, eds., *Revisioning Italy: National Identity and Global Culture* (Minneapolis: University of Minneapolis Press, 1997), pp. 253–274, p. 256.

125 Mary P. Wood, "Italian Film Noir," in Andrew Spicer, ed., *European Film Noir* (Manchester: University of Manchester Press, 2007), p. 243.

126 Martin Clark, *Modern Italy, 1871–1995* (London: Longman, 1996), pp. 350–351, 378–379).

127 András Bálint Kovács, *Screening Modernism: European Art Cinema, 1950–1980* (Chicago: University of Chicago Press, 2007), p. 257.

128 Ibid., p. 257. Kovács's discussion of the film on p. 259 also informs this sentence.

129 See Ned Rifkin's reading of the soundtrack in *Antonioni's Visual Language* (Ann Arbor: University of Michigan Research Press, 1982), p. 18.

130 Kathleen M. Vernon, "Reading Hollywood in/and Spanish Cinema: From Trade Wars to Transculturation," in *Refiguring Spain: Cinema/Media/Representation*, ed. Marsha Kinder (Durham, NC: Duke University Press, 1997), p. 36.

131 Ibid., p. 50.

132 Ibid., p. 40.

133 For a brief overview of Spanish noir under Franco see Rob Stone, "Spanish Film Noir," in *European Film Noir*, ed. Andrew Spicer (Manchester: University of Manchester Press, 2007), pp. 185–209.

134 Kinder, *Blood Cinema*, p. 55.

135 Ibid., p. 60.

136 Stone, "Spanish Film Noir," p. 196.

137 Ibid., p. 196.

138 Ibid., p. 200.

139 Gyan Prakash, *Another Reason: Science and the Imagination of Modern India* (Princeton, NJ: Princeton University Press, 1999), pp. 201–226.

140 Quoted in ibid., p. 210.

141 Quoted in ibid., p. 210.

142 Ibid., p. 201.

143 Ibid., p. 213.

144 Vijay Mishra, *Bollywood Cinema: Temples of Desire* (New York and London: Routledge, 2002), p. 75.

145 Ibid., p. 75.

146 Maithili Rao, "How to Read a Hindi Film and Why," *Film Comment* 38:3 (May/June 2002), p. 40.

147 For a discussion of Hindi cinema's internationalism (and, even before independence, its cosmopolitan talent) see Sangita Gopal and Sujata Moorti, "Introduction: Travels of Hindi Song and Dance," in *Global Bollywood: Travel of Hindi Song and Dance*, ed. Sangita Gopal and Sujata Moorti (Minneapolis: University of Minnesota Press, 2008), pp. 1–60.

148 Hansen, "Mass Production of the Senses," pp. 67, 69.

149 Cory Creekmur, "C.I.D," program notes, http://www.uiowa.edu/~incinema/CID.html.

150 Ali Gheissari and Vali Nasr, *Democracy in Iran: History and the Quest for Liberty* (Oxford, UK: Oxford University Press, 2006), p. 55.

151 Ibid., p. 57.

152 Ibid., p. 61.

153 Ibid., p. 62.

154 Hamid Reza Sadr, *Iranian Cinema: A Political History* (London: I. B. Tauris, 2006), p. 136.

155 Ibid., p. 137.

156 Ibid., p. 137.

157 Ibid., p. 140.

158 Ibid., p. 142.

159 Hamid Naficy, "Islamizing Film Culture in Iran: A Post-Khatami Update," in *The New Iranian Cinema: Politics, Representation and Identity*, ed. Richard Tapper (London: I. B. Tauris, 2006), p. 26.

160 Ibid., p. 27.

161 Ali Mirsepassi, *Intellectual Discourse and the Politics of Modernization: Negotiating Modernity in Iran* (Cambridge, UK: Cambridge University Press, 2000), pp. 10–11.

162 Hamid Naficy, "Veiled Voice and Vision in Iranian Cinema: The Evolution of Rakhshan Banietemad's Films," *Social Research* 67:2 (Summer 2000).

163 Ackbar Abbas, *Hong Kong: Culture and the Politics of Disappearance* (Minneapolis: University of Minnesota Press, 1997), p. 6.

164 Ibid., p. 23.

165 Ibid., p. 25.

166 On Hong Kong cinema's strategies of "cultural androgyny," and their utility for the industry's "pursuit of the global market," see Esther C. M. Yau's introductory essay in her collection *At Full Speed: Hong Kong Cinema in a Borderless World* (Minneapolis: University of Minnesota Press, 2002), pp. 7–8.

167 On these influences, see David Bordwell's discussion of Wong, *Planet Hong Kong: Popular Cinema and the Art of Entertainment* (Cambridge, MA: Harvard University Press, 2000); and Stephen Teo's *Wong Kar-wai* (London: BFI Publishing, 2005).

2

CRITICAL DEBATES

Genre, gender, race

PART I: NOIR'S ONTOLOGY, ORIGINS, AND CRITICAL FUTURES

What is the film noir, exactly? Where and when did it originate, and why? Pools of critical ink have been spilt trying to answer these questions, and several generations of film critics and theorists, caught in noir's web of fascination, have offered a range of different, even contradictory, answers. As we've demonstrated, the question only becomes more complicated when noir is approached as an international phenomenon crossing genre and media, hybridizing local aesthetic traditions and transnational cultural influences. Amidst the global flows of culture and commodities, the specific characteristics of film noir blur into other artistic genres and histories, and become impossible to establish finally. Film noir is no game for purists. In an important sense, film noir – as a stable collection of cinematic objects with identifiable properties – does not exist. Put less certainly, film noir is not any one thing, but rather a heterogeneous phenomenon that tells us as much about the nature of genre and the history of film criticism as it does about the dark essence of melodrama or crime thrillers.

When we speak of cinematic "genres," we generally mean categories of films with identifiable formal patterns that endow the film with a generic "identity" within a broader universe of films with similar characteristics. Such categories acquire labels ("a musical," "a western") used in production, marketing, and distribution, and over time generate an evolving set of expectations for audiences and critics about what kind of film they will be seeing. But the case of film noir is rather different. Hollywood directors in the 1940s did not set out to make a "film noir," but rather a "melodrama," a "thriller," a "mystery," a "red meat crime picture," or a "detective story."[1] Instead, as we've explained, it was the postwar generation of French critics who, viewing these pessimistic American films in very specific historical circumstances, gave them the label that still sells today – "film noir." So, while the American films of the 1940s and 1950s that became "films noir" were made under particular conditions of production (wartime scarcity, relaxed censorship codes, the influx of European talent into Hollywood, etc.), film noir was very much an event of reception. For this reason, many critics today tend not to think of film noir as a genre at all but rather as a "critical category," a "collector's idea," or a "fantasy" that "belongs to the history of ideas as much as to the history of cinema; in other words, it has less to do with a group of artifacts than with a discourse – a loose, evolving system of arguments and readings that helps to shape commercial strategies and aesthetic ideologies."[2] In what follows, we'll explore more carefully the implications of this argument that noir is primarily *discursive* – a way of talking about films more than any kind of film.

We will discuss three important historical contexts in which "film noir" emerged as a talismanic critical object: the midcentury invention of noir; Hollywood's production of so-called "neo-noir" beginning in the late 1960s; and academic debates about postmodernism in the 1980s and 1990s – debates concerned with both noir's very purchase on history and the politics of the nostalgia that noir so often takes as a theme and engenders in its spectators. In the process, we explore how these moments of noir's discursive circulation are also shaped by the methods, archives, and theoretical preoccupations of film noir's critics. Noir's rich critical history develops alongside the formation of academic film studies and the transformations of its methodologies over time. In fact, as Tom Gunning has suggested, film noir may just be "the great achievement of film studies" itself.[3] Because this discipline has, in the last fifteen years or so, taken a pronounced turn toward more careful historicism, we will examine a few important recent examples of noir historiography, and then explain the compatibility of these arguments with our own international approach to noir, itself shaped by a transnational turn in academic culture more broadly. This contemporary angle of vision allows us to see how the history of critical debates about noir's ontology – its curious being – has been consistently informed by transnational transfers of culture, cosmopolitan cinephilia, and critical reckonings with the nature of globalized culture itself.

Genre or Discourse?

We can get a better grasp on the notion that film noir has "no essential characteristics" by briefly surveying the range of critical claims made about noir's ontology in the decade of noir's historical "invention" at midcentury. In Chapter 1, we explained how, in 1946, two French critics, Nino Frank and Jean-Pierre Chartier, discerned in a small group of American crime thrillers and melodramas (*Double Indemnity*; *Laura*; *The Maltese Falcon*; *Murder, My Sweet*; *The Lost Weekend*; and *The Postman Always Rings Twice*) contradictory aspects of American culture in the moment of America's postwar ascendancy. For them, "films noir" portended either signs of American cinema's capacity for an internal critique of capitalism (Frank) or America's moral decay (Chartier). Nonetheless, Frank and Chartier both saw film noir as a stark revision of the "detective film genre," now imbued with a more realistic attention to "psychology" and "lived experience" stylistically evident in these films' "first-person narratives."[4]

But consider a quite different take on some of the same films offered by Siegfried Kracauer, whose essay "Hollywood's Terror Films: Do They Reflect an American State of Mind?" also appeared in 1946. A

German film critic and theorist in exile from the Nazis, first in Paris and then in America, Kracauer also observed a streak of psychological darkness in Hollywood films like *The Lost Weekend*, *Shadow of a Doubt*, and *The Spiral Staircase*. However, from Kracauer's perspective, Hollywood's new penchant for films "saturated with terror," "sadism," "and "psychological aberrations" spoke to the transfer to the American scene of horrors "formerly attributed only to life under Hitler."[5] In these films' sadistic energies, Kracauer discerned roiling in American hearts an "emotional preparedness for fascism."[6] But, unlike Frank and Chartier, Kracauer never uses the term "film noir," and he seems much more interested in the status of democratic life than the detective story, referring to the terror films instead as "thrillers" and "melodramas." Different angles of critical vision insert the film noir into different artistic genealogies and traditions. Frank and Chartier, for example, draw comparisons between the visual and narrative style of the American films noir and the films of French filmmakers and traditions (e.g., Sacha Guitry, or the prewar "French school of film noir" of Prevert and Carné, or the avant-garde tradition of "pure cinema"). Kracauer, on the other hand, compares the politics of the terror film unfavorably to the healthy resistance to fascism offered by Rossellini's neorealist film *Roma, città aperta/Rome: Open City* (1945). He likens these Hollywood films' "unusual interest in the physical environment" and "chance arrangements of inanimate objects" to the German "street" films (*Straßenfilme*) of the Weimar period – in the German 1920s and the Hollywood 1940s, "shots of street life" and monstrous objects are the stylistic hallmarks of "people emotionally out of joint," who "inhabit a realm ruled by bodily sensations and material stimulants."[7]

Just born in 1946, the American film noir is already an unstable object. Generically, it is linked to the detective film, the thriller, and the melodrama. Stylistically, it is singled out for either its subjective narration or its thingly mise-en-scène, which connects it variously to the European avant-garde film, or the French poetic realist tradition, or the Weimar street film. Politically, it is made to mean that America is capable of democratic critique, or that America is morally bankrupt, or that

America plays host to latent fascist tendencies. This confusing midcentury picture of film noir, produced in the matrix of different European visions of America, only got murkier in 1955 with the publication of the first book-length study of film noir, Raymond Borde and Etienne Chaumeton's *A Panorama of American Film Noir*. The authors of this influential study begin by declaring the very contingency of their own, local view: "Film noir is noir *for us*, that's to say, for Western and American audiences of the 1950s. It responds to a certain kind of emotional resonance as singular in time as it is in space."[8] Strongly influenced by the artistic values of French surrealism, Borde and Chaumeton describe film noir as "a series" – one united not by visual style or narration but rather by "a consistency of an emotional sort; *namely, the state of tension created in the spectators by the disappearance of their psychological bearings*."[9] Locating the noirness of noir primarily on the highly subjective level of affect and tone, Borde and Chaumeton are the first critics to embrace noir's mutability as the cinephile's genre – noir is noir "for them," after all. At the same time, the Frenchmen insist that noir actually exists outside the eye of its beholder. In fact, the problem with Borde and Chaumeton's study is not that it offers *too few* explanations for noir's historical origins and aesthetic sources, but *too many*. Noir's origins are described, variously, in the hard-boiled novel, the midcentury popularization of psychoanalysis, and the US's growing tolerance of direct treatments of violence following World War II. Further complicating matters, Borde and Chaumeton claim that noir is "typically American" – that European influence on film noir seems "feeble" – *and* that German expressionism "surely" constitutes "the most marked and persistent influence."[10] So, while German émigré directors like Robert Siodmak and Curtis Bernhardt introduce into the Hollywood thriller a "twin tradition" of expressionism and "surrealist cruelty," the "best sources" of the film noir are the three Hollywood genres of the 1930s it synthesizes: the gangster film, the horror film, and the classical, deduction-based detective film.

Confused yet? Unfortunately, the inconsistencies and internal contradictions of these arguments about noir's ontology and origins have only piled up in the decades following noir's midcentury invention. Take two of the most often cited stylistic sources of American film noir: the hard-boiled American novel and German expressionist filmmaking. Both have been recently challenged as historical determinants for noir's emergence. In the case of hard-boiled fiction, Marc Vernet has pointed to the vexing "chronological gap" between the hard-boiled source fictions of Cain and Dashiell Hammett, many written in the Depression-era culture of the late 1920s and 1930s, and the emergence of film noir in the 1940s.[11] If the success of the hard-boiled novel in the 1930s responds to a particular socio-historical climate, then how can critics claim that adaptations of these novels in Hollywood films noir speak *uniquely* to the ideological environment of the 1940s? What about the spate of 1930s crime films (including the first two Hollywood adaptations of Hammett's *The Maltese Falcon* prior to Huston's famous 1941 version) or 1930s films scripted by hard-boiled writers? By what logic are these *not* films noir? (Of course, we've added our own, international complication to this picture, including as films noir European adaptations or responses to *The Postman* like *Ossessione* and *La Bête humaine*.)

The arguments that noir's low-key, high-contrast visual style is indebted to the chiaroscuro techniques of German expressionism and that Hollywood film noir is a kind of German cinema in exile prove equally tenuous. Many noir directors and cinematographers had no historical connections to Germany; as Edward Dimendberg points out, only fifteen of sixty-two directors listed as makers of 1940s noir in Silver and Ward's *Encyclopedia of Film Noir* have German origins.[12] And the German émigré directors who made some of the most famous Hollywood films noir are, as Thomas Elsaesser puts it, "the 'wrong' Germans" to prove the expressionist argument, since their European careers had little to do with expressionism.[13] German émigrés left Europe for various reasons and arrived in the Hollywood industry at different times, often some years before they ever made their "films noir." Indeed, some of the directors fleeing Hitler (including Siodmak, Lang, and Wilder) stopped first to work in Paris, and were thus also influenced by the French style of poetic realism, its own form of film noir. What's more, noir's distinctive, postwar "expressionist image" was, as Vernet argues, found "at least as frequently in films of the preceding decade."[14] Prevalent in Hollywood since at least 1915, the high-contrast style was not only not *exclusive* to 1940s film noir, but may not even have been prevalent in it. For example, few critics would deny that *Laura*, *The Maltese Falcon*, and *The Woman in the Window* are "films noir," if anything is, but these pictures feature very little low-key lighting.[15]

Reviewing the challenges to the hard-boiled and expressionist origin stories, Stephen Neale has argued exhaustively that similar problems emerge for *every* trait adduced as a signature of the film noir. The supposed hallmarks of noir narration – flashback and voiceover – are common in Hollywood prior to the 1940s (and appear in decidedly non-noir films), and their relationship to "vulnerable interiority" is a widespread 1940s trend, evident in the gothic woman's film, the period thriller, and the melodrama. Critical arguments about the film noir's necessary relationship to postwar anxieties about gender and sexuality, or to left-wing challenges to the politics of Cold War America, founder on similar difficulties: the figure of the femme fatale so tightly linked to noir's pervasive gender trouble was, Neale explains, "by no means restricted to *noirs*," nor, we might add, was it limited to America. Neither can film noir be said to have cornered the market on "liberal and left-wing" sentiments, or even be described as ideologically uniform in its politics.[16] These critical debates about noir's politics – its encoding of historical anxieties about gender, sexuality, domesticity, race, and postwar ideological formations – are quite complex, and will be taken up separately in this chapter. For now, we want to emphasize that it is precisely noir's ontological heterogeneity that leads scholars like Neale to declare that any attempt to "homogenize" the various trends and tendencies distributed across these films "under a single heading, 'film noir,' is therefore bound to lead to incoherence."[17] "Unfortunately," Naremore claims, "nothing links together all the things described as noir – not the theme of crime, not a cinematographic technique, not even a resistance to Aristotelian narratives or happy endings."[18]

At this point, any good film student might be tempted to give up. Plagued with a baffling heterogeneity, what, finally, is film noir good for? Is there, then, no such thing as noir, but only ways of seeing films as noir? Yes and no. The various ways of *seeing films as noir* can themselves be located historically in what we might call a geo-politics of cinephilia, and will be explored more carefully in Chapter 3. For now, suffice it to say that the midcentury is one crucial moment when "film noir" attains a particular coherence on the level of spectatorship, here as European critics grapple with postwar hegemony of US culture and its global spread. As Elsaesser puts it, "*film noir* credits the U.S., at the heart of its belief in progress and optimism, with a fiercely critical, authentically negative view of American society and its institutions, thus flattering precisely those (French) intellectuals whose (left-wing) political convictions and (surrealist) aesthetic predilections obliged them to pay this compliment in the first place."[19]

How Global Culture Remakes Noir

To get a better sense of noir's status as both a fantasy and an actually existing phenomenon of global proportions, let's consider two other important moments in noir's discursive life – the invention of "neo"-noir in the 1960s and 1970s and the naming of "postmodern" noir in the 1980s and 1990s. In the late 1960s, which coincides with the institutional formation of academic film studies, film noir began to consolidate as a scholarly idea among Anglo-American critics. In 1968, the first English-language text to use the term "film noir" was published, Charles Higham's *Hollywood in the 1940s*; and a few years later two of the most influential attempts to define film noir were written, Raymond Durgnat's essay "Paint It Black: The Family Tree of the Film Noir" (1970) and Paul Schrader's "Notes on Film Noir" (1972).[20] At roughly the same time, film noir reemerged as a clear production trend within American cinema, beginning with films like *Harper* (1966) and *Point Blank* (1967), and continuing through many of the most famous films of the so-called "Hollywood Renaissance": *Bonnie and Clyde* (1967), *Klute* (1971), *The French Connection* (1971), *The Conversation* (1974), *Chinatown* (1974), *The Long Goodbye* (1974), *Taxi Driver* (1976), and *The Killing of a Chinese Bookie* (1976). As Robert Kolker has argued, this moment of Hollywood's aesthetic rebirth, while aided by relaxed censorship codes and the industry's desire to cater to an increasingly educated, middle-class audience, was also a function of another transnational transfer – namely, the influence of the European art cinema, especially the French New Wave, on a new generation of American directors.[21]

In the late 1950s and early 1960s, young French filmmakers like Jean-Luc Godard, François Truffaut, and Claude Chabrol, who had first extolled the virtues of American films noir as critics in the pages of *Cahiers du Cinéma*, produced a spate of stylistically experimental crime pictures and thrillers. These New Wave films were at once creative, cinephilic homages to Hollywood B films and genre pictures and the fruit of the postwar Americanization of French culture that, paradoxically, would be the signature of a renewed French national cinema.[22] In films like *À bout de souffle/Breathless* (1960) and *Tirez sur le pianiste/Shoot the Piano Player* (1960), the French showed the world how cinematic style might be renewed and made "modern" through a playful, highly self-reflexive reworking of "low" cultural material imported from America. Such modernist experiments in generic remaking and renewal were a global success, and highly influential for a range of young, cinephilic American directors like Martin Scorsese, Brian De Palma, Francis Ford Coppola, and Peter Bogdanovich – film school products all, who began, in the late 1960s and 1970s, to make their own self-reflexive, revisionist genre pictures that would form the core of the Hollywood renaissance. These directors' nostalgia for noir was also a nostalgia for the genre pictures of the now-vanished studio system more generally, and this taste for the cynical glamour of bygone Hollywood was cultivated in film courses.

In America, then, what critics have called "neo-noir" emerged at this curious moment when, as a result of global transfers of culture, as well as the flowering of an American culture of cinephilia fostered by film cults and the nascent institutionalization of academic film studies, critics and filmmakers began to agree that film noir actually existed, and could now be made "new." Here again, as Naremore argues, "the idea of film noir tends to bridge a gap between Europe and America, between mainstream entertainment and the art cinema. Thus American film noir of the historical period was largely a product of ideas and talent imported from Europe, and neo-noir emerged during a renaissance of the European art film, when America was relatively open to imported culture."[23] Acutely self-reflexive, American neo-noir is a historical artifact of a particular moment in the development of global film culture and cinephilic film literacy. Starting in the 1970s, filmmakers actually set out to make "films noir," and often did so as part of a broader, and critical, demystification of Hollywood's generic myths.[24]

At the same time, we might rightly wonder about the singular status of noir's "newness." Our international perspective has demonstrated that, at least since the 1930s, noir has been consistently made "neo" in a variety of local contexts and national cinemas, where transnational cultural flows have yielded a self-reflexive, generically hybrid, "modern" noir vision acutely sensitive to local crises of urban modernity. In fact, as the editors of a recent collection of critical essays on neo-noir acknowledge, "the simplest explanation of (or retroactive story about) neo-noir requires film noir to be a US phenomenon."[25] But this "too simple and unilinear" history "overlooks the global circulation of Hollywood crime thrillers (both classical and post-classical) and of the term 'film noir' and the images and ideas associated with it." While the subversive, modernist noirs of the Hollywood renaissance are surely part of the neo-noir story of the 1960s and 1970s, a fuller perspective would ask after, say, the stunning films noir made in this period in France by Jean-Pierre Melville, or the noir culture produced by the Argentinian "craze" for hard-boiled fiction between 1946 and 1960, or the postwar vogue for "Spanish-language translations of Hammett, Chandler, and David Goodis."[26] How do we account for film noir inflections in the formal experiments of the Japanese New Wave directors (Masahiro Shinoda's *Kawaita hana/Pale Flower* [1964], Shohei Inamura's *Erogotoshi-tachi yori/The Pornographers* [1966], or even Nagisa Oshima's *Seishun zankoku monogatari/Naked Youth* [1960]) and the subversive, generically heterogeneous action pictures of Seijun Suzuki, from his early gangster films like *Ankokugai no bijo/Underworld Beauty* (1958), to his occupation noir, *Nikutai no mon/Gate of Flesh* (1964), to his more delirious riffs on the yakuza genre, *Tôkyô nagaremono/Tokyo Drifter* (1966) and *Koroshi no rakuin/Branded to Kill* (1967)? In fact, as we'll see in Chapter 3, the yakuza genre's own consolidation in the 1960s bears a more complex relationship to American and European film noir than is generally allowed.[27]

These international complications of noir periodization have been overlooked until quite recently. Instead, the American and Western European foundations of academic film studies in America and Western Europe helped insure the production of histories of film noir centered in the West and, more often than not, restricted to America. Understood as an "American" phenomenon, film noir had emerged by the end of the 1970s as a clear object of academic study and a contested canon of films: E. Ann Kaplan's foundational collection of feminist essays, *Women in Film Noir*, was published in 1978 and marks the beginning of a productive marriage between feminist film theory and film noir that continues to this day. In 1981 there was the publication of several book-length studies and encyclopedias of film noir and hard-boiled fiction: Foster Hirsch's *The Dark Side of the Screen*; the first edition of Silver and Ward's *Film Noir* encyclopedia; and Charles O'Brien's *Hardboiled America*. Also in 1981, Hollywood released two highly reflexive neo-noirs, Lawrence Kasdan's *Body Heat* and Bob Rafelson's *The Postman Always Rings Twice*. The particular mode of self-consciousness of these Hollywood neo-noirs has led critics like Leighton Grist to introduce yet another distinction within the "neo-noir" category itself – that between the subversive "modernist" neo-noirs like *Point Blank* or *Taxi Driver*, in which genre is reworked in the service of social analysis or critique, and the superficial "postmodernist" neo-noirs like *Body Heat*, which seem given over to an empty, apolitical "play of surfaces."[28] At stake here are two ways of understanding the politics of noir style as it is made new – as a sort of biting parody with a satirical intent or as "pastiche," a blank, uncritical mixture or stylistic hodgepodge that ransacks the archives of film culture in the service of fashion, commodification, or nostalgia.

Such distinctions between modernist and postmodern neo-noir, or between critical parody and nostalgic pastiche, are largely indebted to Fredric Jameson's theoretical argument about postmodernism published first in the mid-1980s and later collected in *Postmodernism: Or, the Cultural Logic of Late Capitalism* (1991). Jameson's complex thesis has proven wildly influential in film, literary, and cultural studies over the last twenty-five years, and critics of film noir, including Grist, Naremore, Stanfield, and Spicer, have discerned in neo-noir many of the stylistic features that, for Jameson, are symptomatic of postmodern art and culture – pastiche, depthlessness, inauthenticity, the reign of the simulacrum, "weak" affect, to name a few.[29] But it is also important to recall that for Jameson, a Marxist critic, postmodernism is not just a style, but rather the cultural logic of "the bewildering new world space of late or multinational capital," a space defined by "new forms of business organization (transnationals and multinationals)," new "international divisions of labor," and "novel forms of media interrelationship (global media conglomerates)."[30] In short, Jameson's version of postmodernism is also a theory of globalized culture, and a decidedly noir one: "this whole global, yet American, postmodern culture is the internal and superstructural expression of a whole new wave of American military and economic domination throughout the world: in this sense, as throughout class history, the underside of culture is blood, torture, death, and terror."[31]

What does this picture of globalized culture mean for our present, and film noir's critical future? Does Jameson's triple equation of globalization, American culture, and postmodernity – three synonyms for the same style of world domination – seem useful for understanding noir's global currency? The question is all the more pressing now that film noir has become an inextricable part of the contemporary global "mediascape," circulating through the exploding information technologies of twenty-first-century culture, from cable and digital television to DVDs, graphic novels, and every dark corner of the new media environment. Jameson, for his part, feared that, when "the producers of culture have nowhere to turn but to the past," what is lost is our own "historicity", the "lived possibility of experiencing history in some active way."[32] His concern that postmodern neo-noir is hopelessly nostalgic is echoed in Naremore's claim that noir today is a "worldwide mass memory; a dream image of bygone glamour, it represses as much history as it recalls, usually in the service of cinephilia and commodification."[33]

Post-Postmodernism?: or, The Future is History

These warnings are useful, but they have a way of pitting noir nostalgia and noir history against each other, as if film noir was not always both a global "mass memory" and historically located, as if feelings of nostalgia could not be historicized or themselves work as a kind of historicism. As Paul Young observes, film noir has always tended to transform "all critics into cultural historians just long enough for them to read film noir as a cracked mirror of postwar American culture."[34] And yet, like academic film students more generally, critical accounts of film noir in the last decade or so have taken on the task of producing less fleeting, and more finely grained and nuanced, methods of historical research. In fact, some of the most compelling recent examples of film noir's historical turn, all of them operating within the American context, have in various ways inspired the picture of global noir we've produced. Like globalization itself, this picture can't seem to do without the nostalgia for homes and the uncanny violence of modernity.

Take Vivian Sobchack's important 1998 essay "Lounge Time: Postwar Crises and the Chronotope of Film Noir." Responding directly to arguments like Vernet's, Sobchack asks, "What is the 'there' there of film noir? And what is its 'truth'?"[35] Her answer? American film noir attains historical coherence around particular kinds of transient, anonymous, de-individuated *spaces* – nightclubs, bars, hotel rooms, boardinghouses, dance halls, bus and train stations. These spaces came to dominate both American cultural life and American movie screens during the 1940s. During this period, the US "went off to fight the good fight and to come home after it to a troubled capitalist domestic economy."[36] The homecoming's mood of "domestic anxiety" was produced not just by the wartime economy's widespread challenge to traditional modes of gendered behavior, but also by "constantly rising prices of food, clothing and other necessities," by "increasing rents and a nationwide housing shortage," by labor disputes, and by fears of a renewed Great Depression, which persisted until 1947.[37] For Sobchack, these concrete social conditions produced a cultural tension between the myth of a stable, secure home or homefront and the reality of its loss. In this climate, the transient places so common in the postwar film noir were neither metaphors nor allegories, but instead represented "actual spaces charged with a particular temporal meaning," expressing "the lived sense of insecurity, instability, and social incoherence Americans experienced during the transitional period that began after the war and Roosevelt's death in 1945, lasted through the Truman years (1945–52), and declined as the Eisenhower years (1952–60) drew to a prosperous close."[38]

To connect America's domestic unease and the unhomely cultural products of film noir, Sobchack draws on Russian literary critic Mikhail Bakhtin's theory of the *chronotope* (literally, time-space). For Bakhtin, the chronotope is not a "spatiotemporal backdrop," but rather a historically specific, local *experience of space and time* that itself generates narrative structures, characters, tropes – and in its own spatio-temporal image.[39] Sobchack is especially interested in Bakhtin's description of the dominant, pastoral form of the chronotope that emerges in eighteenth-century literature and is later destroyed by the new individualism of the bourgeois novel in the late eighteenth and early nineteenth centuries. For Sobchack, this idyllic mode of space-time, associated with folklore, is a historical analog for the mythic fantasies of home that became so popular in 1940s American cinema. Both idylls promise "an organic fastening down, a grafting of life and its events to a place, to a familiar territory . . . and one's own home."[40] And on the other side of these idylls – of intimate, organic community, of generational continuity, of intelligible, secure, rooted homes – are the "unfamiliar, unfamilial, and anonymous" spaces of film noir and the temporal experience common to it – lounge time.[41] Noir's "lounge time," Sobchack concludes, is a "perverse and dark response, on the one hand, to the loss of home and a felicitous, carefree ahistoricity and, on the other, to the inability to imagine being at home, in history, in capitalist democracy, at this time."[42]

Is it a problem, methodologically speaking, that Sobchack's attempt to historicize American film noir does so by virtue of Russian literary theory, and through a complex historical analogy between the late-eighteenth-century novel's challenge to the idyllic chronotope and the "lounge time" of postwar American films? She ends by comparing the doomed existentialism of Burt Lancaster's "The Swede" in *The Killers* (Siodmak, 1946) to "the putative hero of the *bildungsroman*."[43] Both are faced with the inadequacy of their organic idyll in light of the new capitalist world – its fragmented social forms, its alienated labor, its egotism, its estranged city life. Sobchack's seeming anachronism in fact reflects a central claim of this book, and of much recent noir scholarship – that postwar American film noir be understood as one historical, national inflection of a transnational historical sensibility of not being at home, "in capitalist democracy, at this time."[44] The missing conceptual term from Sobchack's analysis – and one that joins the malaise experienced in Goethe's novel of bourgeois development (the explicit object of Bakhtin's analysis) to postwar American cinema – is *modernity*, the experience of the new, capitalist world whose uneven processes of disembedding have threatened domestic traditions and organic national culture the world over. "Lounge time," as we've shown, pervades the global itinerary of noir – it connects Cain's vagrants in the 1930s, the drifters of French poetic realism, the way-ward desires of the Mexican *cabaretera*, and the Americanized deca-dence of Kurosawa's nightclubs in *Stray Dog* and *Drunken Angel*.

The concept of modernity, as our own book attests, has made a striking comeback in film studies over the past decade or so, and has proven central to its historical turn. In the case of film noir, the crucial text in this regard is Edward Dimendberg's *Film Noir and the Spaces of Modernity* (2004), an erudite, expansive study of American film noir's response to changes in the built environment of twentieth-century urban modernity. Like Sobchack, Dimendberg understands films noir as documents of specific forms of lived, urban experience in America at midcentury. However, Dimendberg's historical approach is consid-erably more interdisciplinary, drawing together film history and crit-icism as well as the "extracinematic precincts of geography, city planning, architectural theory, and urban and cultural history."[45] For Dimendberg, because Hollywood film noir and the American city are "mutually implicated in the construction of common spatial fantasies and anxieties," both contend with specific transformations of urban space that Dimendberg associates with the period of "late moder-nity."[46] So-called "late modern" space, Dimendberg explains, is situ-ated at a transitional moment at midcentury marked by "the eclipse of concentrated 'centripetal' urban space" and the rise of "dispersed 'cen-trifugal' space."[47] Centripetal space, the holdover of American urban-ism of the 1920s and 1930s, is defined by an ordered, centered, internally differentiated urban environment – one that seems to promise a transparent social structure of mappable space and familiar forms of organic urban community. Centrifugal space, by contrast, is diffuse and decentered, marked by the explosive growth of postwar American suburbia and its forms of serial, homogeneous space – a space of more "opaque social and economic relations."[48] Historically coincident with "unprecedented architectural destruction" in the US, American film noir presides over the waning of local, knowable, seemingly authentic space and the waxing of abstract, serial space – spatiality "in which the simulacra and spectacles of contemporary postmodern culture are clearly visible in retrospect."[49] Film noir is thus marked by a critical nostalgia for disappearing or outmoded forms of local, urban experience sacrificed in the development of postwar modern life marked by the "loss of individual identity and the growing power of a technological society organized by new spatial forms and the mass media."[50]

Notice how Dimendberg's distinction between centripetal and centrifugal spatiality recasts, and more fully historicizes, Sobchack's contrast between the organic idyll of postwar homelife and the noir reality of "lounge time." Both critics understand noir to encode a crisis of dwelling – a form of local, spatio-temporal experience imperiled by the developmental logic of postwar American modernity. But, as we've shown, because modernity develops unevenly across the globe, noir's capacity to articulate crises of local spaces crosses national boundaries and complicates periodizing efforts. Buñuel's parable of non-development in *Los Olvidados*, for example, is also an anatomy of the transition to centrifugal space in the context of Mexican postwar modernization, just as *Chungking Express* explores Hong Kong's local culture of disappearance in the 1990s. The condition of homelessness within capitalist democracy is, we've suggested, the malaise of globalization.

Noir historicism can itself be centripetal – more tightly circumscribing the object of study by theme (Dimendberg's spatiality) or genre, or through focused industrial history – or centrifugal, crossing and contaminating generic, temporal, and disciplinary borders.[51] More contained histories run the risk of sacrificing explanatory power, or erecting arbitrary boundaries around their objects of study, whereas more expansive studies may lose historical detail or precision in the same, noir night where all cows are chiaroscuro. Paula Rabinowitz's *Black & White & Noir: America's Pulp Modernism* (2002) is an important recent example of the latter – a far-flung work of interdisciplinary cultural history that takes noir not as a subject of study, but as a restive political "sensibility" running throughout twentieth-century American culture.[52] For Rabinowitz, film noir is nothing short of a "theory of American modernity," a "template" that has not so much *reflected* American politics as made politics and social experience culturally legible, framed it in a noir idiom.[53] Rather than some ontologically fuzzy group of films in need of more and better contexts and histories, noir performs its own form of national historiography – it is a "political theory of America's problematic democracy disguised as cheap melodrama, with origins in two submerged aspects of American modernity: the contradiction of slaveholding in a democracy and the suppression of working-class organizing."[54] Noir reveals American modernity to be "structured around two poles: each working to suppress a hidden history of state violence: racial codings . . . and class melodrama."[55] And these traumas of class conflict and racial violence chaotically repeat across the landscape of the twentieth century: "just as 50s popular culture refers unconsciously to 30s political culture, recent popular political culture gestures continually to noir."[56] As a popular theory of the uncanniness of American-style capitalist democracy, noir's political sensibility cannot then be neatly periodized, nor limited by media. Instead, Rabinowitz discerns a noir sensibility in the OWI photographs of Esther Bubley in the 1940s, in 1930s images of the rural poor, in the midcentury novels of Ann Petry, Richard Wright, and Ralph Ellison, in the kinds of fetishized objects taken up by feminist theory, and even in women's experimental cinema of the Vietnam era, which offers its own noir version of uncanny domesticity. Rabinowitz's centrifugal methodology, ranging brilliantly among "seemingly disparate fields of inquiry," thus seeks to demonstrate "the wild totality possible through interdisciplinary work."[57]

The Future of Noir Nostalgia: The American Friend

If noir's ontological incoherence has helped fuel a critical return to the archives of American cultural history, such historicism has produced a dazzling variety of contexts (aesthetic, industrial, political) in which the noir phenomenon might be approached. The archivist, searching for the origins of anything, always produces more archive, and more desire to recapture the best story about the past. The archive fever of historiography thus plays out its own noir drama, ever pining after obscured origins. This is much to the gain of film history and criticism, which will always have more to say, and has the added benefit of forcing film historians and film students out of their comfort zones – archival, disciplinary, historical, and linguistic. So, as admirable as these works of noir historicism are, their insights and methodologies are transportable beyond the American context, and this too is good. If noir can be thought of as a problem of the uncanniness of capitalist democracy (Sobchack), one encoded in the history of modernity's built environments (Dimendberg), or one marked by the traumatic returns of a submerged history of state violence (Rabinowitz), then this sensibility is also a global one, which is not to deny its local inflections. As an example, consider Wim Wenders's *Der amerikanische Freund/The American Friend* (1977), a film considered as exemplary of a certain postmodern nostalgia, but one that also delivers a sharply noir account of capitalist modernity's troubled homes.

The American Friend is a German adaptation of the novel *Ripley's Game* (1974), the second in the acclaimed "Ripleiad" written by American novelist Patricia Highsmith. But it is also a highly self-conscious use of film noir as, in Rabinowitz's terms, a critical *theory* of American modernity. The film's hyper-referentiality is most obvious in its casting. Nicholas Ray, a director of several canonical American films noir (*They Live by Night* [1948], *In a Lonely Place* [1950], *On Dangerous Ground* [1952]), and a fetish auteur for the French New Wave, plays an art forger faking masterpieces by a dead painter named Derwatt. Wenders cast Samuel Fuller, American pulp novelist and director of *House of Bamboo* (1955) and a host of other low-budget noir masterpieces, as a mobbed-up American producer of pornographic films. Listed in the credits only as "Der Amerikaner" (The American), this character's attempt to control the German market is one of the film's more overt references to Hollywood's aggressive postwar dominance of German screens. And Dennis Hopper, an actor virtually synonymous with American 1960s counterculture and the Hollywood renaissance (and who received his first Hollywood role in Nicholas Ray's *Rebel without a Cause* [1955]), plays Highsmith's talented psychopath Tom Ripley. In the film, Ripley sells forged Derwatts in Europe and, in the process, fatally contaminates the homelife of an ailing German picture framer named Jonathan Zimmerman (Bruno Ganz). Wenders's cinephilic casting is complemented by the film's many references to Hollywood's past. Tom, who rents an absurd neoclassical villa in Germany that looks like a miniature White House, cavorts in scarlet satin sheets straight out of *Gentlemen Prefer Blondes* (Hawks, 1953); Jonathan's son Daniel has a night-light featuring Buster Keaton's titular train from *The General* (1926); and Jonathan himself collects pre-cinematic optical devices. His nostalgic hobby links his old-world craftsmanship as a picture framer to a certain hankering after cinema's own silent origins, the Golden Age of German cinema.[58] And Wenders, in turn, associates Jonathan's acts of skilled framing with his own in the film's many theatrically framed compositions.

Like German culture itself following America's postwar hegemony, *The American Friend* is flooded with the icons of American popular and mass culture – Hollywood fare (including film noir) and other notorious products of global US culture like Coca-Cola machines. Wenders thus skillfully deploys Highsmith's arty metaphors of forgery and authenticity, fakes and originals, to comment on the unhomely status of German national culture in the 1970s. The young generation of directors who would become known as the New German Cinema were positioned between what they saw as a foreclosed national cultural past, forever stained by Nazism, and the imposition of American mass culture, whose movies served as a kind of surrogate cultural archive for a nation invested in forgetting its own bloody history.[59] *The American Friend*'s titular bond between Tom and Jonathan works as a rather explicit allegory of US–German relations, exploring the way in which, as one of Wenders's other protagonists put it in *Im Lauf der Zeit/Kings of the Road* (1976), "The Yanks have colonized our subconscious." In the process, Wenders makes Ripley a much uglier and more homesick American than in Highsmith's source novel, where Tom – a consummate mimic of manners and taste – has accommodated himself rather nicely to European life. In Wenders's revision, Ripley sports a ten-gallon cowboy hat and drives a vintage white Ford Thunderbird (Figure 2.1). He seems to figure the ahistoricity of postmodern Americanization itself – and its losses. Ripley makes dictaphone recordings of his present self, which he later replays compulsively, and in which he confesses to not knowing who he is; and he later tells Derwatt that he just wants to "go home," a nostalgia he repeatedly connects to the workmanlike substantiality of Jonathan's homelife. He likes the peaceful, homey wood and paint in Jonathan's frame shop, and he admires the fact that Jonathan "actually makes things" and can see the material fruits of his work. Ripley's labor, on the other hand, is the intangible stuff of capital as a mobile force of abstraction: "I make money," Ripley explains, "and I travel a lot."

It's just this kind of international abstraction – linked to money and travel – that Jonathan experiences more acutely the more he becomes entangled in a financial partnership with Ripley. Suffering from a rare, apparently terminal blood disease, Jonathan agrees to serve as a button

FIGURE 2.1   Ripley plays himself (*The American Friend*, 1977).

man for Ripley's French associate Raoul Minot, whose targets are vaguely linked to an international battle for control over the German porno market. With Minot's help, Ripley spreads a rumor that Jonathan is in fact sicker than he really is, and then arranges to fly him to foreign specialists at (not coincidentally) the American Hospital in Paris. It's the "best in town," Minot crows. "Onassis died there. Jean Gabin too." It's Wenders's first cruel joke about America's cultural influence on foreign shores, where hospitality blurs with deathliness; the American hospital is the place where celebrity billionaires and noir icons go to die, although Jonathan hopes to avoid Gabin's legendary forms of cinematic death, protesting "I don't intend to die there." Ripley's hospitality, however, will prove equally fatal. Forging Jonathan's medical reports with Minot's help, Ripley convinces Jonathan that he is quickly dying, and had better turn hit man to provide a stable future for his wife and his son, Daniel. Once Ripley enters Jonathan's homelife, it is hopelessly displaced. Searching after the truth of his medical condition, he becomes a murderer to secure the future of his family. In the process, though, Jonathan only estranges himself from his wife, Marianne (Lisa Kreuzer), who distrusts Ripley, and feels deserted by Jonathan at the hands of his queer new American friend. In Sobchack's terms, the homosocial partnership with Tom stalls Jonathan in the static, repetitive temporality of "lounge time" – anonymous, unfamilial, and abstract, and now operating on European shores.

Wenders's mise-en-scène clarifies Ripley's domestic threat by contrasting the cozy warmth of Jonathan's home with the artificial, abstract space of Ripley's villa. Its hollow center is a pool table over which hangs a Canada Dry light spilling a sickly yellow green glow that suffuses the anonymous modern spaces of Wenders's film – the windows of highrises, the spaces of airports and airplanes, the subterranean light of subway tunnels. In Dimendberg's terms, Wenders stages a contrast between the outmoded, centripetal space of Jonathan's home – a quaint, brick-faced apartment building – and the threat of abstract, serial "centrifugal" space that threatens to engulf it.

Curiously, Jonathan's home is right on the harbor – and this proximity to the abstract flows and movements of capital is noted in an odd top-shot of his apartment building that reveals it as a tiny island adjacent to a void where, apparently, a neighboring building used to be. Centrifugal space proliferates in the film, and confuses national boundaries. We see it in the way the menacing giant crane outside the window of Jonathan's Parisian hotel echoes the horizon of port cranes outside his home window, in the disorienting patterns of Wenders's editing, which refuse establishing shots that would clarify the characters' international movements, and in the sites of mobility and travel in which Jonathan's deadly capers with Ripley are staged (trains, planes, cars, hotels, subway stations).

The film's final sequence is the culmination of this kind of spatio-temporal abstraction. After Jonathan and Ripley have successfully defended Ripley's villa from a siege of "Der Amerikaner's" henchmen, Jonathan's wife improbably appears in a Volkswagen Beetle, imploring Jonathan: "I've looked for you everywhere. Let's go home." In response, Jonathan deliriously mumbles Beatles lyrics: "Baby, you can drive my car." The song is the punchline of a complex audio-visual pun joining two kinds of Beatles/Beetles, both storied transatlantic commodities that here seem to seal the fate of Jonathan's failed home-life. The couple agrees to follow Ripley, who has commandeered Der Amerikaner's ambulance and "wants to get to the sea." At the water's edge, which really could be *anyplace*, so delocalized is the space, the couple abandons Ripley and proposes to get back to Daniel. On the way, Jonathan collapses and dies at the wheel of the car. There will be no going home for Jonathan, and over shots of his dead body Ripley salutes him, singing his eternal exile: "Pity the poor immigrant . . ." We cut abruptly to the streets of New York at sunset as Derwatt, master forger and master capitalist, appraises the Manhattan skyline. As the credits roll, Derwatt/Ray walks toward the World Trade Center, that now tragically destroyed emblem of American-style global capitalism. While its sight conjures a kind of nostalgia today for a lost American innocence that never was, for Wenders, in 1977, the Twin Towers still stood for the power, and violence, of US capital, which dwarfs the romantic allure of American culture. For Wenders, and French *Cahiers du Cinéma* critics before him, one of the names for this promise was "Nicholas Ray."[60] This final image encodes the ambivalent relationship to American modernity that has historically marked noir's global reception.

Positioned in the spaces and flows of late capitalism, Wenders's film is quite historical, even though its story of German culture in the 1970s forsakes the nostalgia for cultural "authenticity" betrayed in Jameson's own reckoning with the postmodern. Moreover, the film's historical sensibility is of a piece with its cinephilia rather than its victim. The film is undoubtedly nostalgic, but in an acutely noir sense – it is nostalgic for a past that it knows never existed. Like Wong's *Chungking Express*, Wenders's *The American Friend* suggests that, rather than ways of finally returning home, nostalgia and cinephilia are also modes of dreaming new, better futures, or of marking out spaces of critical dissatisfaction with the present. Noir's nostalgia is produced by and imaginatively reroutes global apportionings of culture and cultural access. The turn to the past is always contingent, structured by the critical pressures, archives, and methodologies available at any given present. In other words, *The American Friend* begins to suggest how film noir – and criticism of it – might have a future within a global film culture that cannot but return to it. This means thinking about film noir's global culture of cinephilia and nostalgia historically – as richly embedded acts of local perception. As Borde and Chaumeton knew, film noir is always noir *for someone*. Their midcentury insight remains today, for us, as good a description of noir's ontology as any.

PART II: NOIR'S OTHERS

Noir Sexuality and The Politics of Desire

Whether it is considered as a genre, a movement, or a discourse, noir has fascinated critics for the ways it dramatizes irrational, violent desire and puts into play two archetypal figures of modern sexuality: the hard-boiled hero and the dangerous femme fatale. The rise of feminist film theory in the 1970s invigorated debates about noir's gender dynamics and led critics to consider how representations of gender historically responded to and continue to structure social relations. For many critics, as we will see, noir's sexual politics is its most distinctive feature, one that – like noir's politics more generally – may be read as inherently conservative, and even misogynistic, or as a progressive challenge to patriarchal, heterosexual norms, if only because noir lays bare those values that other Hollywood genres seamlessly uphold.

One strand of criticism argues that noir's gender play and the recurrent narrative patterns of the femme fatale's lethal sexuality reflect radical social changes in the US during and following World War II. As men were drafted and fought in the world's most brutal hostilities, women entered the workforce in unprecedented numbers and achieved a new social and financial independence that upset the traditional gender roles and threatened the structure of the American family. Film noir, some argue, emerges as a response to this shift and offers narratives that help men make sense of this new American woman.

During the war, it was women's patriotic duty to work in munitions factories, and Hollywood played its part by promoting the homefront culture. But, as Frank Krutnik argues, beginning in 1944 Hollywood began the cultural reorientation to a postwar domestic order in which women would have to return to previous roles as wives and mothers. Women who resisted this reorientation, who insisted on retaining their economic and social autonomy, would become the social basis for the femmes fatales "who seek to advance themselves by manipulating their sexual allure and controlling its value."[61] In this way, real women's newly acquired social and economic independence was transmuted into a fantasy of their fatal sexual power. Because she is both desired and feared, the femme fatale is the cynosure of imperiled masculinity. The hero must either resist her advances (and in so doing stifle his own desire) or risk real or symbolic death. Typically his resistance results in her demise. "It is, in fact, in the way that it reflects the new status of women in American society that film noir is most closely connected to its period," explains Foster Hirsch. "Like everything else noir touched, it transformed the new role of women into a negative image." The "weak, uncertain, woefully neurotic men and fire-breathing dragon ladies" are "nightmarish distortions of contemporary realities."[62]

According to this view, noir served a social function for its 1940s American audience by expressing and focusing a variety of male anxieties onto an archetype of sexual femininity. If men were anxious about woman, film noir justified the dominant ideology, as Janey Place explains, by "first demonstrating her dangerous power and its frightening results, then destroying it."[63] The larger social danger such films posed, of course, is that these representations would organize our perceptions of actual women. Read as conservative texts that reflect and construct social reality, noir stereotypes of the femme fatale and the virginal wife create rigid and untenable categories of female sexuality. And the narratives themselves seem to authorize violence against women who transgress these stultifying norms.[64]

Yet, as Place argues, the often excessive style of film noir may overwhelm the narrative's conservative message. Because the femme fatale dominates the compositions in which she appears, and because she captivates us with her ambition and sexual allure, her image transcends her cinematic destruction. "The visual style gives her such freedom of movement and dominance that it is her strength and sensual visual texture that is inevitably printed in our memory."[65] After watching The Postman Always Rings Twice (1946), to use Place's example, what we remember is not Cora's death, but her quick-witted plotting, her exposed midriff, and her "turban-wrapped angelic face."[66] In this reading, American postwar film noir emerges as a vexed object for feminists because, while it punished alluring women, it nonetheless "stands as the only period in American film in which women are deadly but sexy, exciting and strong."[67]

For Sylvia Harvey, it is not so much the femme fatale who is under attack in film noir as the institution of the American family and the increasingly corporatized workplace, which fail to provide sexual pleasure and occupational satisfaction, respectively. The noir couple represents radical nonconformity because they turn away from the moribund institutions that governed postwar social relations in the US and seek pleasures and money elsewhere. As Harvey notes, the family in films noir is an institution of loveless feminine oppression. Husbands are crippled, impotent, and angry. Wives are either the desexualized mothers or plotting adulterers. "The expression of sexuality and the institution of marriage are at odds with one another, and . . . both pleasure and death lie outside the safe circle of family relations."[68] If the dominant ideology of postwar America pressured women to forsake their independence by returning to the home as wives and mothers, and if the family was to be the institution of the woman's supreme fulfillment, film noir makes this family strange, perverse, or altogether absent. As we discuss above, Vivian Sobchack's discussion of noir's "unfamilial" space and time, its "lounge time," expands while it also historically grounds Harvey's earlier reading of the missing family. For Sobchack, it is not just the family that is missing in noir; the entire home and homefront of the pre-World War II imaginary have been replaced with rented, dislocated spaces populated by noir predators. Thus, both Harvey and Sobchack read noir not as a conservative backlash to women's emancipation, as Hirsch sees it, but as a counter-narrative that may "encourage the consideration of alternative institutions for the reproduction of social life."[69] In the spirit of Place's essay, Harvey contends that the punishing ending of these films cannot "recuperate their subversive significance."[70]

Indeed, several critics note that, because heterosexual romance is always doomed in noir, hard-boiled heroes find comfort in the company of men; thus, one alternative to which noir points is a queer sociality.[71] Compared to other Hollywood genres, noir is striking not only for its socially sanctioned homoeroticism (a form of male–male intimacy that is not explicitly sexual but can be read as "quasi-gay")[72] but also for its representation of queer characters whose deviance from heterosexual norms has the potential to destabilize those norms as such. How subversive noir is on this score is a matter of critical debate. Richard Dyer, for example, argues that noir's gay characters are those, like Waldo Lydecker in *Laura* (1944) or Ballin Mundson in *Gilda* (1946), who are associated with an effeminate aestheticism evident in their preference for finely tailored clothes, perfume, and *objets d'art*, and enjoy a flirtatious relationship with the hard-boiled hero. These men are coded as evil not only because they resemble the femme fatale, but also because they enjoy an exclusive intimacy with her that is "uncomplicated by heterosexual lust."[73] That is, these gay-coded characters "aestheticize" and "adore" alluring women "without really desiring them sexually."[74] The very idea that queer men share so much with these evil, narcissistic women is inherently homophobic and misogynistic, and thus part of a larger "armoury of gay oppression and indeed of sexual oppression generally."[75] Noir is potentially subversive, however, in the way that it defamiliarizes and denaturalizes the bewitching properties of womanhood. In these films, the perfumed and coiffed queers are merely an "exaggeration or parody of femininity."[76] Because they share an effeminate culture and look with the femme fatale, noir's homosexuals foreground noir womanhood as a kind of performance, or what other scholars have called a masquerade.[77]

Take, for example, the parallels between the enthralling Laura Hunt (Gene Tierney) and Lydecker (Clifton Webb), the queer art critic, in Otto Preminger's *Laura*. We are first introduced to Lydecker through his possessions and disembodied voiceover narration. The camera smoothly tracks through his lavish apartment revealing shimmering glass collectibles, an ornate freestanding clock, a sparkling chandelier, and exotic masks on the wall. Finally the camera rests not on Lydecker, but on our detective hero, McPherson (Dara Andrews), who is waiting to interview him about a murder. McPherson sneers at this refinery, feeling himself out of place and perhaps outclassed. But the sneer returns to McPherson's face when finally he sees Lydecker in the flesh, or, shall we specify, in the nude. For Lydecker is bathing in his equally ornate bathroom during their first exchange. As the two men discuss the murder case, Lydecker towels off and dresses with meticulous attention to his silk pocket square and fragrant boutonnière. It is both the objects and the "overall fussiness [of his toilet] process itself" that style Lydecker as queer.[78] As Lydecker explains to McPherson that evening over a candlelit dinner, he is a self-proclaimed, self-absorbed connoisseur of women, of art, and of true crime, who has molded Laura into the successful advertising executive she's become – that is, until her alleged murder.

In keeping with Dyer's reading, Lydecker does not love Laura or sexually desire her so much as he prizes her as an object reflecting his good taste. McPherson, a working-class and uncultured gumshoe, has little access to this world of high refinery. Yet, when he becomes intimate with Laura's equally lavish apartment (which boasts an exact replica of Lydecker's freestanding neo-baroque clock), McPherson becomes romantically obsessed with this "dead" woman. In one scene, he moves around her apartment handling her effects: a silk scarf, her perfume, her clothes, and her letters (some written to her by Lydecker). McPherson pours himself a drink and gazes at a portrait of her that he plans to buy from the estate. As Lydecker asserts, McPherson has fallen in love with a corpse. While this desire is meant to convey the power of Laura's appeal, we may read this necrophilia as a statement about noir femininity. Even in the absence of a flesh-and-blood woman, McPherson is seduced by the products that *produce* her and that materially *connect* her to a gay-coded character. In this way, *Laura* suggests that femininity is not any more "natural" than sexuality.

That Lydecker and Laura share so many objects in common, moreover, implies that McPherson's heterosexual fixation on things could easily find him amorously attached to other (male) bodies. The candlelit dinner that McPherson and Lydecker share, at the exact table where Lydecker and Laura used to dine, constructs Lydecker as both McPherson's romantic rival and his romantic interest. The connections between people and things, and between things and desire, reveal how sexual longing in this film circulates through a polymorphous range of deviant object choices that cut across hetero- and homo-subjectivities. Critic Robert J. Corber argues not only that Lydecker is associated with the femme fatale, but that he is the femme fatale. It is Lydecker, and not Laura, who kills out of jealousy, and who seductively deceives McPherson to keep Laura out of his grasp.[79] Just before he attempts to kill her again, Lydecker admits to Laura his deranged passion for her: "The best part of myself – that's what you are. Do you think I'm going to leave it to the vulgar pawing of a second-rate detective who thinks you're a dame? Do you think I could bear the thought of him holding you in his arms, kissing you, loving you?" Here Lydecker offers a vicious declaration of self-love in the form of a homoerotic fantasy. Laura is his better part, one that he would sooner destroy than allow to be pawed by an uncultured dolt. In the final scene, however, we are once again drawn back to the film's erotic economy of things. Lydecker is shot by one of McPherson's men just as Lydecker fires his rifle, and, missing the cop, instead hits the face of the freestanding clock. This is the exact replica of the clock we first saw in his apartment; and the shot in the face is precisely how he intended to kill Laura, and how he had already killed and defaced Diane Redford. And yet, it is as if, in shooting the clock, Lydecker also shoots himself. It is he, and not Laura, who now lies on the floor with a belly full of buckshot. As the camera pans from Lydecker, to Laura, to the clock, Lydecker says goodbye. It is over the image of this now-destroyed timepiece that Lydecker utters his last: "my love." The clock both stands for the fallen Lydecker and substitutes for Laura as the lost object of his love.[80]

For Dyer, noir is interesting precisely because it detaches gender from biological sex (and, in *Laura*, detaches it from bodies altogether), and reveals varieties of "undomesticated femininity" as the source of the hero's anxiety.[81] This threat is embodied in several characters: the femme fatale, the queer rival, and even the butch lesbian, who in films like *Farewell, My Lovely* (aka *Murder, My Sweet*, 1944) and *In a Lonely Place* (1950) are mannishly represented but fail to live up to hard-boiled standards. "Film noir's queerness suggests that the feminine is not coterminous with womanhood – that there are different ways of being feminine, that some men can be feminine, and that some women can be effeminate."[82] Though the coding of queer characters is homophobic (they are always evil), noir still challenges gender norms because it intimates that the distinctions between straight and gay, between feminine and masculine, and even between people and things – distinctions essential to a conservative understanding of sexual politics – are themselves fictions.

Reading noir's codes in this way may seem like a perverse stretch of the imagination. Yet, because the Hollywood Production Code forbade explicit representation of gay characters and homosexual (and for that matter explicit heterosexual) desire, such subplots could only be intimated.[83] In fact, it may be that only by connecting gay characters to criminal types could such veiled representations of homosexuality pass the Production Code Administration's (PCA) scrutiny. It is one project of queer theory in film studies to bring to light the repressed and closeted narratives in Hollywood films, however much they are manifested in negative stereotypes, by returning to the film's hard-boiled sources (many of which, like *Laura*, are much more explicit about the character's sexual orientation), researching the PCA's archive to better understand censored content, and excavating the biographies of gay Hollywood talent.

One of the few known gay stars of the 1940s, Clifton Webb, was instrumental in "outing" his character, Lydecker, through his virtuosic performance (what one critic praised as his "auntyish effeminacy"[84]), which earned him an Academy Award nomination. But the PCA demanded that Preminger modify the film's explicitly homosexual content. Based on his on- and off-screen persona, spectators could read the film for signs of a queer subtext. Other Hollywood noirs likewise routed the representation of homosexuality through criminal characters. Take, for example, *The Maltese Falcon*, whose criminal gang is replete with queer signifiers. Joel Cairo (Peter Lorre) is first introduced in the film when the secretary presents Sam with Cairo's "gardenia"-scented calling card. Cairo then enters the office adorned in a tuxedo, with coiffed hair, polished nails, a flirtatious manner, and glamorous edge-lighting. His gay-coded style is seemingly confirmed when Sam searches Cairo's wallet and finds opera tickets and a perfumed handkerchief. Working with Cairo is the British criminal mastermind Gutman (Sydney Greenstreet) and his "gunsel," Wilmer (Elisha Cook), as Sam refers to him.[85] As numerous fan-sites note, the ambiguity of the term "gunsel" – meaning both "homosexual youth" and "hired gunman" – is slyly exploited in *The Maltese Falcon*'s criminal milieu. Wilmer, we gather, is just one in a series of boys Gutman keeps in tow, although little of the film's homoeroticism is explicit (Figure 2.2). Moreover, queer characters are also associated with foreignness. Lydecker, as Leonard Leff notes, speaks "social French" and boasts a "near British accent"; his queerness is further conveyed through his "continental table manners."[86] Joel Cairo, whose last name announces a foreign, "oriental" origin, holds three different passports, none of them American. And Gutman is marked by Greenstreet's distinct

FIGURE 2.2 Gutman pets his "gunsel" (*The Maltese Falcon*, 1941).

British accent and his treasure-seeking adventures in the Middle East. It would seem that noir's construction of American hetero-manhood imagines homophobia as a form of xenophobia.

More to the point, for Corber, is that film noir made gay characters visible during the Cold War era when the right-wing consensus argued that homosexuality, like communism, was the invisible threat to American security.[87] Film noir challenges the Cold War consensus on many fronts, not only for making the gay male body visible, but also because noir invites a mode of queer spectatorship, as is most evident in *Laura*. Corber argues that *Laura*, like many noirs, privileges stylistic innovation and formal excess over narrative coherence in contrast to most plot-driven Hollywood narratives and earlier detective films.[88] Noir's ornamental camera angles and often embellished mise-en-scène may obscure narrative comprehension for the sake of visual play. In this regard, noir creates spectacles out of style that distract from narrative absorption, which is the dominant, presumably hetero-normative, mode of spectatorship. In Corber's reading, the gay character has a similarly disruptive function. Lydecker arrests the narrative when he makes a spectacle of his own body, especially in the bathroom scene described above, and he is a collector of spectacular objects to boot. Just as these objects distract us from the linear narrative, McPherson too is enthralled by the commodity culture Lydecker and Laura represent. The more he gives in to his fascination with her objects and then to her, the less he attends to the murder case at hand. This distraction applies equally to McPherson and *Laura*'s spectator. In fact, insofar as gays and women are presumed to be drawn to commodities and the "purely visual aspects of cinematic experience," the film promotes a feminized, even queer, mode of spectatorship.[89] By the end of the film, McPherson and Laura are recuperated into a heterosexual domesticity, and thus the film's oppositional politics are foreclosed. But, with its many instances of cinematic excess and narrative detours, *Laura* opens a space for gay male, and even camp, pleasure.[90] Whether reading the film as queer camp or misreading the film altogether, audiences in a small Connecticut town reportedly laughed during *Laura* at all the wrong places. "Could the trigger," Leff wonders, "have been Waldo's queerness, or the actor's?"[91]

Such arguments about noir's gender politics agree that these films represent a uniquely American, *postwar* response to an imperiled hetero-masculinity. However, Christopher Breu has recently argued that film noir has its foundations in the pulp literature of the 1920s. Noir's "resolutely negative cultural fantasy" should be understood as a response to the rise of corporate capitalism and the waning of artisanal and entrepreneurial capitalism in the interwar period.[92] The hard-boiled hero in pulp magazines like *Black Mask* struggles to maintain his autonomy in the face of these economic changes and the impact they have on gender and race relations. Cultivating a "prophylactic toughness," he stifles his affect and projects his desires onto sexual and racial others with whom he has an antagonistic, if not downright violent, relationship.[93] At the same time that it dramatizes an antagonism between white and non-white men, hard-boiled fiction borrows "in disavowed ways" from representations of black manliness in order to define the white hero against "both older forms of Victorian manhood and the larger social order of which it is a part."[94] Black masculinity becomes an unacknowledged source for an invigorated and transgressive white manhood. Thus Breu argues that changes in early-twentieth-century economic relations brought about a new form of masculinity that rejected the civilized refinement of the Victorian era in favor of a muscular brute who clings fiercely to his autonomy. The hero's ritual rejection of the femme fatale, Breu claims, is not only another means by which he resists conforming to the corporate order by refusing marriage and romance. Simultaneously attractive and repellent, the femme fatale represents the hero's "larger sense of cultural loss and betrayal," and thus toward her "he directs his displaced aggression and self-loathing."[95] The sexual dynamics of noir have their roots in the postwar moment not of World War II but of World War I, and the femme fatale is more properly understood as a character whose complex sexuality has more to do with what the hero represses than with actual, empirical women who lead nontraditional lives.

If, as Breu suggests, we take a longer view of noir's origins, it may be that masculinity has always been in crisis, and not only in the US. We have shown in Chapter 1 that the crisis of masculinity attributed to American noir protagonists – prompted by shifts in economic life, world war, the problems of postwar adjustment, and the forever-altered homefront culture – was global in scale and experienced even during the interwar period, as explained in our discussion of *The Postman*'s interwar migrations. Mary Ann Doane likewise notes that the femme fatale is the most persistent character of urban modernity, beginning in the nineteenth century. She is a storied figure in French Symbolist literature and proto-Expressionist German theater, and is strongly associated with the Decadent and Art Deco movements of the early twentieth century. In cinema, she makes appearances in Weimar "street" films, French poetic realism, Scandinavian and Italian silent melodrama, and, of course, American film noir. Coincident with the rise of psychoanalysis and a new public awareness of unconscious desires and sexual difference, the femme fatale symbolizes male anxiety and is the "articulation of fears surrounding the loss of stability and centrality of the self, the 'I,' the ego."[96] In the Freudian economy, male subjectivity is produced positively as the possessor of the phallus in opposition to the woman's lack of the phallus. Her lack, however, also represents the possibility of his loss. In 1975, Laura Mulvey famously argued that mainstream Hollywood cinema offers modes of visual pleasure that subvert the threat of castration represented by the woman's body by either reducing female characters to fetishized objects or punishing them as active subjects.[97] The point is that Hollywood structures sexual difference in ways that are strikingly similar to Freudian scenarios, which have a longer history. In noir, the femme fatale, writes Doane, is punished in a "desperate reassertion of control on the part of the threatened male subject."[98] But, more than this, she is an object of investigation. The drama of detection has less to do with crime and more with revealing and neutralizing the power of the unknowable woman. The femme fatale is thus an epistemological puzzle. Rather than view this figure as a *postwar* feminist icon, as

Place does in her earlier assessment of this strong, sexually charged character, Doane reads her "as a symptom of male fears about feminism" that are as old as modernity itself.[99] Film noir, then, is a perfect place to analyze this dynamic between the unknowable woman and the puzzling world she inhabits. At the same time, Doane reminds us that American film noir is not the only genre or national cinema to register these fears.

Where other Hollywood fictions present us with a realist image and a mappable diegesis, noir "flirts with the limits of this system," and it is the femme fatale who "confounds the relation between the visible and knowable at the same time that she is made into an object for the gaze."[100] Doane points to the famous "modified striptease" in *Gilda*, "the perfect iconography of film noir."[101] Before an enthralled audience, Gilda (Rita Hayworth) sings while disrobing only her gloves and necklace. Johnny (Glenn Ford), her frustrated ex-lover, stops the performance before she can expose any more of her body. Though it would seem that the performance would reveal a truth of her identity, the entire tease is, itself, just an act. Gilda is actually a good girl pretending to be bad. For Doane, the process of revealing and concealing the woman's body in order to get at the truth of her character (which, in this film, is already a fiction within a fiction) is similar in structure to the layers of the narrative itself. In *Gilda*, people are never what they appear to be (least of all Gilda!), and Johnny is no more in command of Gilda's body than he is of the international cartel or Ballin's dastardly plotting. At every turn, Johnny is duped and rendered impotent. In fact, his failure to know the truth – about his boss, about Gilda, about the cartel – is explicitly tied to his frustrated sexual desire, as expressed through the film's numerous double entendres. This film, for Doane exemplary of noir technique, elaborates how "the visual representation of the woman carries with it the potential to provoke a crisis in the codification and coherency of ideological systems."[102] Noir's unknowable woman is connected to other inscrutable truths that, in turn, prop up larger ideological systems.

But is film noir an inherently masculine, misogynist genre? Do these scenarios speak only to male audiences who feel their

subjectivity and place in the world are in jeopardy? Glossing the critical debates on noir's representation of sexuality, Stephen Neale
reminds us that there are other genres that dramatize a crisis in male
subjectivity and that there are noirs without femmes fatales, and non-
noirs with fatal women.[103] If defined by the presence of these sexual-
ized characters, noir becomes an even more elusive "genre" to track.
Here, Elizabeth Cowie has offered a useful corrective, arguing that the
trope of dangerous female sexuality and the lure of self-destructive
desire are fantasies that men and women share equally; "its pleasures
lie precisely in its forbiddenness."[104] Cowie, however, reads noir not as
a specific genre about male desire for the femme fatale, but as a stylistic and narrative inflection of psychological melodrama featuring
male and female protagonists compelled by an irrational, perverse,
destructive, and possessive desire – an amour fou or "mad love" that fascinated the surrealists.[105] Cowie's psychological definition of noir as a
dark and porous form of melodrama thus helps to explain how noir
could travel internationally and be easily adapted by other national
cinemas. In the US, Cowie argues, film noir was a strategy Hollywood
adopted to reinvent older genres, including the detective film and the
women's gothic; and these two gendered genres are really different
sides of the same coin. Cowie reminds us, moreover, that women
authored a number of noir screenplays and novels adapted for the
screen (including Laura, written by Vera Caspary), and that there are
noirs that absent the femme fatale or that focus on self-destructive
heroines, such as Fritz Lang's Secret Beyond the Door (1948). In this film,
Celia (Joan Bennett) abandons her engagement to a safe but dull man
when she visits Mexico. There she meets the exciting but murderous
Mark (Michael Redgrave), whom she impulsively marries and then
fears. In contrast to gothic heroines, Celia is not innocently duped into
marriage; she knowingly seeks romance with this potentially homicidal stranger because he is dangerous. In order to escape her death, she
must help Mark overcome his neurosis. His cure, which is necessary
for her survival, also signals the end of his allure. The plot replays the
paradoxical attraction–repulsion the noir hero feels towards the

femme fatale. *Secret Beyond the Door*, writes Cowie, brings Celia "to a position where, instead of fearing death, which is equivalent to her desire, Celia . . . fears the loss of desire, or Mark, in preference to which she would rather die."[106] Seen in this light, Celia is a classic noir protagonist. As with Walter Neff in *Double Indemnity* or even the noir couple in *The Postman Always Rings Twice*, the protagonist's sexual desire is tantamount to her destruction. *Postman*'s Cora and Frank fall into dull and desexualized routines once they are married and the court case is behind them. But their love is rekindled once the danger of death returns. It is not the illicit sexual relations of noir that are so controversial, but the nature of sexual desire that is inextricably bound to – indeed cannot survive without – danger and the threat of death.

Cowie's reading demonstrates that how we define noir as a genre, and as a specifically *masculine* genre, determines and delimits how we read noir's sexual politics. If it is only for men, then noir's misogyny is its most legible feature. But if we acknowledge the affinities between hard-boiled noir and melodrama, and the role of women as both authors and characters in these narratives, we cannot reduce noir to a simply masculine fiction. Driven by the erotics of death and the dark side of *human* nature, noir dramatizes the dead ends of modern sexual longing and the desire for violence that no one gender may exclusively claim.

Noir as The Refuge of Whiteness?

The literal "darkness" of film noir – its shadows, chiaroscuro lighting patterns, and many night scenes – conveys thematic pessimism and the characters' moral ambiguity or, in some cases, their unambiguous turpitude. Manthia Diawara reframes this observation, attending to the genre's racial signification. Noir, as it was first discovered as a style, "uses the tropes of blackness as metaphors for the white characters' moral transgressions and falls from grace."[107] For most noir critics, he observes, "film noir is black because the characters have lost the privilege of whiteness by pursuing lifestyles that are misogynistic, cowardly, duplicitous, and that exhibit themselves in an eroticization of violence."[108] Building on Diawara's observation, Eric Lott writes that the "black" of film noir is both "literalized" in the visual style and "dissipated" through the marginalization of black characters whose presence in these films is, for this reason, all the more interesting and symptomatic of midcentury racial fantasies.[109] Using characters of color metonymically to signal white pathology, "film noir rescues with racial idioms the whites whose moral and social boundaries seem so much in doubt. 'Black film' is the refuge of whiteness."[110] That is, because noir represents white immorality as darkness, and because immoral characters are associated with people of color, "whiteness" in film noir is preserved as the province of upstanding morality. When white characters cross into darkness, and move literally into shadow, they depart from both the stylistic conventions of Hollywood three-point lighting for its white actors, and the social norms of white bourgeois culture.

We can see this signifying process at work through Lott's brilliant reading of *Double Indemnity*. Both Walter (Fred MacMurray) and Phyllis (Barbara Stanwyck) are associated with racial others. Walter refers to the "colored" woman who cleans his apartment, and Phyllis is first introduced in her once-trendy Spanish-style house, where she is tanning herself, a hobby that Lott describes as the "new interest in self-othering."[111] When Walter and Phyllis first plot her husband's murder and discuss the insurance benefits, they move into his unlit kitchen, where they appear to us as sinister silhouettes. But the idea of insurance fraud has already been introduced in the film when Keyes (Edward G. Robinson) discovers that Sam Garlopis (a Greek American character, played by the Spanish actor Fortunio Bonanova) set fire to his own truck in order to collect fraudulently on his policy. "Garlopis's Greekness suggests his potential for moral lapse as his duplicity defines his excessive ethnicity."[112] And, as Lott explains, after they carry out Mr. Dietrichson's murder, it is people of color – the black garage attendant, and Walter's Jewish partner, Lou Schwartz – who serve as his alibis and unknowingly as accomplices. When white characters transgress the law, they do not taint whiteness because, according to the film's narrative and visual logic, they are becoming more like black/ethnic Others.

As in *Out of the Past*, so too in *Double Indemnity* Mexico and national borders become spaces of refuge from the white bourgeois order these characters both desire and long to escape. In fact, black culture, in *Out of the Past*, is the gateway to the southern border: Jeff is tipped to Kathie's Mexican whereabouts when he interviews her black maid, Eunice (Theresa Harris), in an all-black, Harlem jazz club (Figure 2.3). Similarly, in *Double Indemnity*, Walter takes a bereft Lola to a Mexican restaurant to keep her from turning in her evil stepmother Phyllis. At the end of the film, Walter, shot by Phyllis, pleads for Keyes's help in escaping to Mexico. Lott observes that the integrity of Walter's bodily boundary has been compromised by a bullet; his bleeding, which darkens his body, also signals his own compromised moral and legal status. This legal compromise, in turn, compels him to flee the US for Mexico. In this way, Walter transgresses boundaries of morality, body, and nation. "Villainizing the desires that drive the narrative,

FIGURE 2.3   Harlem: gateway to Mexico (*Out of the Past*, 1947).

utilizing racial codes implied in moral terminologies and visual devices, [*Double Indemnity*] preserves the idea of whiteness" and, we might add, white *Americanness* "its own characters do not uphold."[113]

Of what, exactly, are such representations symptomatic? Eric Lott and Julian Murphet both link noir's racial and racist metaphorics to the period's social upheaval. During World War II, African Americans migrated en masse from the Jim Crow South to what would become the segregated US cities in the North and on the West Coast for work in the munitions factories. Others enlisted in the military with the hopes of fighting fascism abroad and realizing social, racial justice at home.[114] During the "long hot summer" of 1943, scores of US cities witnessed civil unrest by African Americans protesting the country's persistent racism. Just as women in the workplace threatened to upset male dominance, so did the presence of African Americans in the cities threaten a white order, encouraging white flight to the suburbs under influence of the Federal Housing Act of 1949.[115]

Film noir's representation of empty urban streets, observes Julian Murphet, belies the fact of vibrant African American life and culture in American cities in the 1940s and 1950s. For Murphet, what is striking is not the marginalization of black characters per se, but their fundamental absence in noir's lonely, mean streets. This absenting of black people, combined with noir's signature misogyny and fearful investment in urban space, "comes dangerously close to exhibiting the logic of U.S. racism," and thus, as a genre, noir is uniquely poised to "clear room for the critique of that logic."[116] Murphet writes that "white America is ceaselessly cajoled into reading the black body as the site of its most potent threat, whereas that body is in fact the bearer of the displaced violence of whiteness itself."[117] This displaced racial violence is the very stuff of film noir. Because the Production Code forbade it, and because it contradicted the democratic ideology of the period, racism could not be explicitly represented in Hollywood films. So, noir absents the black body and invests the streets with the fear that black culture produces in white men, as signaled obliquely through the use of jazz music, the black-and-white cinematography, and even the darkness of the femme fatale herself. In fact, film noir's misogyny is perhaps a more culturally acceptable alibi for its racism. The hero hates and punishes the woman who, also absent from the street, stands in for the missing black subject. This suppression is also evident in the formation of the white hero himself; recall Breu's argument that hard-boiled masculinity is built on unacknowledged and repressed black manhood. The twist is that the noir hero experiences the threatening urban space as a black person would fear it owing to white racism. That is, the noir hero identifies with the violence directed at blacks, but fails to recognize that the source of this violence is white power. The hero fears the very violence he enacts on others. This repression, directed at other, ideologically acceptable targets – women, communists, queer characters – is consolidated in what Murphet calls noir's "racial unconscious," which produces a new white male subject who can handle the terrain of the changing American city.

Fritz Lang's first US film, Fury (1936), about a lynching in a small American town, illustrates noir's modes of racial displacement. But, as a prewar film, it is interesting for the ways it signals, without repressing, noir's racial unconscious. Spencer Tracy plays Joe Wilson, who is wrongly accused of kidnapping a child. When he's taken into custody to await his trial, the townspeople, eager for justice and convinced of his guilt, conspire to burn down the prison. Their violence erupts into frenzied celebration as the prison goes up in flames, all of which is captured by a newsreel cameraman and later used against the townspeople in court. According to Anton Kaes, though Lang wanted his hero to be African American, the studio mandated that the main character be white. So Lang devised ways to convey indirectly the story's racial content, namely, white lynching of blacks (many episodes of which had occurred around the time of the film's release).[118] In contrast to what happens in the noirs Murphet describes above, Lang does not absent black people, nor do black characters serve as metonyms for white guilt. Rather, at key dramatic moments, they remind us that this tale about a *white* mob lynching a *white* man is literally off-color. Kaes points to the following scene. In the local bar, a group of men plan their assault on the jail. The rallying cry? "Say, come on, let's have some fun!" At this moment, Lang cuts to the door outside the bar, where a black shoeshine man, who has been listening to the vigilante merry-making, jumps back to his stand "to make way for the whip-cracking white men" who spill out.[119] This "visual marker" highlights the "real tragedy to which Fury only subtextually refers," both here and in several other examples in the film where black characters signify white American racism.[120]

Yet Fury does not end with the guilty townspeople being brought to justice. Unlike the black victims to whom the film indirectly refers, Joe survives the fire and then plots his revenge against the townspeople by keeping his survival a secret. Twenty-two of the guilty are sentenced to hang for his murder. In the process, Joe becomes a scary, drunken monomaniac – a double of the crowd's irrational passion – until, at the very end, he's convinced to come clean. In this way, the attempted lynching of a black-coded man only nearly results in the hanging of twenty-two whites. In Joe's quest for vengeance, the "fury" that begins as a white rage against an innocent man is redirected back onto those very white people, as if, in 1930s America, twenty-two white citizens would be hanged for killing a black man. Perhaps it is not so much that Fury displaces white racism as that it improbably dramatizes its legal consequences.

For Murphet, American noir's racial logic is partly what attracted French critics to this cycle of films after the war, when France not only experienced global consumerism as a form of Americanization, but was about to be embroiled in its own colonial battle in Algeria. American racism and the history of slavery find their analog in French colonial racism. The American hard-boiled hero seems to be physically and psychically equipped to manage the changing racial topography of the increasingly globalized, multiracial city. Giving noir its "racially overdetermined name," French critics' fascination with noir's existentialist individuality was also a response to this genre's racial coding, which resonated with fears of immigration and decolonization.[121] Murphet points briefly to Godard's Breathless, whose Bogart-worshipping thug,

Michel, attests to French enthusiasm for this new white man "who seems already to bear within himself all of the rising existential dread about otherness that has yet to be encoded in any acceptable French idiom."[122] And yet, within France's own noir tradition, there was an idiom of colonial dread expressed in Julien Duvivier's *Pépé le Moko* (1937), a film made at the height of French colonialism that we may read productively through Murphet's formulation of noir's "racial unconscious."

The film is set in the Casbah of French-controlled Algiers and focuses on the titular character (played by Jean Gabin), a carpenter-turned-jewel thief who takes refuge in the native Algerian quarter, hunted by the French police. The Casbah and its nefarious inhabitants both protect and incarcerate Pépé, and, as the film opens, he longs to return to Paris. But to go back home and to leave the Casbah would mean certain imprisonment, and the Paris for which he pines has, in any case, already largely disappeared. So he bides his time until he meets the radiant Gaby (Mireille Balin), who dons Parisian haute couture, but is, herself, of working-class origin (Figure 2.4). She is "kept" as a tourist in Algiers by an overbearing champagne magnate who prevents Gaby from meeting Pépé once their affair is brought to his attention. At the end of the film, a love-struck and homesick Pépé is lured out of the Casbah, ratted out by his jealous "native" lover Ines (Line Noro), and caught by the Algerian police officer Slimane (Lucas Gridoux). Rather than go to jail, however, Pépé kills himself on the pier as he watches Gaby's boat depart for France.

Janice Morgan notes that the popular readings of the film pin Pépé's downfall on the racial and cultural Others – Ines and Slimane – who entrap him. And yet, in the end, the real winners are the "unem pathetic authority figures": the inept colonial police, who will take credit for Pépé's long-elusive capture, and the chubby champagne tycoon, who gets Pépé's girl. The popular reading improbably blames the colonial subjects for subjugating the French working class.[123] Murphet's reading of noir's racial logic is consistent with Morgan's insofar as the tragedy of Pépé, a white Frenchman, is to be treated

FIGURE 2.4 Longing for Paris in the Casbah (*Pépé le Moko*, 1937).

more like a colonial Algerian by his own government. Rephrasing Murphet's theory of noir, we could call this narrative formulation *Pépé le Moko*'s colonial unconscious. Moreover, as Ginette Vincendeau notes, the film exoticizes the Casbah as an oriental phantasmagoria and all but erases Arabs (see, for example, the travelogue-like introduction to the Casbah in the film's first scene).[124] Thus Arabs, like blacks in most American films noir, are erased, while their cultural signifiers are conveyed geographically, musically, and in the body of fatal, dark women. In both the French and American noirs, white heroes fear violence from oppressed racial minorities that their own culture enacts on these minorities. That an American version of *Pépé le Moko* entitled *Algiers* (1938) premiered just one year later suggests that the American hard-boiled type owed something to its French cousin. After all, French film critic André Bazin rather famously compared Bogart to Jean Gabin in his well-known elegiac essay in Bogart's honor.[125]

Maybe Michel in *Breathless* then is mimicking more than just American masculinity.

American "neo-noirs," especially those written and directed by African Americans, desublimate noir's racial unconscious by making it the explicit content of the film.[126] Or, as Diawara puts it, "the redeployment of noir style by black film-makers redeems blackness from its genre definition by recasting the relation between light and dark on the screen as a metaphor for making black people and their cultures visible."[127] *Devil in a Blue Dress* (1995), for example, directed by Carl Franklin and adapted from the novel by Walter Mosley, is set in Los Angeles in 1948 and follows an African American vet-turned-detective (Denzel Washington) as he tracks down the white-passing mulatta fiancée (Jennifer Beals) of LA's corrupt mayor. The film takes us to the jazz clubs and lingers on the quotidian black street culture of postwar LA. Justus Nieland remarks that, in contrast to the white midcentury hard-boiled fiction and films that absent blacks and black culture, *Devil* "documents the racially marked spaces of modernity" and the dynamics of racism in which white noir participated.[128] Franklin's film, along with other African American noirs, is not merely a corrective to classic noir – it enables us to read the missing spaces and absent people in noir's first wave, and to unpack the racist psychopathology of white masculinity.

The Lady from Shanghai, Touch of Evil, *and Noir's Exaggerated Types*

To better understand the connection between noir's intertwined sexual and racial logics, we conclude this part by looking at Orson Welles's *The Lady from Shanghai* (1948). In their compelling reading of the film, Kelly Oliver and Benigno Trigo note that Welles made the film in order to explode noir's stereotypes by intensifying the clichés of femininity and ethnicity the genre proffers.[129] They argue that, while this strategy makes stereotypes more visible (at times even parodic), the types remain relatively unexamined in the film's visual and aural style.

The film's story is actually quite straightforward, though the manner of its telling is anything but. Our hero, the Irish sailor Michael O'Hara (Orson Welles), encounters the enchanting Elsa Bannister (Rita Hayworth) one night, quite by chance, in New York's Central Park. He saves her from robbers and shortly thereafter, and against his better judgment, is lured to work on her husband's yacht. A smarmy, crippled, and vicious criminal lawyer, Mr. Bannister (Everett Sloane) seems to encourage Michael and Elsa's intimacies, knowing that Elsa will never leave him. What he has on her, we never learn. The Bannisters, Michael, his friend, and Mr. Bannister's partner, the equally smarmy and strident Grisby (Glenn Anders), sail from New York to San Francisco via Mexico. When they finally hit the US shore, Michael is duped into playing the fall guy. A farcical trial followed by a manhunt through San Francisco's Chinatown ends in an abandoned fun house where Elsa and Bannister confront each other in the hall of mirrors. Shooting at their reduplicated images, they manage to kill each other. Michael walks off into the sunset, leaving Elsa for dead.

Welles cast his own wife, Rita Hayworth, as Elsa when she was at the apex of her "pin-up" celebrity status, thanks, in part, to her titillating striptease number in Gilda. To prepare her for the Shanghai role, Welles cut Hayworth's famous auburn hair (in front of news cameras, in fact), and dyed it platinum blonde. As Dyer might note, Welles displayed for the public the artificial construction of the femme fatale and the Hollywood star playing her. Of white skin and nearly white hair, Hayworth's new look literalized Elsa Bannister's heritage as the daughter of White Russians and further whitewashed Hayworth's own Spanish heritage. Elsa's dark and evil disposition, however, is connected to her birthplace, Chefoo, and the place where she later worked, Shanghai.[130] This is the modern Chinese city that Josef von Sternberg exoticized for film audiences in the proto-noir Shanghai Express (1933) starring Marlene Dietrich and Anna May Wong, and the delirious noir The Shanghai Gesture (1941) starring Laura's Gene Tierney. By 1948 Shanghai was shorthand for noir's orientalism, and any female character associated with this city was sure to be wicked. Elsa's mystery, in noir fashion, is further conveyed through her association with the black maid Bessie (Evelyn Ellis), who suffers Mr. Bannister's insults because, she says of Elsa, "Somebody's got to take care of her." Playing "the black mother to Elsa's 'whiter than white' Asian femme fatale," Bessie both confounds and reinforces Elsa's otherness, and this intimated relationship between the women sets into motion the melodramatic possibility that Elsa is "passing" as white.[131]

Of course, Elsa is no child, and, in contrast to Gilda, who pretends to be bad, Elsa, femme fatale that she is, pretends to be good. We learn in the end that it was she who set Michael up and who also planned to kill her husband and collect his insurance. As is standard in noir's sexual optics, the femme fatale's sexual danger is constructed through foreign, racialized, and exoticized others. But this film goes to great lengths to make these connections explicit. Indeed everything in this film is so over-the-top that we must see even this standard characterization as an elaborate fiction, a strategy Welles would use again in creating and conflating American and Mexican types in Touch of Evil. In Shanghai, for example, Welles plays Michael with a bad Irish brogue and with a poetic language that connects him pretentiously to modern literature; Bannister and Grisby speak in theatrically odd cadences and are often framed in jarringly extreme "choke" close-ups when they speak. And the film's settings move from the touristic Mexico, à la Out of the Past, to Wild Kingdom-like views when the group travels inland in rowboats for a picnic; they spy water snakes, crocodiles, and menacing flora. Later, Elsa and Michael meet in the aquarium (recommended because only schoolchildren and tourists go there), where they declare their love while huge octopi and strange fish swim just behind them. But the film takes its most bizarre turn when Michael, drugged and barely conscious, flees his trial and takes refuge in the Chinese opera house, where a performance is underway. Elsa follows him, and shocks us with her fluent Cantonese first when she buys her ticket and then again when she calls her servant, Lee, from the opera house phone. As Oliver and Trigo write of this sequence: "The condensation of both languages compounds the condensation of both races in her evil character and has a predictable effect on the English-speaking audience. How, it asks, can Elsa look so white and speak an Asian language so fluently?"[132] It is a question the same audience might have phrased differently when, during the trial, two Chinese women speak in Cantonese, and one woman concludes the exchange by saying in unaccented vernacular English: "You said it, sister!" Bilingualism speaks, literally, to the inadequacies of appearances as signs of national or ethnic belonging. Significantly, in both instances, it is women who express this cultural-linguistic fluency, which the film codes as duplicity.

For a non-Cantonese-speaking audience, the untranslated language combined with the exoticism of the Chinese performance on stage reinforces Elsa's evil (because unknowable) character. Yet, as Oliver and Trigo note, for the Cantonese and bilingual audiences, another story emerges. Elsa has a Chinese name; she is called Xinlin Zhang. Perhaps, then, Chinese is her "mother tongue." Though he does her bidding, Lee is hardly in her thrall, as is evident in his untranslated Cantonese response to her plea: "Do I owe you something, red-haired foreigner? You are giving me a hard time. Why should I help you?"[133] Elsa is Other to these Others, as foreign to them as she is to us. And the reference to her red hair suggests that he either sees her differently or knows something about her past (though surely this also a reference to Hayworth's pre-*Shanghai* makeover). Meanwhile, on stage, the Chinese troop performs an opera about the mysteries of female identity. Oliver and Trigo translate the scene: "It performs the trial of a woman accused of being a sinner by a judge who asks her, 'what is your given name and surname?' When the woman answers, 'Li Yulan,' the judge asks, 'Li Yulan, what is the origin of your story? Spit it out!'"[134] Elsa finds her double in this mysterious stage woman on trial in San Francisco (and the very fact that this trial is a form of entertainment is, itself, parallel to Michael's own show trial). Likewise, the English-speaking audience of the film shares with Lee and the Chinese audience in the film watching the opera the same question about a woman's true identity. This characterization is consistent with Mary Ann Doane's reading of the femme fatale as the unknowable woman. Were it translated, this scene would produce a comity between different linguistic audiences, de-exoticizing, and thus rendering less sinister, the trappings of Chinese culture. That is, if Welles wanted to exaggerate the stereotypes of noir to expose and explode their meaning, he may, in fact, have only rapturously reinforced the genre's sexist and racist tropes. Further, given noir's familiar detours, excesses, and exaggerated sexualities, is it even possible to make a noir with heightened stereotypes that can signify as something other than the genre's familiar types? When does noir seriousness cross the threshold into farce or parody? Is *Laura* still a noir if it makes Connecticut audiences laugh? What of Billy Wilder's satiric/musical noir *A Foreign Affair*? As James Naremore observes, when it comes to noir "we cannot say exactly when parodies of noir began, and we cannot distinguish precisely between parody, pastiche, and 'normal' textuality."[135]

Pitched on the tonal boundary between parody and tragedy, Welles's *Touch of Evil* (1958) is set in a fictional, dizzyingly squalid border town between the US and Mexico, and thematizes the artificiality of borders that mark genres, nations, and ethnicities. Cast as the Mexican narcotics agent Miguel Vargas, Charlton Heston donned "brown face" for the role but did nothing to alter his unmistakably American accent, while Marlene Dietrich, as the Mexican prostitute Tanya, seems right out of her Weimar cabaret days, German accent intact. Orson Welles cast himself as the corrupt, racist, American cop Hank Quinlan, who frames a Mexican for killing a white American big-shot whose car blows up in the film's opening sequence. Featuring actors cast against "type," *Touch of Evil* dispenses with the verisimilitude between actor and character. And, populated with cameos (Zsa Zsa Gabor, Joseph Cotten), the film seemingly eschews the hermeticism of fiction altogether. Perhaps even more than in *The Lady from Shanghai*, Welles brings our attention to how ethnic types are constructed. As Quinlan says of Vargas: "He don't talk like one, a Mexican, I mean." This line could be taken as a sign of Heston's bad acting, or an acknowledgment that Mexicans do not always "sound" like Hollywood fictions.

   These meta-fictional nods and exaggerated characterizations make *Touch of Evil* equal parts pulp noir and modernist political critique, a drama and, perhaps, a farce.[136] Furthermore, this film crosses the national border so many times that we cannot keep the localities straight. The border – so essential to America's security state – is at once phantasmagoric and perversely real because, even in this film, it determines legal jurisdiction and the rights of citizens. In exposing the seemingly arbitrary boundaries of the state and the violence of the law, *Touch of Evil* dramatizes more than just genre mixing: the film puts into play what Jonathan Auerbach calls "noir citizenship," "a condition of statelessness or nonexistence," that "sheds light on the psychological contours of *film noir* as well as the anxieties of the nation-state at mid-century intent on policing itself against uninvited outsiders."[137] As a place where Mexican and American cultures mix and become perceptually indistinguishable, the border is also the site of racial hybridity.[138] Quinlan, obsessed with the "half-breed" who murdered his wife years ago, sees all around him "mixed" couples, including the Mexican suspect Sanchez and his white American girlfriend. Searching Sanchez's apartment on the US side of the border, Quinlan plants evidence that will secure Sanchez's guilt in the car bombing. Though Vargas pleads on Sanchez's behalf, this is Quinlan's jurisdiction, where he makes up the rules as he goes along. But, at the end of the film, Quinlan is himself subject to Vargas's extra-legal measures when he is entrapped into confessing and is illegally recorded. Walking right through the border between the two countries, Quinlan is, in a sense, alienated from his so-called inalienable rights and due process. The border itself becomes a kind of legal no-man's-land. It is in the polluted river that separates one country from the other that Quinlan's corpse finally floats. In his overzealous efforts to police the borders and regulate ethnic distinctions, Quinlan becomes victim to another form of "borderline justice."[139] In fact, *Touch of Evil*'s status as a borderline noir is itself symptomatic of the very border control it dramatizes and frustrates. As Oliver and Trigo succinctly put it: "Just as film noir can be interpreted as a manifestation of anxieties over the arbitrary and blurred borders of race, sex, and nationality, so noir criticism with its debates over definitions and origins displays a similar anxiety over the breakdown of the borders of genre and national origins."[140]

NOTES

1 In fact, Janet Staiger has argued convincingly that Hollywood films "have never been pure instances of genres." See "Hybrid or Inbred: The Purity Hypothesis and Hollywood Genre History," in *Film Genre Reader III*, ed. Barry Keith Grant (Austin: University of Texas Press, 2003), pp. 185–199, p. 185.

2 See, respectively, Stephen Neale, "Film Noir," in *Genre and Hollywood* (London: Routledge, 2000), p. 153; Marc Vernet, "Film Noir on the Edge of Doom," in *Shades of Noir: A Reader*, ed. Joan Copjec (London: Verso, 1993), pp. 1–32, p. 26; Elizabeth Cowie, "Film Noir and Women," in *Shades of Noir: A Reader*, ed. Joan Copjec (London: Verso, 1993), p. 121; James Naremore, *More than Night: Film Noir in its Contexts* (Berkeley: University of California Press, 1998), p. 11.

3 Tom Gunning, Review of James Naremore's *More than Night*, in *Modernism/Modernity* 6:3 (September 1999), p. 151.

4 Nino Frank, "The Crime Adventure Story: A New Kind of Detective Film," in *Perspectives on Film Noir*, ed. R. Barton Palmer (New York: G. K. Hall & Co., 1996), pp. 21–22; Jean-Pierre Chartier, "The Americans Are Making Dark Films Too," in *Perspectives on Film Noir*, ed. R. Barton Palmer (New York: G. K. Hall & Co., 1996), p. 26.

5 Siegfried Kracauer, "Hollywood's Terror Films: Do They Reflect an American State of Mind?," first published in *Commentary* 2 (1946), pp. 132–136, reprinted in *New German Critique* 89 (Spring–Summer 2003), pp. 105, 109, 110.

6 Ibid., p. 110.

7 Ibid., p. 109.

8 Raymond Borde and Etienne Chaumeton, *A Panorama of American Film Noir, 1941–1953*, trans. Paul Hammond (San Francisco: City Lights Books, 2002), p. 5.

9 Ibid., p. 13.

10 Ibid., pp. 22, 24.

11 Vernet, "Film Noir on the Edge of Doom," p. 14.

12 Edward Dimendberg, "Down These Seen Streets a Man Must Go: Siegfried Kracauer, 'Hollywood's Terror Films,' and the Spatiality of Film Noir," *New German Critique* 89 (Spring–Summer 2003), pp. 113–143, pp. 115–116.

13 Thomas Elsaesser, "A German Ancestry to Film Noir? Film History and its Imaginary," *Iris* 21 (Spring 1996), p. 136. Fritz Lang is an exception.

14 Vernet, "Film Noir on the Edge of Doom," p. 8.

15 Neale, "Film Noir," p. 171.

16 Ibid., pp. 163, 159.

17 Ibid., p. 174.

18 Naremore, *More than Night*, p. 10.

19 Elsaesser, "A German Ancestry to Film Noir?," p. 130.

20 Both Schrader and Durgnat's essays are collected in *Film Noir: A Reader*, ed. Alain Silver and James Ursini (New York: Limelight Editions, 1998).

21 Robert Kolker, *The Cinema of Loneliness: Penn, Kubrick, Coppola, Scorsese, Altman* (New York: Oxford University Press, 1980). For a great discussion of how French postwar cinematic culture fueled the rebirth of Hollywood in the late 1960s and 1970s, see Louis Menand's "Paris, Texas: How Hollywood Brought the Cinema back from France," *New Yorker* (February 17, 2003), pp. 168–174.

22 For a good example of *Cahiers'* noir cinephilia, see Claude Chabrol, "Evolution of a Thriller," in *Cahiers du Cinéma: The 1950s: Neo-realism, Hollywood, New Wave*, ed. Jim Hillier (Cambridge, MA: Harvard University Press, [1955] 1995), pp. 158–163. On France's rapid postwar modernization, see Kristin Ross, *Fast Cars, Clean Bodies: Decolonization and the Reordering of French Culture* (Cambridge, MA: MIT Press, 1999). For a recent account of the New Wave that situates its formal innovations in the broader dynamics of postwar modernization, see Richard Neupert's *A History of the French New Wave Cinema* (Madison: University of Wisconsin Press, 2002).

23 Naremore, *More than Night*, pp. 202–203.

24 See John Cawelti, "*Chinatown* and Generic Transformation," in *Film Genre Reader III*, ed. Barry Keith Grant (Austin: University of Texas Press, 2003); for another account of film noir's increasingly generic self-consciousness in the 1970s, see Todd Erickson's "Kill Me Again: Movement Becomes Genre," in *Film Noir: A Reader*, ed. Alain Silver and James Ursini (New York: Limelight Editions, 1998), pp. 307–329.

25 Mark Bould, Kathrina Glitre, and Greg Tuck, eds., *Neo-noir* (London: Wallflower Press, forthcoming).

26 On Spanish translations of American hard-boiled fiction, see Naremore, *More than Night*, p. 28.

27 Shinoda has described the influence of the American film noir on his *Pale Flower* in Chris D., *Outlaw Masters of Japanese Film* (London: I. B. Tauris, 2005), pp. 122–123; and yakuza director Kinji Fukasaku has acknowledged the impact both of Billy Wilder and of the tradition of 1930s French film noir on the postwar yakuza cycle. See Mark Schilling, *The Yakuza Movie Book* (Berkeley, CA: Stone Bridge Press, 2003), pp. 47, 50. At the very least, these statements cast doubt on Paul Schrader's attempt to draw clear generic and national boundaries between the yakuza film and the "American and French film noir" in his "Yakuza-eiga: A Primer" (*Film Comment*, January–February 1974, pp. 10–17), which was published only a few years before his canonical "Notes on Film Noir." This generic purity was also belied by Schrader's own script for the Hollywood yakuza–film noir hybrid *The Yakuza* (1975), co-starring noir icon Robert Mitchum and Japanese yakuza icon Ken Takakura.

28 Leighton Grist, "Moving Targets and Black Widows: Film Noir and Modern Hollywood," in *The Movie Book of Film Noir*, ed. Ian Cameron (London: BFI, 1994), p. 281.

29 See ibid.; Naremore, *More than Night*; Peter Stanfield, "Film Noir Like You've Never Seen: Jim Thompson Adaptations and Cycles of Neo-noir," in *Genre and Contemporary Hollywood*, ed. Steve Neale (London: BFI, 2002), pp. 251–268; Andrew Spicer, *Film Noir* (Harlow, UK: Longman, 2002).

30 Fredric Jameson, *Postmodernism: Or, the Cultural Logic of Late Capitalism* (Durham, NC: Duke University Press, 1991), pp. xviii–xix, 6.

31 Ibid., p. 5.

32 Jameson, *Postmodernism*, pp. 17–18, 21.

33 Naremore, *More than Night*, p. 39.

34 Paul Young, "(Not) The Last Noir Essay: Film Noir and the Crisis of Postwar Representation," *Minnesota Review* 55–57 (2002), pp. 203–221, p. 203.

35 Vivian Sobchack, "Lounge Time: Postwar Crises and the Chronotope of Film Noir," in *Refiguring American Film Genres: History and Theory*, ed. Nick Browne (Berkeley: University of California Press, 1998), p. 137.

36 Ibid., p. 165.

37 Ibid., pp. 131–132.

38 Ibid., pp. 147, 131.

39 Ibid., p. 151.

40 Ibid., p. 160.

41 Ibid., p. 160.

42 Ibid., p. 166.

43 Ibid., p. 166.

44 Ibid., p. 166.

45 Edward Dimendberg, Film Noir and the Spaces of Modernity (Cambridge, MA: Harvard University Press, 2004), p. 9.

46 Ibid., p. 12.

47 Ibid., p. 6.

48 Ibid., p. 4.

49 Ibid., p. 3.

50 Ibid., p. 14.

51 For important examples of more restricted approaches to noir as a genre, see Frank Krutnik's landmark study of the Hollywood "'tough' thriller" of the 1940s, which he distinguishes from the "semi-documentary policier" and the social-problem crime drama that emerge in the later 1940s, In A Lonely Street: Film Noir, Genre, Masculinity (London and New York: Routledge, 1991); see also David Andrews's careful history of the noir tradition of nontheatrical erotic thrillers, "Sex Is Dangerous, so Satisfy your Wife: The Softcore Thriller in its Contexts," Cinema Journal 45:3 (2006), pp. 59–89. A good recent example of tightly focused industrial history is Sheri Chinen Biesen's Blackout: World War II and the Origins of Film Noir (Baltimore, MD: Johns Hopkins University Press, 2005).

52 Paula Rabinowitz, Black & White & Noir: America's Pulp Modernism (New York: Columbia University Press, 2002), p. 15.

53 Ibid., pp. 9–10.

54 Ibid., p. 18.

55 Ibid., p. 18.

56 Ibid., p. 22.

57 Ibid., p. 21–22.

58 On this Wenders complication of the opposition between a pure German tradition embodied by Jonathan and a corrupt American influence represented by Ripley, see Paul Cooke's "German Neo-noir," in European Film Noir, ed. Andrew Spicer (Manchester: Manchester University Press, 2007), pp. 164–184.

59 On the New German Cinema's vexed relationship to American cultural imperialism, see Eric Rentschler, "How American Is It? The US as Image and Imaginary in German Film," German Quarterly 57:4 (1984), pp. 603–620; and Robert Kolker, The Films of Wim Wenders: Cinema as Vision and Desire (Cambridge, UK: Cambridge University Press, 1993).

60 For a good sense of the Cahiers critics' investments in Ray, see "Dossier: Nicholas Ray," in Cahiers du Cinéma: The 1950s: Neo-realism, Hollywood, New Wave, ed. Jim Hillier (Cambridge, MA: Harvard University Press, 1985), pp. 104–125.

61 Krutnik, *In a Lonely Street*, p. 63.

62 Foster Hirsch, *The Dark Side of the Screen: Film Noir*, 2nd edn. (Cambridge, MA: Da Capro Press, 2001), pp. 19–20.

63 Janey Place, "Women in Film Noir," in *Women in Film Noir*, ed. E. Ann Kaplan, revised and expanded edn. (London: BFI Publishing, 1998), p. 56.

64 See, for example, Richard Dyer, "Introduction" and "The Role of Stereotypes," in *The Matter of Images: Essays on Representations* (London: Routledge Press, 1995, reprinted 2000), pp. 1–5, 11–18, respectively; see also Molly Haskell, *From Reverence to Rape: The Treatment of Women in the Movies*, 2nd edn. (Chicago: University of Chicago Press, 1987). For Haskell, film noir marks the transition signaled in her title.

65 Place, "Women in Film Noir," p. 63.

66 Ibid., p. 54.

67 Ibid., p. 63.

68 Sylvia Harvey, "Woman's Place: The Absent Family of Film Noir," in *Women in Film Noir*, ed. E. Ann Kaplan, revised and expanded edn. (London: BFI Publishing, 1998), p. 42.

69 Ibid., p. 45.

70 Ibid., p. 45.

71 See, for example, Krutnik, *In a Lonely Street*, p. 63; Harvey, "Woman's Place," p. 45.

72 Richard Dyer, "Resistance through Charisma: Rita Hayworth and Gilda," in *Women in Film Noir*, ed. E. Ann Kaplan, revised and expanded edn. (London: BFI Publishing, 1998), p. 115; Dyer, "Postscript: Queers and Women in Film Noir," in *Women in Film Noir*, p. 127.

73 Dyer, "Postscript," p. 125.

74 Ibid., p. 124.

75 Richard Dyer, "Homosexuality and Film Noir," in *The Matter of Images: Essays on Representations* (London: Routledge, 2000), p. 52.

76 Dyer, "Postscript," p. 125.

77 For a discussion of the masquerade and its implications for film theory and spectatorship see Mary Ann Doane, "Masquerade Reconsidered: Further Thoughts on the Female Spectator," in *Femmes Fatales: Feminism, Film Theory, Psychoanalysis* (London: Routledge, 1991), pp. 33–43.

78 Leonard Leff, "Becoming Clifton Webb: A Queer Star in Mid-century Hollywood," *Cinema Journal* 47:3 (Spring 2008), p. 7.

79 Robert J. Corber, *Homosexuality in Cold War America: Resistance and the Crisis of Masculinity* (Durham, NC: Duke University Press, 1997), p. 62.

80 Our clock-watching is indebted to Lee Edelman's chapter "Imagining the Homosexual: *Laura* and the Other Face of Gender," in which he reads the face and effacement of the clock as a comment on the film's own work of inscribing and effacing Waldo's homosexuality. In *Homographesis: Essays in Gay Literary and Cultural Theory* (London: Routledge, 1994), p. 231.

81 Dyer, "Postscript," p. 127.

82 Ibid., p. 129.

83 See Vito Russo, "Who's a Sissy? Homosexuality according to Tinseltown," in *The Celluloid Closet*, ed. Vito Russo, rev. edn. (New York: Harper & Row, 1987), pp. 4–59.

84 Quoted in Leff, "Becoming Clifton Webb," p. 10.

85 Naremore, *More than Night*, pp. 60–61.

86 Leff, "Becoming Clifton Webb," p. 7.

87 Corber, *Homosexuality in Cold War America*, pp. 10–11.

88 Ibid., pp. 61–62.

89 Ibid., p. 60.

90 For another interesting reading of Cold War noir and homosexuality see Robert Lang, "Looking for the 'Great Whatzit': 'Kiss Me Deadly' and Film Noir," *Cinema Journal* 27:3 (Spring 1988), pp. 32–44.

91 Leff, "Becoming Clifton Webb," p. 9.

92 Christopher Breu, *Hard-Boiled Masculinities* (Minneapolis: University of Minnesota Press, 2005), p. 24.

93 Ibid., p. 1.

94 Ibid., p. 15.

95 Ibid., p. 71.

96 Mary Ann Doane, *Femmes Fatales: Feminism, Film Theory, Psychoanalysis* (New York and London: Routledge Press, 1991), p. 2.

97 Laura Mulvey, "Visual Pleasure and Narrative Cinema," in *Feminism and Film*, ed. E. Ann Kaplan (Oxford, UK: Oxford University Press, 2000), pp. 34–47.

98 Doane, *Femmes Fatales*, p. 2.

99 Ibid., pp. 2–3.

100 Ibid., p. 103.

101 Ibid., p. 105.

102 Ibid., p. 116.

103 Stephen Neale, *Genre and Hollywood* (London: Routledge Press, 2000), pp. 162–163.

104 Cowie, "Film Noir and Women," p. 136.

105 Ibid., p. 130.

106 Ibid., p. 148.

107 Manthia Diarawa, "Noir by Noirs: Toward a New Realism in Black Cinema," in *Shades of Noir: A Reader*, ed. Joan Copjec (London: Verso, 1993), p. 262.

108 Ibid., p. 262.

109 Eric Lott, "The Whiteness of Film Noir," *American Literary History* 9:3 (1997), p. 544.

110 Ibid., p. 546.

111 Ibid., p. 546.

112 Ibid., p. 546.

113 Ibid., p. 550.

114 These historical pressures fueled the very noir, hard-boiled LA protest fiction of African American writer Chester Himes, especially his first two novels, *If He Hollers Let Him Go* (1945) and *Lonely Crusade* (1947).

115 Lott, "The Whiteness of Film Noir," pp. 550–552; Julian Murphet, "Film Noir and the Racial Unconscious," *Screen* 39:1 (Spring 1998), pp. 28–30.

116 Murphet, "Film Noir and the Racial Unconscious," p. 24.

117 Ibid., p. 24.

118 Anton Kaes, "A Stranger in the House: Fritz Lang's Fury and the Cinema of Exile," *New German Critique* 89, Film and Exile (Spring–Summer 2003), p. 54.

119 Ibid., p. 49.

120 Ibid., p. 49.

121 Murphet, "Film Noir and the Racial Unconscious," p. 32.

122 Ibid., p. 32.

123 Janice Morgan, "In the Labyrinth: Masculine Subjectivity, Expatriation, and Colonialism in *Pépé le Moko*," in *Visions of the East: Orientalism in Film*, ed. Matthew Bernstein and Gaylyn Studlar (New Brunswick, NJ: Rutgers University Press, 1997), pp. 266–267.

124 Ginette Vincendeau, *Pépé le Moko* (London: BFI, 1998), pp. 58–59.

125 André Bazin, "The Death of Humphrey Bogart," in *Cahiers du Cinéma: The 1950s: Neo-realism, Hollywood, New Wave*, ed. Jim Hillier (Cambridge, MA: Harvard University Press, 1985), pp. 98–99.

126 This is Murphet's claim at the end of his essay.

127 Diawara, "Noir by Noirs," p. 263.

128 Justus Nieland, "Race-ing Noir and Re-placing History: The Mulatta and Memory in *One False Move* and *Devil in a Blue Dress*," *Velvet Light Trap* 43 (1999), p. 72.

129 Kelly Oliver and Benigno Trigo, *Noir Anxiety* (Minneapolis: University of Minnesota Press, 2003), pp. 49–72.

130 Borde and Chaumeton observe that Elsa has likely worked in the brothels of Shanghai, but it would have been "contrary to good manners" to say this in the film. *A Panorama of American Film Noir*, p. 17.

131 Oliver and Trigo, *Noir Anxiety*, p. 63.

132 Ibid., p. 64.

133 Quoted in ibid., p. 69.

134 Ibid., p. 70.

135 Naremore, *More than Night*, p. 201.

136 James Naremore, *The Magic World of Orson Welles* (Dallas, TX: Southern Methodist University Press, 1987), p. 147.

137 Jonathan Auerbach, "Noir Citizenship: Anthony Mann's *Border Incident*," *Cinema Journal* 47:4 (Summer 2008), pp. 102–103.

138 See, for example, Jill Leeper, "Crossing Musical Borders: The Soundtrack for *Touch of Evil*," in *Soundtrack Available: Essays on Film and Popular Music*, ed. Pamela Robertson Wojcik and Arthur Knight (Durham, NC: Duke University Press, 2001), pp. 226–243.

139 Donald E. Peace, "Borderline Justice/States of Emergency: Orson Welles' *Touch of Evil*," *New Centennial Review* 1 (2001), pp. 75–105.

140 Oliver and Trigo, *Noir Anxiety*, p. xv.

3

FILM NOIR STYLE AND THE ARTS OF DYING

Because film noir is not any one thing, it has no stylistic signature that persists across time, no abiding formal unity, no aesthetic core. As a global phenomenon, noir style is a kind of ghost – a phantom of ideas that film critics and spectators have about the now-vanished past of film technique (and of cinema itself) that uncannily returns in times and places far removed from its imagined American origin. For this reason, film noir is a Frankenstein's monster of technique, a heterogeneous assemblage of formal strategies killed off with the obsolescence of certain media technologies, only to be nostalgically brought back to life, revivified in surprising new media environments. Because noir style has no coherent, stable set of parameters, it tends to circulate instead as "a nexus of fashions in hair, fashions in lighting, fashions in motivation, fashions in repartee."[1] Linked with the temporal cycles of fashion, noir style is bound to commodification, fatally reified. But, by the same logic, noir style never really dies, but is ever reanimated in local acts of cinephilia, where spectators, critics, and filmmakers world-wide have always found something new to love about noir's death-bound plots.

In their landmark *Panorama of American Film Noir* (1955), Borde and Chaumeton observed film noir's fascination with "the ceremony of killing."[2] In this chapter, we propose two ways of thinking of noir style itself as a similar ritual, an art of dying. In the first part, we discuss a few exemplary technological innovations and intermedial exchanges film noir has witnessed over the years, offering a materialist history of some key technical developments that have put noir style to death and brought it uncannily back to life, helping to make film noir an exemplary object of cinephilia in the process. In the second part, we pursue noir cinephilia as a means of offering a different, idiosyncratic kind of global film history, one that proceeds through loved moments, iconic gestures, and transportable fashions. By retroactively reactivating lost episodes in film history, noir cinephilia is not so much ahistorical or apolitical fashion as it is a way of producing new, fractured genealogies of cinema's past.[3] This, we think, befits a style that never really was.

PART I: TECHNOLOGIES OF NOIR STYLE

Noir Style as History

A standard story about American film noir's distinctiveness is that it arose as an "aesthetic innovation" that had to "differentiate itself from the dominant conventions of Hollywood style."[4] The signatures of noir — the dark, rain-slicked city streets, the low-key lighting, the claustrophobic compositions, jarring, canted angles, the hard-boiled voiceover narration, as well as the convoluted and dark plots — mark its break from classical Hollywood's "invisible" or "seamless" style that subordinated (and thus hid) elements of technique to the demands of narrative action. According to this view, what French critics called noir was a response to a new style in American cinema they had not seen before World War II. Vivian Sobchack, for example, asserts that, while noir was indebted to the American cinema of the 1930s, it was a specifically postwar American phenomenon.[5] However, recall also Marc Vernet's claim that the wartime and postwar hard-boiled films in fact continued in the vein of the American detective films and fallen woman melodramas from the 1930s, many of which were based on hard-boiled fiction and had some of the visual markers of the noir style.[6] What we call noir was not a decisive break from the Hollywood system – after all, it was developed *within* that system and it was quite compatible with its norms. And many of the "new" techniques had a long history in US filmmaking. For example, we find low-key, expressive illumination in *Conscience* (Vitagraph, 1912) and more famously in Ralph Ince's *His Phantom Sweetheart* (1915) and Cecil B. DeMille's *The Cheat* (1915).[7] Barry Salt finds a few instances of canted angles in 1930s Hollywood films such as *The Adventures of Robin Hood* (1938).[8] Noir's urban mise-en-scène is found in gangster and detective films of the 1930s, and its signature cynicism is anticipated in the economic ruthlessness and sexual pragmatism found in a Depression-era musical like *42nd Street* (1933).

Yet arguments for noir's stylistic distinction die hard. In one of the more provocative recent arguments for the novelty of noir's visual style, Sheri Chinen Biesen describes a convergence of circumstances that facilitated a decisive shift toward thematically and stylistically darker films in Hollywood during World War II.[9] Responding to the exigencies of wartime shortages and taking advantage of a less restrictive censorship code, US film studios ventured into the "red-meat crime" cycle, a mode of filmmaking that was linked to both the material and the social conditions of America at war. For example, the darkness of Hollywood noir was not only expressive of the world of urban crime, but it was a *fact* of low-budget production that spared rationed electricity and made the most of limited building materials. Low-key illumination, shadows, mist, and other atmospheric special effects could hide recycled and under-constructed sets, while canted and unusual camera angles could make such scenes more visually interesting. Location shooting at night was necessary to save on electricity needed during the day. In fact, noir's dark streets (sometimes shot in tarped-over studio backlots) were themselves emblematic of the city "blacked out" at night to prevent enemy bombers from finding military targets. Los Angeles, officially designated as a "theater of war," was constantly subject to blackouts that affected shooting on and off the set.[10] While the use of low-key and expressive lighting was not without precedent in Hollywood (as Vernet and Salt demonstrate), the arrival of faster, light-sensitive film stock in the early 1940s facilitated night shooting and the more widespread use of dark cinematography. Furthermore, because the nitrate it contained was also needed for weaponry, film stock was rationed, thus encouraging cinematographers and directors to cultivate more efficient shooting and what they called the newsreel style of realism.[11] In some respects, then, noir may be described as an "aesthetic of scarcity" in the wartime US. This creative response to economic and material constraints also helps to explain the emergence of film noir in newly liberated and impoverished postwar Europe and Japan, as we discussed in Chapter 1.

As Biesen observes, noir may also be seen as a move toward enhanced verisimilitude. For example, the low-key lighting schema that critics often describe as an expressive departure from Hollywood style could just as easily be understood as a move toward greater Hollywood realism. The authors of The Classical Hollywood Cinema write that "such 'weird lighting' was often considered realistic in contrast to three-point studio glamour lighting, and the effect could be plausibly motivated as coming from a single, harsh, source – say a street light, or a feeble lamp." Realism, as we've seen, is itself a convention with a complex stylistic history across the range of media with noir traditions, including, but not limited to, cinema. Thus, the authors continue, "the German influence upon Hollywood lighting during the 1920s and 1930s re-emerged in films noir because current [that is, 1940s] conceptions of realism came to reinforce existing generic norms."[12] It stands to reason that "noir" elements are found then not only in detective/gangster films, but also in horror films, westerns, and melodramas. Of course, though not considered musicals, hardboiled films often featured musical performances, and, as James Naremore reminds us, the famous "Girl Hunt" sequence in the Technicolor musical The Band Wagon (1953) captured, for Borde and Chaumeton, "the very essence" of the noir series (Figure 3.1).[13]

FIGURE 3.1 "Girl Hunt" (*The Band Wagon*, 1953).

"Hence," Elizabeth Cowie argues, "the term film noir names a set of possibilities for making existing genres 'different,'" as opposed to naming a distinctly different genre.[14] In this view, noir style describes another set of aesthetic possibilities that are consistent with the ever-evolving American mode of production.

If noir's visual aesthetic may be adapted into a variety of darkly themed genres, what we take to be paradigmatic of "film noir" is itself very adaptable to new technologies and easily translated into other media. This suppleness begins to explain how noir continually reinvents itself both in the US and around the world. Take just one example. Noir is typically imagined as a black-and-white style of cinematography. In the 1950s, color film stock and the widescreen aspect ratio allowed Hollywood producers to differentiate the cinematic image from television, while at the same time demonstrating Hollywood's "global domination of world film culture" and technology.[15] Before and during the war, color films were scarce because they were made using the expensive three-strip Technicolor process. But when the Allied forces confiscated Nazi Agfa color film stock at the beginning of the occupation, film manufacturing companies in the US soon began to develop a similar single-strip process that would become an industry standard.[16] In this light, it is interesting to revisit *House of Bamboo*. As we discussed in Chapter 1, this film noir was shot in impoverished US-occupied Japan. It sumptuously captures the street life in Tokyo, marrying noir techniques with what Fuller called a "Japanese" style. He did this by exploiting the compositional possibilities of colorful mise-en-scène using Fox's single-strip color film stock, Deluxe, and the widescreen, CinemaScope aspect ratio, and thus departed from noir's stylistic norms. That is, Fuller tells his story of occupation racketeering using technology that was itself indebted to the spoils of occupation. But there were few noirs made in color during the 1950s and 1960s.[17] Indeed, as more Hollywood films were made in color, black-and-white noirs seemed initially to be a holdover of the wartime aesthetic, further marking this chiaroscuro visual style as the genre's *signature* feature. By the 1970s, however, when color film stock was the production norm owing to the rise of color TV, directors and cinematographers adapted the noir look to color cinematography.[18] Films like *Point Blank* (1967), *The Long Goodbye* (1973), *Chinatown* (1974), and *The Conversation* (1974), to name only a few, were shot in color and achieve a noir look in which color and shadow interact to produce the psychological tensions we associate with these stories.[19] Today not only is black-and-white stock more expensive because it is so infrequently used, but its payoff is cultural capital, signifying "artiness," prestige, retro-chic, or cultivated nostalgia. Contemporary producers of black-and-white noirs for such films as the Coen brothers' Cain tribute *The Man Who Wasn't There* (2001) must pay more today to recreate yesterday's "aesthetic of scarcity." Such is the rising price of noir cinephilia. More recently, Steven Soderbergh revives noir's black-and-white cinematography and resurrects a number of its character types and narrative tropes (especially those found in *A Foreign Affair* and *The Third Man*) to revisit and critique the politics of occupation in *The Good German* (2006). If *House of Bamboo* departs from noir norms in its interpretation of an ongoing occupation in Japan, in Soderbergh's film classic noir style returns in the form of occupation history. These stylistic and historical gestures are meant not only as a quasi-nostalgic look back. Given the time of *The Good German*'s release, this noir also nods to America's then-current occupation of Iraq.

But who says "noir" has to be black to be dark? J. Hoberman traces an alternative aesthetic history in what he calls "sunshine noir."[20] For him, this phrase conjures noirs made in and about Los Angeles, where the city that produced dark films becomes its own cinematic subject. It also captures the "high-noon surrealism" represented by the experimental work of Maya Deren and Alexander Hammid's *Meshes of the Afternoon* (1943) and Kenneth Anger's magnificent ode to silent-era stardom, *Puce Moment* (1949), which ends in broad daylight.[21] Hoberman's "sunshine noir" unfolds the secret, ghostly history of LA by immortalizing it on film and bringing it, as it were, into the light of day. But the title of his essay, "A Bright, Guilty World," is a nod to that moment in *The Lady from Shanghai* when Michael (Orson Welles) beholds the touristic beauty not of LA, but of Acapulco, from a hilltop in the radiant midday sun. After passing numerous laboring locals, he muses: "'Tis a fair face to the land, surely, but you can't hide the hunger and guilt. It's a bright, guilty world." In this illuminated landscape, the city and its crimes are not tucked away in dark alleys or cast shadows. Nor, for that matter, is the hunger or poverty a mystery in this "third-world" country where rich, mean Americans take their vacations. As the saying goes, these crimes are hidden in plain sight, and the light itself becomes unbearable.

Christopher Nolan's *Insomnia* (2002) turns on a "negative" image of classic noir. The story follows a criminal investigator (Al Pacino) who travels from LA to Alaska, where legendary white summer nights mean that the sun never sets. He's there to help solve the case of the mysterious death of a seventeen-year-old girl, but more than battle a killer he must learn to handle the sun that won't let him sleep. He's nearly driven mad in the process. Though the film has plenty of darkness, it's what is outside and in daylight that terrifies the most. We are told that the evidence – the brutalized body of the teenage girl – is found in an empty garbage dump left to rot in the sun. That this film is a remake of the 1997 Norwegian original by the same name (directed by Erik Skjoldbjærg), which takes place in the white nights of far-northern Norway, suggests that sunshine noir is a shared transnational longing for urban darkness, where criminal human nature can remain hidden from view. Thus is the signature darkness of noir expressed in brightness.

Lost Voices and Other Ghosts of Noir Media

Another way to understand noir's stylistic fluidity is through its relationship to other media. We have discussed at length the relationship between global noir and the culture of literary migration, tracking, for instance, the way that hard-boiled literature from the US, Britain, France, and Japan was translated into other languages and adapted for the screen. But there is also the process by which noir's style takes its cues from and adapts for the eye and ear the prose rhythms of the literature on which it's based. This is not to say that the literal darkness of film noir is explicitly spelled out in the novels. For example, in the film *Double Indemnity*, when Walter first explains to Phyllis how insurance murders in the past have gone wrong, Wilder moves them into the almost total darkness of the kitchen to convey the immorality of the plot they're hatching, and he casts them in darkness again when Walter formally offers his help. In Cain's novel, however, the couple sit by the fire and discuss the murderous scenarios in far more gruesome terms "just as casually as if it was a little trip to the mountains."[22] The point, as Borde and Chaumeton explain it, is that the process of translation, combined with the pressures of censorship, meant that the Hollywood films "had to proceed by allusion more than by direct description."[23] Making use of off-screen space, hiding sexually or criminally explicit elements in the shadows, and intimating violence and sexual perversion through gestures, costuming, or camped-up performances, Hollywood's noir style was developed in part to convey the novels' scandalous material in a way that would pass muster with the Production Code. For Borde and Chaumeton, noir's suggestiveness is what makes it such a fascinating and forceful genre, and that, in some cases, serves as an important reality check on the novels' gratuitousness. Quite simply, "It's easier to describe a series of ten murders by pen than it is to film them." But, "a single act of violence, artfully suggested, has more impact than a text in which the crimes mount up."[24] Filming actual bodies in existing (if constructed) locations, moreover, tempered the novels' excesses through a more enduring documentary realism. "In a few years, all those hard-boiled novels will be mixed up or blurred in our memory, but we'll still remember the close-up of that criminal hand [in *The Enforcer* (1955)] and its professional ways."[25] We can see here that it is not in spite of their deathly consequences, but perhaps because of them, that noir gestures begin to take on a life of their own.

The stylistic influence, of course, moved between these media. Hard-boiled fiction has taken many of its cues from cinema, as, for that matter, did the broader modernist literary tradition. French literary critic Claude-Edmonde Magny compared Hammett's "perfect objectivity" to that of a cameraman "who has been placed [in the scene] for our benefit."[26] Frank Krutnik remarks that, where Hammett's "cold-blooded, imagistic deadpan" derived its cool objectivity from the cinema, other hard-boiled novelists, including Cornell Woolrich, whose work has been widely adapted into noirs, ventured into a more "avowedly Expressionistic" atmosphere and psychology "apparently influenced by the capacity of film to generate expressive effects rather than its ability to record reality."[27]

Of course, the most direct transcription of fiction to film is the dialogue and tale-telling voiceover narration, the latter of which cements us to the hero's fractured subjectivity and often implicates us in his crimes.[28] Where images typically signify in the "present tense," the voiceover commonly associated with noir sets the action in the past tense and thus accompanies images that have, in a sense, already occurred. In these cases, there is a temporal disjunction, generally, between sound and image, which helps to produce noir's characteristic sense of fate, anxiety, and melancholy. At the same time, and similar to noir's visual style, the voiceover narration may also be understood as a turn to documentary-style objectivity in the spirit of the newsreel's "voice of God" that reports on the images' content. For Fredric Jameson, however, the fact that noirs narrate the crime and investigation "as a completed adventure" is, for him, the genre's most distinctive feature, and one that connects both the films and the novels to a "new reproducible oral aesthetic," or what he also calls a "radio aesthetic," of the 1930s, "which has no equivalent in the earlier novels or silent cinema." This voiceover "allows the novel's past tenses to resonate with doom and foreboding and marks the detective's daily life with the promise of adventure."[29]

Double Indemnity's voiceover, for example, tells us that the seemingly banal act of calling on Mrs. Dietrichson to renew her husband's auto insurance is, in fact, a founding and fated event of a violent story that both has already transpired and is about to unfold. When Walter walks around the Dietrichsons' living room, he describes the smell of the room and interprets in detail the objects we see there before us. In so doing, the voice compensates for the paucity of the image, which cannot fully convey the texture and feel of this room. But, in describing a scene in which he himself figures (and offering a description that is not in the original novel), Walter's voiceover also conveys his objective, almost third-person, relationship to these already-transpired events as well as his detachment from his almost-expired body. The voiceover ghosts Walter, turning him into a living phantom. After he murders Mr. Dietrichson, Walter saunters nervously to the drugstore along a dark sidewalk in order to secure his alibi. He remarks in voiceover, "I couldn't hear my own footsteps. It was the walk of a dead man." Though we see Walter put one foot in front of the other, his footsteps are in fact inaudible. His death is aurally foreshadowed.

The connection to radio and to audio reproduction also helps us to consider how noir travels across radio, print, and film. Indeed, film noir takes its cues from crime radio programs (which were themselves concurrent with pulp fiction). A great example is *The Shadow*, a radio series that began in 1930 with CBS's *Detective Story Hour* and then became its own program in 1937, running in prime time for seventeen years and spinning into films, comic books, daily cartoons, and pulp novels. As Jason Loviglio describes the titular character, The Shadow is a super-hero/detective/mesmerist who polices a dark urban world, protect-ing its denizens, who are constantly threatened by foreign evildoers.[30] The program was striking for how it evoked the metropolis through the sounds of the city, its public spaces, and its ethnically diverse pop-ulation. *The Shadow* is one example where the milieu of film noir is aurally prefigured in city soundscapes. This sound montage would become a common feature in many early sound films such as *The Public Enemy* (1931), as well as in later procedural noirs like *The Naked City* (1948). In keeping with what would become the hard-boiled tradition, this series routinely marked characters' racial, ethnic, and gender differences through aural cues, tutoring audiences to attach disembodied speech to a body marked as "different." Repeating noir's penchant for constructing immorality through racial and gendered cues, *The Shadow* conflated "foreignness, criminal activity, 'feminiza-tion,' and the occult," and thus "overdetermined what it means to be an outsider."[31]

For the first season, Orson Welles was the voice of The Shadow, and through him we learned of the hero's mind-controlling powers and his ability to outwit his antagonists when, in one episode, he manipu-lates shortwave and broadcast radio, taps into phone lines, and influ-ences the radio news. That is, The Shadow defeats his enemy by manipulating the very radio technology that transmitted his voice into American homes.[32] Welles, who began his career working in theater and radio (most famously in his *War of the World* broadcast), brought his own radio aesthetic to his canonical noirs. On this score, *Touch of Evil* is interesting not only for its impressive opening sound montage (accompanying its famously long tracking shot), but also for its use of radio technology in the final showdown. Vargas manages to wire Menzies (Joseph Calleia) in order to record the confession of corrupt cop Quinlan. As we cut from the source of the sound, to the device recording it, to various distances from these two sources, Welles provides a tour de force in sonic perspective filmed as the three men cross the border. At one point, Vargas hides under the bridge that Quinlan and Menzies cross. The feedback from the recorder creates a distinct echo, a kind of "audio house of mirrors" similar to the baroque fun-house shootout in *The Lady from Shanghai*.[33] Indeed, tipped by his own excessive voice, Quinlan realizes he's been framed and shoots his partner. Recalling our discussion of noir's borderlands, this scene shows the ease with which sound travels, or how voices may cross borders that bodies may not. After Quinlan and Menzies have been shot, an officer plays back the tape, and we hear Menzies's voice even as we see his corpse. This moment exposes the unsettling aspect of sound technology that lies at the heart of noir's voiceover narration, and perhaps also its uncanny ideas about citizenship. Not only are voices disembodied and mechanically reproduced: recorded they easily cross national borders and, once murdered, come back from the dead.

Appropriately, one episode of *The Shadow* was entitled "Can the Dead Talk?"[34] Film noir's best affirmative answer, and one of its more perverse experiments in voiceover narration, is *Sunset Boulevard* (1950), a "sunshine noir" (in Hoberman's sense) that chronicles the moribund culture of silent cinema in the age of the talkies. Joe Gillis (William Holden) plays a down-on-his-luck screenwriter who describes in voiceover his descent into Norma Desmond's (Gloria Swanson) decrepit Hollywood world. It is only at the end of the film that we realize he has been speaking to us from his grave, or, to be precise, from Desmond's pool, where he lies floating, face down, as the police take photographs (Figure 3.2). This scene, he reminds us, is where the film began. Here, with his corpse, we are "back at the pool again." As in *Double Indemnity*, Joe narrates for us the events we see on

FIGURE 3.2 Back at the pool again (*Sunset Boulevard*, 1950).

screen, but his deadpan here turns noir into black humor. Almost jocularly he says: "It's dawn now, and they must have photographed me a thousand times. They got some pruning hooks from the garden and fished me out, ever so gently. Funny how gentle people get with you once you're dead." *Sunset Boulevard* creates a radio aesthetic of pastness, but also enacts the haunting property of audio recording, which of course is the technology that enabled Hollywood's transition to sound and signaled the death of silent cinema. This silent film culture is uncannily preserved in the ghosts of Hollywood's silent past that populate Norma's mansion and in the silent films she herself screens for her own viewing pleasure. If sound put to death silent cinema, it also created nostalgia for this technological past.

As Jonathan Sterne explains, because audio recording makes possible the preservation of the voice even after the body departs this world, the recording itself is "a resonant tomb." Where telephones "facilitated the hearing of a voice physically absent to the listener," the phonograph and later recording devices "took this a step further by dramatically facilitating the audition of voices absent to themselves."[35] This absence is a fact of audio technology that reifies and revivifies the human voice, as we've already heard above; it is also an aesthetic of alienation that is quintessentially noir, but not, we stress, uniquely cinematic.[36]

If so-called classical noir is already intermedial, Mark Bould writes, contemporary noir is hypermedial in the way it foregrounds its process of cross-media translation – or what Bould, borrowing from David Bolter and Richard Grusin, refers to as "remediation" – and its own technology. Sin City (2005), the digitally animated film noir, is a key example. The film is based on Frank Miller's serial comic noir of the same name (originally published 1991–1992), which combines a visual style indebted to American comics, Japanese manga, and film noir, with the prose style of hard-boiled fiction.[37] The hypermediality of the graphic novel returns us to some of the uncanny image–voice relations raised by Walter Neff's voiceover in Double Indemnity. Bould explains that, "as Miller remediates the hardboiled novel in comic book form, the visual image claims a greater immediacy even as the intermittent excesses of text point to the inadequacies of the visual image at capturing aspects of the hardboiled novel."[38] That is, as Bould reads it, Miller's comic exemplifies the problem of translating prose into images through its graphically represented excess of writing on the page. The film Sin City "remediates Miller's written text as voiceovers which become so excessive" that one character "seamlessly takes over his internal monologue, speaking it aloud within the diegesis."[39] On the one hand, the film version translates the comic's graphic excess into vocal excess that cannot be contained through the convention of voiceover narration. On the other hand, in returning the disembodied voice to its now-digital body, it may be that both voice and body have themselves become the remediated, alienated ghosts of noir.

PART II: STYLES OF NOIR CINEPHILIA

The surrealists, whose sensibility helped to invent the American film noir in postwar France, were also mad scientists of cinematic spectatorship. In 1951, they conducted an "irrational enlargement" of Josef von Sternberg's *The Shanghai Gesture* (1941), a nightmarish film noir set in a Shanghai gambling den (Figure 3.3). The decadent casino is run by Mother Gin Sling (Ona Munson), who is being forced to close her establishment under pressure from Sir Guy Charteris (Walter Huston), a British financier. But Charteris's wayward daughter Poppy (Gene Tierney), a lovely girl with an inborn taste for evil, has become a regular at Gin Sling's place, running up gambling debts and getting romantically entangled with Omar, one of Gin Sling's smarmy cronies. Late in the film, Mother Gin Sling reveals herself as Charteris's former wife (whom he thought he had killed) and Poppy's mother. Poppy, incredulous, denounces her new-found mom, and Gin Sling shoots her in a fit of rage. The film takes noir's preoccupation with fate and

FIGURE 3.3 Spectatorship as fetishism (*The Shanghai Gesture*, 1941).

uncanny families to outrageous extremes, and its dreamlike visual style is wildly overdone, even for Sternberg. The surrealists, however, adopt the film's excesses of style as the basis for their research in spectatorial fetishism. Their "irrational enlargement" consists of asking their members very specific questions about what particular details – both in the film and fantasized *outside* the diegesis – mean to them, individually, on a libidinal level: "What ought to happen when Mother Gin-Sling comes down to the gaming room after the revolver is shot?"[40] The group's various answers attest to the subjective poetry of cinema, its irrational power to move and disorient its spectators, to carry them away: "Fire breaks out in a mountain hut"; "Mother Gin-Sling masturbates ferociously over the suicide's corpse"; "A lion drops from the ceiling in to the gaming table"; "Everyone drips and melts like candles."[41]

The surrealists were a kinky bunch. But their game-playing with the excesses of noir style reminds us of those personal, obsessive, erotic dimensions of spectatorial experience that constitute cinephilia – the love of cinema, or the desire for cinema. In cinephilia, as Paul Willemen suggests, "there is always the fetishizing of a particular moment, the isolating of a crystallisingly expressive detail."[42] Cinephilia operates less through attachment to plot or narrative than to particular details of mise-en-scène – to gestures, styles of clothing or performance, emotionally charged moments in our experience of cinema. In these moments, "what is being revealed is subjective, fleeting, variable, depending on a set of desires and the subjective constitution that is involved in a specific encounter with a specific film."[43] Film noir, as it circulates globally, remains today a hotbed of cinephilia. But the kinds of attachments noir has sparked in spectators – affinities signaled through style – still get a bad rap. While noir cinephilia is easily dismissed as a form of ahistorical nostalgia, we prefer to consider it as itself a kind of eccentric historical practice.

Moved by the surrealists, we propose our own game: to write a micro-history of noir style that begins through the sheer suggestiveness of one man's cinephilia, and that reanimates – for him and us – an eloquent series of loved moments in the history of film noir, creating a different noir history in the process. Our presiding cinephile will be Jim Jarmusch, and his work of cinephilic history, *Ghost Dog: The Way of the Samurai* (1999), a film about the violent life and death of a young African American hitman living in some unnamed American inner city, and a generic hash Jarmusch described as a "samurai-gangster-hip-hop-Eastern-Western." As we are told in *Ghost Dog*, "the end is important in all things," so we'll begin our history with an ending: the moment late in *Ghost Dog*'s credit sequence when Jarmusch "personally thanks" the following: Tsunetomo Yamamoto, Mary Shelley, Ryunosuke Akutagawa, Seijun Suzuki, Jean-Pierre Melville, Miguel de Cervantes, Akira Kurosawa, and the Wu-Tang Clan. As both a cinephilic gesture and an act of auteurist self-fashioning, the list assembles a motley crew of writers, directors, and musicians, and moves between Western and Eastern cultural sources, much like Ghost Dog himself. We'll begin with just one of these names, Jean-Pierre Melville, a French master of the film noir, and see where Melville takes us, before returning to *Ghost Dog*. Along the way, some of the protagonists of Jarmusch's story, like Melville, will be enlarged, surrealist style, while the import of other players will be reduced to make way for new paths opened by our own cinephilia. Our reading will fracture Jarmusch's own genealogy a bit, but that, *Ghost Dog* insists, is its own act of love.

Gestures, Hats, and Contract Killers: Noir Fashion in France

A legendary cinephile, Melville makes a famous cameo as the pretentious writer Parvulesco in Jean-Luc Godard's *Breathless* (1960), a landmark film of the French New Wave, a playful film noir, and a superb example of French postwar cinephilia. The sequence opens under the sign of cinematic nostalgia, as we iris in to the film's famous lovers, Michel (Jean-Paul Belmondo), a French petty thief on the lam for killing a policeman, and Patricia (Jean Seberg), a young American correspondent for the *New York Herald Tribune*. Michel drops Patricia at the airport, where she will participate in a press conference for Parvulesco, who has just published a new novel. As the couple says goodbye for a time, they do so in gestures that, by now in the film, are familiar tokens of intimacy, both for them and for Godard's spectator. Michel goofily shadowboxes, as he has just done in front of a mirror in Patricia's apartment, and then draws his thumb over his lips – the loving homage to Humphrey Bogart, first performed earlier in front of a poster for Bogey's final film, *The Harder They Fall* (1956). Parvulesco-Melville enters through the same door that Michel-Belmondo exits, and bumps into him in the process. More inside baseball in a highly self-reflexive movie: Parvulesco and Michel are strangers, but Belmondo will shortly appear in Melville's *Léon Morin, prêtre/Leon Morin, Priest* (1961), and star both in two of his great film noir, *Le Doulos/The Finger Man* (1963) and *L'Aîné des Ferchaux/An Honorable Young Man* (1963), another homage to American cinema.

During the press conference, held on an outdoor platform above an active Orly runway, Melville-Parvulesco is a lovable snob, an impossibly cool mixture of charm and condescension. The reporters roll their cameras, scribble notes, and press their mikes to the mouth of the master, asking Parvulesco a series of fawning questions about the state of modern life, and the fate of romantic love and feeling within it. Parvulesco is unflappable; he has an answer for everything. Patricia, more tentative, gets no response to her first question, and later tries again with another: "Do women have a role to play in modern society?" Removing his Ray-Bans to stare at the lovely Patricia, wearing sunglasses and a striped dress, Parvulesco responds, "Yes, if they're charming and wear striped dresses and dark sunglasses." Patricia smiles, appreciating the compliment, and gains the confidence to re-ask her first question: "What is your greatest ambition?" Parvulesco replies: "To become immortal, and then die." Struck by the answer, Patricia removes her glasses, and looks directly at the camera, as the scene ends.

Parvulesco's answer is neither profound nor absurd, but instead a cinephilic paradox. It conjures the secular afterlife of the movie star, perhaps one of noir's doomed heroes, the type played by Bogart or Jean Gabin. Such stars die tragically only to live again, and be again put to death, in cinematic repetitions, and for viewers who can relive the pathos and pleasure of such tragedy, knowing how noir protagonists tend to die. This knowing, gratuitous sequence does nothing to advance *Breathless*'s scant plot, but serves instead as an instance of exuberant cinephilia. Foregrounding technological recording devices, it's a meta-cinematic interlude, packed with a pile of citations, aphorisms, and references to other artists (not just Melville, but also Rilke, Casanova, Brahms, Chopin, and Cocteau) that lets you know you're in a Godard movie. It's thus a nested example of *Breathless*'s own famously disjointed narration, built less on continuous plotting or careful characterization than on fragmented gestures to a virtual world of films and texts.

Of course, Parvulesco's *bon mots* about women are also cinematic clichés about film noir's femmes fatales, and Patricia will later play just that role for Michel, giving him up to the police, and to his death: "Feelings are a luxury few women indulge in," Parvulesco proclaims, forecasting the end of *Breathless*; or, in a more hard-boiled key, "Two things matter in life: For men, it's women, and for women, it's money." Parvulesco's words and gestures in the episode speak to the contagious circulation of signs in *Breathless*'s semiotic universe. When asked by a reporter how many men a woman can love, physically, in a lifetime, Parvulesco answers by counting on his fingers, recycling the very motions recently made by Michel and Patricia in her apartment when they ask each other about past loves. Similarly, the word Parvulesco chooses to express his disgust for Chopin (*dégueulasse*) is mouthed again by Michel in his last, dying breaths, and famously mistranslated to Patricia by the police. Patricia, for her part, responds by citing Michel's Bogey gesture, looking straight into the camera as she does so, and thus echoing at the film's end her breaking of the fourth wall at the conclusion of the Melville-Parvulesco scene (Figures 3.4 and 3.5). These noir gestures never die. Nostalgically reactivated by the cinephile, or passed on to other films, they will always be made anew.

FIGURE 3.4 Michel does Bogey's gesture (*Breathless*, 1960).

Such, at least, was Godard's plan for Breathless, a film he hoped would "give the feeling that the techniques of film-making had just been discovered or experienced for the first time."[44] The style of American film noir is reborn through its reduction to cliché, stereotype, and gesture, and its cinephilic reinvention in postwar France – here, through the formal hallmarks of early Godardian modernism: elliptical narration, discontinuous editing, and a quick, rough-and-ready shooting style. As discussed in Chapter 2, the New Wave's reflexive riffs on Hollywood cinema were part of a broader geopolitics of French cinephilia energized by the postwar Americanization of French culture. This cinephilic era began in earnest while the major players of the nouvelle vague were not yet directors, but rather film critics at the journal Cahiers du Cinéma. There, the Cahiers group, under the guiding spirit of André Bazin, developed a highly cinephilic brand of film

FIGURE 3.5 Patricia does Michel's gesture (*Breathless*, 1960).

criticism. The connoisseurship would later fuel their filmmaking (Godard always insisted on the continuity between his film criticism and his filmmaking, each versions of each other), and depended on the access to world cinema they were granted at Henri Langlois's Cinémathèque Française. There, they regularly saw Hollywood films noir, and other genre films, on double or triple bills with films from other countries, and marked by a range of different styles, periods, and sensibilities. As Christian Keathley has recently argued, the Cinémathèque's screening practices produced a particularly ahistorical kind of cinephilia among the *Cahiers* cadre, one based on a decontextualized, comparative approach to international filmmaking.[45] In Langlois's museum of world cinema, all films (high and low) and directors (independent visionaries and studio hacks) became contemporaries on the level of spectatorship. This comparative approach helped to foster the *Cahiers'* famous *politique des auteurs* (auteur theory), in which the *Cahiers* critics discerned, even in the most formulaic Hollywood product, the evidence of authorship – stylistic signs of the director's presiding sensibility, as expressed in the deft manipulation of mise-en-scène. French and American films noir were privileged sites for *Cahiers'* critical cinephilia: Godard, no stranger to hyperbole, proclaimed Renoir's *La Nuit du carrefour* "the only great French thriller," and waxed rhapsodic about Nicholas Ray in the *Cahiers* "dossier" on that auteur; Jacques Rivette found in selected, enigmatic moments of Otto Preminger's noir melodrama *Angel Face* (1952) "the door to something beyond intellect, opening out onto the unknown"; Claude Chabrol mourned the growing "mediocrity and slovenly formulae" of the American thriller from the interwar period through Robert Aldrich's *Kiss Me Deadly* (1955); and Bazin wrote a moving elegy for Humphrey Bogart.[46]

As the epitome of an independent auteur and a master of mise-en-scène, Melville was lionized by the *Cahiers* group in the 1950s; most importantly, he shared their love of American cinema, an Americanophilia of a piece with France's modernization in the American model. During the war, Jean-Pierre Grumbach, the son of a bourgeois, Jewish family, took the name "Melville" (after his favorite American author) as a member of the French Resistance. Melville's American persona, donned in the theater of war, would be later supplemented by fashion: his Ray-Ban sunglasses, and his trademark hats, preferably trilbies or Stetsons. However, Melville's critical favor among the *Cahiers* group, so tightly bound to his American style, would fall as French cinephilia itself seemed to die through the radicalization of French film culture in the late 1960s and early 1970s, which rethought the political nature of the media environment. If "Melville" stands in for the postwar heyday of French cinephilia, then, as Paul Willemen suggests, "1968 was more or less the end of cinephilia."[47] Following the turbulent political events of that year, in France and around the globe, *Cahiers'* approach to cinephilic pleasure shifted drastically once American cinema could no longer be separated from US economic imperialism. As Hollywood became a bad object, cinephilic desire was theorized as a mechanism of ideological mystification, and Melville's fey genre cinema was decried in the pages of *Cahiers* as thoroughly, if unselfconsciously, imbued with dominant ideology.[48]

Made on the cusp of this sea-change in French film culture, *Le Samouraï* speaks directly to the cultural politics of Melville's signature style. A loose remake of the Hollywood noir *This Gun for Hire* (1942), itself adapted from the British novel by Graham Greene, *Le Samouraï* was Melville's first in a series of three gangster movies starring Alain Delon, then perhaps the biggest male movie star in France. The plot is simple: Jef Costello (Delon) is a hit man who spends the first portion of the film constructing an elaborate alibi for the murder of Martey, the owner of a stylish deco nightclub. After killing Martey, Jef is spotted leaving the club by a number of witnesses, including Valérie (Caty Rosier), a beautiful Afro-French pianist, who plays jazz at the club. The police suspect Jef, but are unable to get the pianist to finger him for the killing. In the meantime, Jef is double-crossed by the mysterious employer who hired him for the hit, pursued by the police, and eventually shot by them at the nightclub where he has returned to deliver on a second contract – presumably the pianist Valérie. However, after Jef is killed on the stage of the nightclub, we learn that his gun was empty, and his death a ritualistic suicide.

The film's beauty and power reside in its formal austerity and painstakingly controlled mise-en-scène, of which Delon's impassive performance is a central piece (Melville claimed to match the film's restricted blue-grey palette to the color of his star's steely eyes). In other words, it's a masterpiece of style and atmosphere, and received some unfavorable reviews in a critical climate that had begun to rethink the politics of such formalism. *Cahiers* critics thought it a tired exercise, "yet another" gangster flick. A few years later, *Cahiers*' Serge Daney and Jean-Pierre Oudart would describe the extravagant style of Melville's late gangster pictures as "pseudo-films," their aesthetics closer to advertising for "a style in raincoats."[49] Such comments are especially telling because the New Wave, whose influential stylistic innovations are easily romanticized in hindsight, always courted fashion and objecthood. An exuberant cinematic modernism, the New Wave was also a product of postwar modernity, a celebrated Gaullist export commodity "promoted like a new brand of soap" (as Chabrol put it) and catering to a new market niche for an international cinephilic audience brought into being by the postwar expansion of the middle class.[50] Making the common pleasures of genre entertainment like Hollywood noir more "arty" for upwardly mobile bourgeois cinephiles, New Wave style, as Colin Crisp has argued, was a "necessary response" to the "changing consumer and leisure routines" of the 1950s and 1960s.[51] Like pornography and widescreen technologies, the New Wave films responded to cinephiles looking for the kinds of pleasure TV was unable to provide. In these terms, Melville's Le Samouraï, by "pushing the figure of the gangster to the limits of its archetype," works as a self-conscious investigation of the end of this phase of French cinephilia.[52] The film examines the proximity between film noir as style – its reduction to fashion, objecthood, and image – and the controlled, planned, procedural environment of 1960s modernity. The trick of Melville's minimalist style – at once spare and nostalgic – is to show just how much cinephilic pleasure depends on a modern culture of seriality.

Melville's minimalism is excessive: less is always more. That's the central paradox of style in Le Samouraï, and the heart of the cinephile's pleasure in small details. Consider the film's famous line-up sequence (Figure 3.6). As our plot summary indicates, this sequence is incidental – another filmmaker could have delivered the scant narrative information of the scene much more efficiently: Jef is hauled into a police line-up; his alibi holds; Jef is released. But Melville is less interested in efficiency than procedure, and he spends nearly twenty minutes on this sequence. It feels like a lifetime. When it finally ends, Melville stamps the frame with the time, "Sunday, 5:45 a.m.," underscoring the sequence's duration. Ginette Vincendeau, Melville's best critic, notes the way Melville eschews the speed and violence of Hollywood thrillers for a more ritualistic pacing: "Action and movement instead materialize in the carefully planned and professionally executed

FIGURE 3.6 Melville's line-up (*Le Samouraï*, 1967).

gestures, either the heist . . . or the contract killing."⁵³ In these terms, the sequence *has* to be long so as to compare and balance the inspector's thorough, repetitive procedures for testing Jef's alibi with Jef's own painstaking gestures and motions in constructing it in the film's opening, equally procedural scenes. We see this also in Melville's fetishistic attention to the ring of visually identical keys Jef uses to steal cars; the police, we later learn, have a similar ring. When Jef tries his ring to boost a car, he places the keys in a row (another line-up), and Melville allows us to feel the time it takes Jef to locate the one that will start the car. The contract killer and the cops are bound in their shared professional routines; their repetitive actions are certain, but cool and unreflective. "What do you think about Jef Costello?," the Inspector (François Périer) is asked at the line-up sequence's conclusion. "I never think," he answers.

On another level, the temporal dilation of these scenes offers a specific kind of cinematic pleasure – the banality, slowness, and redundancy of action on the diegetic level produces a stalled temporality for the spectator, and allows us to obsess upon the details of the mise-en-scène, our own way of killing time. (Jarmusch, we'll see, has had the time to notice these details, and *Ghost Dog* will expand and redeploy them.) This lingering in process is one upside of noir's characteristically suspended temporality, opening *Le Samouraï*'s cinephilic dimension. Melville cues us to this right away in the framing of the initial line-up, a homage to John Huston's film noir *The Asphalt Jungle* (1950), a caper film loosely reworked in Melville's next Delon film, *Le Cercle rouge/The Red Circle* (1970) (Figure 3.7). Consider also Melville's curiously extended sight gag in this scene, in which the inspector seeks to discern whether the other nocturnal visitor to the apartment of Jef's girlfriend Jane (Nathalie Delon) can recognize Jef in a crowd. The inspector stands Jef among rows of cops, dressed in similar trenchcoats and hats; but he asks one of his policemen to trade coats with Jef, and the other to swap hats, effectively disassembling Jef's gangster image into fragments of noir style. Scanning the line-up, the man from Jane's apartment, who has only briefly seen Jef exit and has confessed

FIGURE 3.7 Huston's line-up (*The Asphalt Jungle*, 1950).

to being "not very observant," tells the Inspector: "I have a composite image. A trenchcoat like that, a hat like this or that, and a face like his," correctly reassembling the scattered pieces of an icon. The gag speaks to Delon's star image, and his unmistakable face, but it also underscores the centrality of memory and nostalgia in cinephilia, and to film noir's tendency to deconstruct – through exaggeration – its own types. Memory is built on just such "composite images," snatches and fragments of the irretrievable past that we reassemble in recollection, losing parts of the experience in the process, and charging others with feeling in excess of their initial import. Le Samouraï is itself a rebus of noir style crafted in nostalgia: its emotional yield, however, is not the spontaneity, novelty, or playfulness of Breathless, but something more mournful, flattening feeling through iteration.

Le Samouraï insists on the deathliness of its own stylish repetitions – both within the diegesis (Jef's two killings, his two stolen Citroëns, his repeated trips to Martey's, his ritualistic dressing in front of the mirror, tracing the brim of his hat) and on the level of its own compulsive style, which everywhere proclaims the end of film noir, and its afterlife in memory and myth. Melville described the film's steely palette as "an attempt to make a black-and-white film in color," and, in an early sequence, used xeroxes of banknotes rather than real ones to keep the color scheme muted. Jef's inner life is also drained of vitality: in Tuttle's Hollywood version, the contract killer is psychologized, Raven's violence explained as the traumatic result of childhood abuse. For Melville, Jef Costello remains a cipher to the end, a beautiful, cool image, more object than person. His deadliness, like the film's powerfully moribund tone, points to the inherent necrophilia of cinephilia, its way of "relating to something that is dead, past, but alive in memory."[54] Melville thus acknowledges how cinephilic pleasure – the lure of the contingent, unplanned, excessive detail – promises the outside of an overly planned world of technocratic modernity, but cannot escape its fatal dialectic with the systematic and coded. The dark irony of Le Samouraï lies in the way Jef Costello is emphatically *not* a nostalgic holdover of another, prewar time, but very much of a piece with the film's grey, procedural world. On one hand, as the newly politicized *Cahiers* critics sensed, Melville's style is ideological, the product of a society of spectacle; on the other, it offers a subversive mimicry of a world that has collapsed excess and control, nature and myth. The film's mournful, minimal style is not "a flight from the historical," as Vincendeau has it, but Melville's way of being historical, of owning up to the death of cinephilia, or its blurring with systematicity, which, in France of the late 1960s at least, would amount to the same thing.

Making Asian Gangsters Modern

We've barely mentioned the Asianness of *Le Samouraï*, which is precisely to the point. The film opens with a quotation from the *Bushido, Book of the Samurai* — "There is no greater solitude than that of the samurai, unless it is that of the tiger in the jungle . . . perhaps" – but it is a bogus line, concocted by Melville in a fit of orientalist pique. The bit of forgery encourages us to understand "Asia," like Delon's Citroën DS, as another signifier of style in the film's modern collection. As a connoisseur of style, Melville's double in *Le Samouraï* is Olivier Rey, the film's mysterious arch-villain, whose ultra-chic home contains modern paintings of faceless, ghostly figures as well as classical still lifes, Asian statues, and atomic-age chairs, in which Valérie sits, clad in a lovely black kimono. Doubling the exoticism of Valérie's Africanness, Asia is a design element in Melville's attempt to modernize the film noir. This act of cultural appropriation in the service of noir style, however objectionable on the surface, would be performed in Hong Kong in the 1980s in John Woo's *Dip huet seung hung/The Killer* (1989), an homage of sorts to Melvillian style. Indeed, a similar transfer of sensibilities was at work in Japanese cinema's own noir attempts to modernize the contract killer – by putting him to death – in the 1960s. We can see this in Masahiro Shinoda's *Pale Flower* (1964), at once a landmark film of the Japanese New Wave and a stylish gangster film often compared to Melville's own, and Seijun Suzuki's *Branded to Kill* (1967), a flamboyant, avant-garde genre picture, and one that American director Jim Jarmusch would later, in an act of cinephilia, place in Melville's company in *Ghost Dog*, his own cine-textbook of style.

Generically, *Pale Flower* and *Branded to Kill* are *yakuza-eiga*. The term "yakuza" means gambler or outlaw, and refers to popular films about Japanese gangsters and organized crime. The yakuza have existed in Japan for centuries, already appearing as signs of a dead, but destructively resuscitated, tradition in Kurosawa's postwar occupation noir *Drunken Angel* (1948). But the yakuza mythos flowered again in the 1960s when the Japanese film industry, which had undergone a second Golden Age in the 1950s, began a period of decline amidst rising competition for the leisure dollar of Japan's growing middle class. The yakuza film represented an attempt to lure young, male audiences away from television by updating the older genre of the period samurai film and its traditional moral code of *giri-ninjo* (duty and humanity) – in other words, by reviving precisely the code Kurosawa hoped to bury with *Drunken Angel*. This conservative morality would, as the genre evolved and grew in popularity in the 1960s and 1970s, become increasingly uncertain and ambiguous, and more situational and internally fraught. The early wave of "B" yakuza pictures were highly ritualistic, rule-bound, production-line films set in the prewar period, and their righteous protagonists held to an ancient moral code as a cynical protest against the bankruptcy of a modern world in which they were outcasts. For different reasons, Shinoda and Suzuki's yakuza films of the 1960s anticipated, or hurried along, the decadence and death of this style of gangster picture not, like Kurosawa, by stressing its outmoded code of values, but by making it modern.

Shinoda's career as a director was launched when the prestigious, but old-fashioned, Shochiku studio where he was under contract decided to create its own "Shochiku *Nouvelle Vague*." By allowing young directors like Shinoda and Oshima Nagisa to make films from their own scripts (à la Godard and Truffaut in France), Shochiku hoped to capitalize on the Japanese audience's new appetite for youthful, modern films, as evidenced by the phenomenal success of two 1956 pictures, *Kurutta kajitsu/Crazed Fruit* and *Taiyo no kisetsu/Season of the Sun*, both based on popular novellas by Shintaro Ishihara. Also adapted from an Ishihara story, Shinoda's *Pale Flower* is a brooding, melancholy noir about the unlikely relationship between Muraki (Ryo Ikebe), an unflappable aging hitman for the Yasuoka mob, and teenage Saeko (Mariko Kaga), a beautiful Tokyo socialite. Both characters, in their own way, are overcome by the unchanging emptiness and boredom of their lives, and by despair with humanity in general. Saeko seeks kicks and thrills in the company of illegal gambling dens, heroin, and, in the film's bravura final sequence, the witnessing of Muraki's final contract killing, his self-professed way of feeling alive in a meaningless world. In *Pale Flower*, the yakuza's traditional *giri-ninjo* code is, as Shinoda puts it, "total nonsense"; instead, Shinoda uses Muraki's suspension between the baffling webs of contradictory obligations typical of later yakuza films as a national allegory of Cold War-era Japan, "trapped" between superpowers, and hungry "to find [its] spirit and purpose in life."[55] Asked of the stylistic similarity between *Pale Flower*'s classicism and the work of Melville, Shinoda explained that, while a fan of Melville and film noir in general, he hadn't yet seen any of Melville's work when he made *Pale Flower*. He was inspired instead by Robert Wise's classic American noir *Odds against Tomorrow* (1959), particularly the way the gangsters kill time by the riverside before their big heist: "The daily life of an assassin interests me more than the assassination, the routine of coming home and daydreaming or sitting still and thinking about what you'll do next is what I wanted to capture in *Pale Flower*."[56] Shinoda's yakuza picture is a film noir because its character's moral universe is as empty and purposeless as its view of time, stalled in the futile void of the present, and with no faith in the past. In one memorable moment, the Yasuoka mob kills time in a bowling alley like *Double Indemnity*'s Walter Neff, while listening (ironically enough) to a Japanese version of Elvis's 1960 hit "It's Now or Never": "lounge time," Japanese style.[57]

Like that of the French New Wave, the noir modernism of *Pale Flower* combines the style of Hollywood crime thrillers, the burgeoning youth culture of postwar modernity, and the existential anxiety of a

nation in the shadow of the American superpower. The stylistic innovations of Suzuki's *Branded to Kill* are of a more vernacular sort. Suzuki
has explained his unconventional genre pictures less as avant-garde
subversion or heady technical experiments than as an attempt to distinguish his films from the gamut of cheap genre pictures churned out
by Nikkatsu studios, where he worked as a contract director. His formal novelty, he insists, was a function of boredom with the formulaic
scripts he was handed. In the 1950s and 1960s, Nikkatsu specialized
in low-budget action pictures that were "neither foreign nor
Japanese," but rather a cosmopolitan inflection of a range of Western
influences (jazz, pop music, American cars) and genres (westerns,
detective pictures, rock-and-roll musicals, teen delinquent pictures,
hoodlum flicks) oriented toward a young market with a taste for
Westernized cool, and featuring a stable of teen-idol pop stars.[58] Like
Shinoda or Oshima, Suzuki would eventually become an independent
director, leaving Nikkatsu to make quirky, ambitious art films for the
international market. Unlike Shinoda, however, Suzuki was forced
out, and the film that spelled the end of his twelve-year, forty-film
career grinding out genre quickies was *Branded to Kill* (1967), which the
studio head pronounced "incomprehensible" before canning its
director.

The kind of film that makes less sense with each viewing, *Branded to
Kill* is, to the *yakuza-eiga*, what Ornette Coleman is to Lawrence Welk.
What plot there is concerns an aspiring yakuza hitman named Hanada
Goro (Joe Shisido), "the number three" killer in the Tokyo underworld. Over the course of the film, Hanada, who gets off on the smell
of boiled rice, performs outrageously choreographed killings for the
Yabuhara gang, and is tormented by the mysterious "Number one
killer," who eventually murders him – all while ministering to the
sadistic sexual appetites of his wife and an alluring female client
named Misako, who lives in a room filled with dead butterflies. In
Branded to Kill, the solemn duty of yakuza warriors gives way to human
weakness, cowardice, and paranoia. The tragedy of heroic self-sacrifice
descends into absurd farce. And the ritualized codes of the genre

dissolve into unmotivated fragments of action and behavior, visually dazzling, but meaningless. Matching the eccentric fetishes of his characters with his own astonishing compositions, Suzuki offers a cinephilic disorientation of the genre. If Suzuki is a kind of surrealist, his surrealism lies in his belief in the unruly, emotional power that lies within the most banal forms of mass-produced cinematic fantasy; and *Branded to Kill* is an irrational enlargement of the *yakuza-eiga*. The stunt got him fired from the Nikkatsu, but it made him a countercultural hero for 1960s student radicals in Japan, who protested his firing by picketing the studio, and would later "stay up late to see revivals of his masterpieces at all-night showings in the Tokyo area."[59] Suzuki, in other words, had managed to inspire the kind of devotion among Japanese cinephiles that Henri Langlois had sparked in Paris; at roughly the same time, Langlois would be removed from his post as head of the Cinémathèque Française, an act which led to a major protest by New Wave cinephiles, and anticipated the current of student unrest that would shortly explode in events of May of 1968. In moments like these, cinephilic attachments dovetail with countercultural resistance, another way of marking style's politics.

Unlike the critics-turned-filmmakers of the French New Wave, whose cinephilia was part of an exploding leisure culture of Europe's postwar economic miracle, Hong Kong filmmaker John Woo learned to love movies in the impoverished shantytown of Guangzhou, on mainland China. Born Woo Yu-sheng, the boy who would become "John Woo" was taken to the cinema by his mother, a "huge fan of American classics."[60] Movies were free for kids, and Woo loved them, in part, for providing the dreamy outside of slum life, for "helping [him] escape from that hell."[61] In interviews, Woo is emphatic about the dreamlike status of his own films, especially the celebrated Hong Kong gangster films he began making in the late 1980s: "they take place in a world of their own, a world of my dreams. That world isn't just the world of the American gangster film; it's a hybrid of the worlds of all the films I loved, an imaginary place recreated from the gangster films I saw when I was young. I'm a dreamer."[62] Cultivated in his childhood,

Woo's cinephilic appetite grew and became more voracious. Too poor to attend university, Woo started a film club after graduating from high school to see art films, and, inspired by them, began shooting his own (now lost) experimental films on Super 8mm. He was thus exposed to a range of the explosive new European cinemas of the 1960s, including the work of Bergman, Bertolucci, and especially the French New Wave. In the 1970s, he devoured the gangster pictures of the Hollywood renaissance, captured by the stylized mythologies of male violence offered by Martin Scorsese, Sam Peckinpah, and Arthur Penn.

At this time, Woo's Western cinephilia was hybridized by his apprenticeship in the Hong Kong film industry. Woo began his film career working for the Shaw Brothers studio, and before making the series of gangster pictures that would make him internationally famous, he served as an assistant director to Chang Cheh, a master of the *wu-xia-pian* – epic films of chivalric martial arts; he worked for Golden Harvest studios making low-budget kung-fu movies in Korea like *Haoxia/Last Hurrah for Chivalry* (1979); and he also directed several romantic comedies in Taiwan's Cinema City in the 1980s. The result of this varied early career as a lover of cinema and young filmmaker is Woo's wildly international cinematic idiom. "Movies," Woo claims, "are my major language," and it's a complex mother tongue:[63] from China, the cinematic tradition of the *wu-xia-pian*, and of the legendary heroes of ancient China before that; from Japan, the samurai tradition, the work of Kurosawa, and the codes of the *yakuza-eiga*, especially the films of Takakura Ken; from the West, Hollywood musicals and gangster movies, old and reborn, and the spaghetti westerns of Sergio Leone; and, from France, not only Woo's beloved New Wave, but also the tradition of the French *policier* so important to it, and of Jean-Pierre Melville in particular:

> Melville is God to me. *Le Samourai* was the first of his films that I saw. It was released commercially in Hong Kong in the early seventies and immediately turned Alain Delon into a major star in Asia. . . . In fact, it changed a whole generation of filmgoers. Before that movie, younger audiences in

Hong Kong just enjoyed Cliff Richard, Elvis Presley, and the martial arts film; life seemed simple and easy. . . . When *Le Samouraï* was released, however, it was such a huge hit among the young that their whole lifestyle began to change. The film had an impact on fashion, too. Take myself, for instance: I was almost a hippie, wearing long hair. . . . Right after I saw *Le Samouraï*, I decided to cut my hair like Delon and started wearing white shirts and black ties. . . . What Melville and I have in common is a love for old American gangster films.[64]

What dream of film noir might follow from Woo's conversion to the Church of Melville? A good place to look is Woo's influential Hong Kong gangster film The Killer – at once a homage to Le Samouraï and an exercise in style of a radically different sensibility than Melville's own. Melville's Jef is replaced by Woo's Jeff (Chow Yun-fat), a natty hired gun who accidentally blinds a nightclub singer named Jenny (Sally Yeh) in the film's opening contract killing, and develops an unlikely friendship with Inspector Li (Danny Lee), the cop tracking Jeff. Beyond a shared love of American gangsters, Melville and Woo have in common a taste for the sartorial cool of their male stars: in every loving frame, Delon and Chow are positioned as icons of masculine stardom and style, spectacularized for our pleasure. Both directors are also obsessed with themes of male friendship and loyalty, and Le Samouraï and The Killer in particular share an interest in the doubling between the professional ethos of contract killers and cops. At the same time, it would be hard to imagine a film farther removed from the affectless modernity of Le Samouraï than The Killer, whose mise-en-scène is everywhere as hot and romantic as Melville's is cold and classical.

Take two exemplary scenes from The Killer, both of which showcase the audacity of Woo's style of feeling. In the first, Inspector Li arrives at Jeff's apartment after Johnny Weng's henchmen have ransacked it. Having begun to identify with Jeff, Li now haunts his space like dreamy Dana Andrews in Laura, examining Jeff's photograph of Jenny.

Here, Li puts himself in Jeff's position by virtue of Jeff's romantic relationship with Jenny, as he has just done in an earlier sequence in which he sees Jenny perform in the nightclub, and is mistaken by her for Jeff. Now, as Li examines the photograph, he plays a cassette tape of Jenny's theme – the lush, romantic song that consistently accompanies her performances in the film. The sentimental lyrics forbid remorse and foreswear memory and tears; they ask to be freed of a reverie that "dwells deep in my heart and soul. As if we are made for each other." As the song plays, Woo repeats the same slow-motion tracking shot that we first saw after Li heard Jenny sing at the club – of Jeff, seated, impeccably dressed, and holding perfectly erect a burning cigarette. Now, Woo repeatedly intercuts this shot with a matching shot of Li, seated and holding his cigarette just like Jeff. The swooning romanticism of the accompanying lyrics about a couple "made for each other" applies not so much to Jeff and Jenny, whose love is chaste, as it does to Jeff and Li, whose bodies are brought together in increasingly erotic ballets of masculine violence as the film mounts to its bloody, beautiful climax.

A second, more comic sequence echoes the way Jenny triangulates the powerful homosocial intimacy between Jeff and Li. Jeff returns to Jenny's apartment, where Li has come to question her. Unbeknownst to Jenny, now nearly blind, Jeff and Li have their pistols aimed directly at each other's faces. Making every effort to preserve her innocence, Jeff explains that Li is his "old football buddy," and the three dance about the room in a stand-off. Bound by their still-raised pistols, the two men joke about their nicknames for each other ("I'm Dumbo. He's Mickey Mouse") and their common determination ("That's my style! Mine too!"). It is impossible not to see Jeff and Li as doubles, and Jenny as a prop for their intimacy, not just because of Woo's relentless visual and narrative parallels, but because the men proclaim their affinities to each other so frequently, and so sincerely.

As with his heroes, Woo's style wears its heart on its sleeve. For Western critics, this has raised questions about the extent to which Woo's stylistic bravado and sentimental excess are to be taken seriously. Of course, what binds Jeff and Li, and what joins them to the other men in their lives (Jeff to his old friend Sydney, Li to his partner) is a shared chivalric code of loyalty, honor, and a common nostalgia for a world less given over to mercenary capitalism, a better world where such humane values were the norm rather than the heroic exception. In a conversation with Sydney, set dramatically against the backdrop of the Hong Kong skyline, Jeff muses, "Our world is changing so fast. It never used to be like this! Perhaps we're too nostalgic," and Sydney responds, "Nostalgia is one of our saving graces." As we've seen, nostalgia is also a founding sentiment of film noir's modernity, and has proven essential for interpreting its ambivalent politics. Chow, a close friend of Woo's, characterizes him as "a very traditional Chinese"; and Woo has described his status as a devout Christian (though much of his imagery is Catholic, Woo was raised Lutheran), as well as his desire in *The Killer* to "make a film that would emphasize traditional values: loyalty, honesty, passion for justice, commitment to your family. Things I felt were being lost."[65] In this light, Woo's exuberant sentimentality and taste for melodrama would buttress a fairly conservative model of nostalgia that ministers to the loss of a traditional moral order.

On the other hand, and given the very hybridity of Woo's style, one is forced to ask: nostalgia for which tradition, exactly? The premodern China of ancient chivalric legend? Or, as in Wong's *Chungking Express*, nostalgia for Hong Kong culture itself on the cusp of the 1997 handover to China? Or for the moral order encoded in Melville's masculine genre pictures? If so, how would this loss translate? Melville's particular brand of mourning has been read as a quite specific return to the historical trauma of the Nazi occupation of France, and thus as nostalgia for the structures of loyalty and friendship prized by Melville in the Resistance. But Woo's own comments about his films as oneiric assemblages of other movies emphasizes the transportability of meaning across generic and cultural codes: "To me," Woo explains, "the gangster films are just like Chinese swordplay pictures. To me, Chow Yun-fat holding a gun is just like Wang Yu [star of Chang Cheh's *Golden*

Swallow (1968)]." And, if this is true, then Wang Yu is just like Alain Delon, from whom Chow learned the finer points of noir style – how to carry a gun, and look great while doing it. In other words, Woo's heart problems seem to follow from the gap between his hybrid style, which generates equivalences between cultural and cinematic codes, and his nostalgic appeal to a single, traditional code.

Woo's nostalgia is in service of the future. His film's tonal and stylistic shifts, drenched in pathos one moment and breaking into absurd comedy the next, encourage us to think of noir as a utopia of cinematic style, radically open to new, unforeseen combinations. This, too, is an effect of cinephilia, which, as the surrealists saw early on, turns spectators into dreamers of mass culture. The affinities between Wang Yu's swordsman, Chow's gangster, and Delon's hitman are, Woo insists, true for him. In the process of Woo's cultural code-swapping and exchange, the original cinematic object – American film noir? – is estranged from itself. Transformed by Woo's way of feeling, some of the properties critics have deemed most essential to film noir – the femme fatale, say – drop out of *The Killer*'s dreamscape entirely; Woo, like Griffith, prefers his women impossibly pure. Other recurring features of the film noir, for example the romantic sentiments beating in the hearts of noir's most hard-boiled men, or noir's eroticization of violence, or noir's queer currents of desire, are accentuated – and then some.

In this sense, *The Killer*'s wildly divergent meanings for a range of audiences underscore film noir's inherent instability as an object of international cinephilia. Not a huge hit in Hong Kong, *The Killer* traveled well elsewhere in Asia. As Jinsoo An explains, the film was a major success in South Korea, dubbed by local critics as a cynical brand of "Hong Kong noir."[66] Chow's Delon performance wowed young South Korean male audiences, who saw in Chow an authentic mode of South Korean manhood and "traditional masculine values" at a time when the country's film industry was reacting aggressively to Hollywood's incursions in the national film market and was therefore newly open to Hong Kong imports.[67] In fact, the box-office success of Hong Kong masculinity in Korea in the late 1980s prompted local filmmaker Im Kwon-taek to make his own gangster film – the 1990 blockbuster The General's Son – to speak to "a distinct and authentic Korean masculinity."[68] Around the same time, The Killer was circulating in poorly subtitled versions in the West, where it became a cult film, and where Woo's sentimentalism was read ironically as camp. This tendency amongst Western critics to view Hong Kong films like The Killer as camp has come under some fire because it risks ignoring the cultural specificities of the films, or domesticating the otherness of the foreign text.[69] But, of course, such critiques underestimate the hybridity of Woo's sensibility, whose origins are multiple. Woo, for his part, has publicly celebrated the variety of meanings, camp and otherwise, viewers have found in his films. He even wrote a letter to the author of an academic essay exploring the homoerotic subtext of his films, saying "how much he had enjoyed" the article.[70] Much like Woo, once overcome by the stylishness of Le Samouraï, so too for Alain Delon, who, having witnessed the international success of The Killer, is reported to have penned a note to Chow Yun-fat, thanking him for keeping in circulation his signature style. Whether this style was ever fully his, or Chow's, is another matter entirely.

Ghost Dog: Love, Theft, and The Afterlife of Cinephilia

Jarmusch's Ghost Dog is a film about just this impropriety of noir style, the way it is never fully owned, but only ever appropriated locally. You can bite somebody's style, or nod to the source from whom you're lovingly stealing, but you'd better do something new with it in the process. These are lessons of cinephilia and hip-hop, two nostalgia-bound practices that share a love of the old school and a drive for novelty based in a skilled sampling of the dead forms. And Jarmusch's film writes these lessons into the gestures of its titular hero, Ghost Dog (Forest Whitaker), an African American hitman who, once saved from a vicious street killing by Louie, a mafioso underboss, has adopted the ancient ascetic code of the samurai, and dwells in the film's anonymous American ghetto as both a devout reader of the *Hagakure* and a skilled contract killer for Louie's crime family. In an extended homage to Melville's *Le Samouraï*, Jarmusch begins his film as Ghost Dog prepares for a hit on Handsome Frank, a member of the Vargo family who has made the unhealthy choice of sleeping with the boss's fetching young daughter. Jarmusch updates Delon's stolen silver Citroën – once the vehicle of the future – with a boosted black Lexus, which Ghost Dog opens with a magical electronic gizmo that seems to know the code to every possible carlock.[71] The device magically condenses two Melvillian visual fetishes, Delon's keyring and the policeman's bug. Once inside, and wearing Delon's white gloves (film editors' gloves, Melville insisted), Ghost Dog removes a disc, and his fingers flip it into the CD player like the mechanical arm of a record player or jukebox, which had to turn to the B-side the old-fashioned way. The gesture, repeated in Ghost Dog's three journeys in stolen cars in the film, is a loving echo of Delon's fetishistic dressing rituals in *Le Samouraï*, and his own brooding death drives. But the gesture also sketches one of the film's major themes: the ghosting of new codes and styles by the old, here as the phantom-limb of outmoded technology persists, or is nostalgically remembered, in a digital present. Ghost Dog will perform a similar gesture with his gun, which he insists on reholstering by first swinging it like a sword in obeisance to the samurai tradition, the ancient Eastern cultural code this Western city kid has taken as his own.

Such gestures are cinephilic rites, attentive, like *Ghost Dog* and its maker, to the origins of films in other texts. Melville, recall, is "personally thanked" in the film's credits; so too are: Seijun Suzuki, whose bizarrely choreographed hits in *Branded to Kill* are cited directly in Ghost Dog's baroque acts of violence (Figures 3.8 and 3.9); Akira Kurosawa, modern master of the samurai film and early Japanese films noir; Ryunosuke Akutagawa, Japanese modernist and author of *Rashomon*, the source text for Kurosawa's great film of that title, which circulates promiscuously in the film; Miguel de Cervantes, father of *Don Quijote*, a highly metafictional, seventeenth-century novel about an overread

FIGURE 3.8　The nature of violence (*Branded to Kill*, 1967).

Spaniard's absurd attempts to revive the lost code of knights errant; Tsunetomo Yamamoto, the eighteenth-century samurai who assembled the commentaries on the warrior code that constitute the *Hagakure*; and Mary Shelley, of *Frankenstein* fame, whose famous romantic monster, much like *Ghost Dog*, is an assemblage of dead parts brought back to life. Like the cinephilia of the *Cahiers* group, Jarmusch's is fueled by a seemingly ahistorical jumble of dissimilar

FIGURE 3.9　The nature of violence (*Ghost Dog*, 1999).

texts. Like Woo's gangster films, *Ghost Dog* is a cinematic dream hybrid; its relentlessly textual world is populated by local references to other Jarmusch movies and characters, and a host of cinematic citations and clichés spanning the globe.

Only here, love for movies and love for music mix. At one point, Ghost Dog buys more seed for the pigeons he keeps in his rooftop coop at a store called "Birdland," the name of a movie about the legendary jazz saxophonist Charlie "Bird" Parker, starring *Ghost Dog*'s own Forest Whitaker. Later, on another nocturnal ride through the city streets, Ghost Dog passes a nightclub illuminated by a glowing blue neon sign, a nod to a similar sign outside "Martey's" in *Le Samouraï*, only here the club is "Liquid Swords," the title of an album by GZA of the Wu-Tang Clan. RZA, another Wu-Tang member, scored the film, and makes a cameo in a film full of them, greeting Ghost Dog on the street while clad in camouflage. The clothing of hunters and warriors alike, camouflage is lifted by RZA as street fashion, and underscores the tendency of Jarmusch's style to blend, mimic, and assume different forms. But RZA's haunting score also helps Jarmusch restore to this film the missing history of black urban culture ghosted from an earlier tradition of film noir. He does this through a kind of cinephilic dilation of dead time. When Ghost Dog is cruising (like Alain Delon) through the darkened streets en route to his hits, his CDs help him kill time; this is much like Shinoda's bowling yakuza, or Mr. Vargo's outmoded heavies, who hang out in their club reading the paper, lampin' with nothing to do. But Jarmusch and RZA fill these moments with a noir counterhistory of African American culture that unfolds sonically, from Killah Priest's opening "From Then Till Now," which connects contemporary street life to the long memory of slaveships, to Willie Williams's "Armagideon Time," a reggae song about urban suffering and poverty, to the atonal, wordless free jazz that accompanies Ghost Dog's ride to his final hit – equally silent, equally wild.

No doubt about it: Jarmusch is a stylish director, and a practiced thief of cultural codes. But, as these musical gestures begin to suggest, *Ghost Dog* understands style and fashion as quite serious matters: the

raw fragments of identity, and the synthetic tissue of cultural genealogy. Melville, remember, took his American name as a member of the
French Resistance. This was more than just style; it was his way of sig-
naling loyalty to a threatened democratic future through a borrowed
cultural past. Ghost Dog has performed a similar gesture in choosing
an ancient, Asian lifestyle that is not, organically or culturally speaking, his own. Through this choice, Jarmusch nods to the rich history
of the appropriation of Asian martial arts culture *as style* by minority
subcultures, and specifically by young, urban African American men.
This story of subversive borrowing dates back to the early 1970s,
when inner-city movie audiences enthusiastically embraced the Hong
Kong martial arts pictures made by the Shaw Brothers and Golden
Harvest, and starring the iconic Bruce Lee: first *Tang shan da xiong/Fists of
Fury* (1971) and *Jing wu men/Fist of Fury* (1972), and then the legendary
Enter the Dragon (1973). The phenomenal success of *Enter the Dragon*, and
the untimely death of its young star, would inaugurate a minor cycle
of Hollywood exploitation films mining, as Juan Suárez puts it, "the
resemblance between the ancient martial artist and the contemporary
slum survivor," including two Jim Kelly vehicles, *Black Belt Jones* (1974)
and *Black Samurai* (1977), and the more subtle infusion of martial arts
style in the blaxploitation pictures like *Superfly* (1972).[72] Hip-hop
artists, especially the Wu-Tang Clan, picked up this stylish affinity
where blaxploitation left off, and transformed it into a baroque
mythology deserving its own history and philosophy, *The Wu-Tang
Manual* (2004). Wu-Tang's first album, 1993's *Enter the Wu-Tang (36
Chambers)*, pays its debts to Hong Kong cinema in its title and throughout the album, which contains samples from RZA's extensive personal
collection of martial arts films, and hinges on a series of analogies
between the codes of Asian martial artists, the violent slum life of the
American city, and the extravagant verbal styles of Wu-Tang's clan of
gifted rappers.

   Ghost Dog is everywhere attentive to the fluidity of style as a process of
cross-cultural adaptation, a pervasive survival strategy within the film's
urban environment. In one of the film's many overt exchanges of texts,

it is noted that the bear, Ghost Dog's animal totem, is "adaptable to all types of environments"; Jarmusch shows us several young kids on rollerskates, drafting on the movement of a car they've attached themselves to, unseen, like sucker-fish on a shark; a group of gang members freestyling on the corner rap about their "Black Mafia" and call each other "my De Niro," an overt nod to *The Godfather*, but also a more subtle riff on the actor's performance as a reactionary racist in Scorsese's noir *Taxi Driver*. This last example demonstrates how cross-cultural adoption and adaptation proceed by specific analogies between codes of masculine violence – martial artists, urban gangsters, noir vigilantes, and Italian American mafiosi, whose storied mythologies in American cinema have also found their way into hip-hop culture. In many ways, this analogical process of code-swapping seems to reveal what Jarmusch sees as the truth about the inauthenticity of cultural identity itself. As Suárez argues, the relentless artifice of *Ghost Dog*

> may also be interpreted as a survivalist aesthetic whose main concern is not the recovery and cultivation of the authentic – what may once have been – but what to do with what is left: a messy present, and a heterogeneous cultural archive. The aesthetics of artifice affirms the possibilities of the synthetic, the hot house mix, the lateral identifications and projections that make cultures and identities always plural and derivative.[73]

If Jarmusch reveals culture to be a giant "translation machine," he also notes the inevitable mistranslations committed in sympathetic acts of love and theft;[74] this, at least, seems to be the point of the film's running gag about Ghost Dog's unlikely friendship with Raymond, a cheerful Haitian ice-cream truck owner. Raymond speaks only French, and Ghost Dog only English, and yet they communicate effortlessly, their language uncannily echoing each other's statements and feelings nearly word for word.

In other sequences, even when Jarmusch plays games of translation and mistranslation for laughs, he also asserts the violent work of masculine identity and cultural identification between men. Consider the sequence in which Louie explains his relationship to Ghost Dog to Mr. Vargo, his henchman Sonny Valerio, and a much older consigliere with a hearing-aid and cane. As Louie recounts Ghost Dog's exotic name and lifestyle, Sonny, a walking quotation of a mobster, outs himself as a hip-hop connoisseur ("they all got names like that"), and explains his knowledge of personae donned by rappers "like Flavor Flav from Public Enemy," his personal favorite. Sonny comes by this fascination with extravagant names honestly enough, and will shortly summon into the room his henchmen: "Sammy the Snake, Joe Rags, and Big Angie." Mr. Vargo, ignorant of hip-hop names, notes that Ghost Dog's odd name reminds him of Indian warriors: "Red Cloud, Crazy Horse, Running Bear, Black Elk." But, just as Jarmusch has assembled this playful series of analogies between the funny monikers of rappers, Indians, and mobsters, identity reasserts itself violently as the third mobster, the oldest one with the longest memory, responds, "Indians, Niggers, same thing." In a way, the scene reworks Melville's gag with Delon's disassembled clothes in Le Samouraï, only here identity reasserts itself as a "composite image" forged through a long memory of racial prejudice. Something similar happens when Vargo's mobsters begin to hunt Ghost Dog, murdering indiscriminately another "big black guy" they find on the roof of a building ("I don't think that's him. It could be him."). Later they encounter – on yet another rooftop – an Indian man whom Jarmusch fans will recognize as "Nobody" (Gary Farmer) from Jarmusch's noir western Dead Man. The mobsters are flummoxed: "Yo, what the hell are you? Puerto Rican?" "Cayuga," Nobody answers. "Puerto Rican. Indian. Nigger. Same thing," they reply, and Nobody retorts with his famous, recurring line from Dead Man, "Stupid fucking white man." Steeped in the styles of cultural translation, Ghost Dog shows how flexible patterns of stylistic adaptation persist alongside more intransigent ideas about race with a long and violent history in the West. Sonny, in other words, can love Flavor Flav and still be a racist; just as playful, novel analogies between cultures and cultural codes can also collapse into violent, ignorant equivalences: "Puerto Rican. Indian. Nigger. Same thing."

This deadly allegiance to identity, Jarmusch insists, is ancient. And *Ghost Dog*'s noir edge depends on its attitude toward the near-extinct codes of masculine violence. Shared and subversively appropriated across different cultures, the codes seem to produce a single nightmare of violence in ever greater quantities, as shown by one of the film's cleverly inserted Tom and Jerry cartoons, where a standoff between the pair produces the brandishing of ever larger weapons that ends in a global apocalypse. This millenarian insight is the upshot of the film's melancholy discourse of extinction and nostalgia, best exemplified when Ghost Dog, after killing Mr. Vargo and his henchmen before they do the same to him, stops along the roadside, where two white, camouflaged hunters have just killed a large black bear out of season. The leering hunters explain that they shoot bears "because there ain't too many of these big black fuckers around here," or "colored people either," they add, making the racist equivalence between dead animals and dead black men overt, and unwittingly placing their violence in the West's bloody history of racial murder. Ghost Dog, an animal lover and a practitioner of violence sanctioned by a code, is disgusted by the lawless slaying, and offers his own equation: "In ancient cultures, bears were considered equal to men." "This ain't no ancient culture," they sneer, before Ghost Dog shoots them both, quipping "Sometimes it is." The point – the *noir* point – is not that Ghost Dog's killing is noble and the hunters' unjust, but that hunting, like America's foundational history of racial violence, or the ancient code of the samurai, depends upon entirely arbitrary rules for distinguishing between lawful putting to death and unlawful murder. In the act of killing, Ghost Dog authenticates ancient law by revivifying it, in much the same way that Vin and Louie, the only gangsters to have escaped Ghost Dog's massacre at Mr. Vargo's, describe their perverse pleasure in being hunted *because* it authenticates their identities: "Ghost Dog is sending us out in the old way. Like real fucking gangsters."

Jarmusch, of course, has no truck with such nostalgia for the arbitrary codes of male violence, authenticity, and honorable death – codes his film mocks by scrambling them deliriously, or sending them

FIGURE 3.10   A wounded Belmondo (*Breathless*, 1960).

up, Suzuki style, as cartoonish, ironic farce. "It is said," Ghost Dog reads from one of the film's many inserted quotations from the *Hagakure*, "that what is called 'the spirit of the age' is something to which one cannot return." All the better. *Ghost Dog*'s ironic putting to death of the gangster mythos acknowledges the real cycles of violence that have produced this Frankenstein monster, who must every day "meditate on inevitable death"; thus the repeated flashbacks to Ghost Dog's "birth" when saved by Louie's violence, as well as Ghost Dog's repeated gestures of respect to the graveyard he passes daily on the street. But it also hinges on a Melvillian emptying or hollowing out of the gangster code and its cross-cultural repetitions, a theatrical coming to the end evident in the palpable sense of exhaustion pervading its climactic "final shootout scene" between Louie and Ghost Dog. Everyone – the film's cinephilic audience, its characters, its director – is aware that they are going through the motions of both a classic

FIGURE 3.11 A wounded Louie (*Ghost Dog*, 1999).

western showdown and the suicidal end of *Le Samouraï*. Tellingly, the future of this broken genealogy of noir violence rests in the hands not of another man, but of the bookish young girl Pearline, the daughter of a Caribbean immigrant, who hauntingly picks up Ghost Dog's empty gun in this sequence, and mock-fires at Louie, who mock-stumbles, struck by her virtual bullet and running like a wounded Belmondo (Figures 3.10 and 3.11). If Louie and Ghost Dog, like Godard's Michel, trade in noir's ceremonies of killing, Pearline is Jarmusch's Patricia, left with a corpse and uncertain what do about it. The final object in her hands, however, is not a gun, but Ghost Dog's copy of the *Hagakure* (Figure 3.12). The lessons of texts and films are wildly subjective – call this principle the Rashomon effect, or the Shanghai gesture. They are given to unaccountable appropriations, infinite future acts of love and theft. For this reason, as Jarmusch's credit sequence ironically notes, the copyrighting of translated texts, or the call of the "pileated woodpecker," is patently absurd. *Ghost Dog*'s final hope for Pearline is that her impassioned reading of the *Hagakure* produces a different, less violent story, and not yet another film noir.

FIGURE 3.12   The Rashomon effect (*Ghost Dog*, 1999).

NOTES

1 James Naremore, *More than Night: Film Noir in its Contexts* (Berkeley: University of
   California Press, 1998), p. 168.
2 Raymond Borde and Etienne Chaumeton, *A Panorama of American Film Noir*,
   1941–1953, trans. Paul Hammond (San Francisco: City Lights Books, 2002),
   p. 10.
3 As Laura Mulvey has recently argued, these dimensions of cinephilic pleasure
   have been enhanced significantly by the development of video and now
   DVDs, technologies which have helped produced a reinvigorated spectatorship of temporal delay and the fragmenting of narrative continuity. See especially her chapter "The Possessive Spectator," in *Death 24x a Second: Stillness and the
   Moving Image* (London: Reaktion Books, 2006), pp. 161–180.
4 Andrew Spicer, *Film Noir* (London: Longman, 2002), p. 45. Drawing on Janey
   Place and Lowell Peterson's "seminal account of noir," Spicer argues that noir
   was an "anti-traditional" and unconventional departure from Hollywood
   norms. He offers a useful periodization of Hollywood noir style through its
   development beginning in 1940 to what he calls its fragmentation and decay
   in 1958 (pp. 45–63).
5 Vivian Sobchack, "Lounge Time: Postwar Crises and the Chronotope of Film
   Noir," in *Refiguring American Film Genres: History and Theory*, ed. Nick Browne
   (Berkeley: University of California Press, 1998), pp. 129–170.

6 Marc Vernet, "Film Noir on the Edge of Doom," in *Shades of Noir*, ed. Joan Copjec (London: Verso, 1993), pp. 1–32.

7 Barry Salt, *Film Style and Technology: History and Analysis*, 2nd edn. (London: Starworld, 1992), pp. 119–120.

8 Ibid., pp. 206–207.

9 Sheri Chinen Biesen, *Blackout: World War II and the Origins of Film Noir* (Baltimore, MD: Johns Hopkins University Press, 2005).

10 Ibid., p. 63.

11 Ibid., pp. 6, 96.

12 David Bordwell, Janet Staiger, and Kristin Thompson, *The Classical Hollywood Cinema: Film Style and Mode of Production to 1960* (New York: Columbia University Press, 1985), p. 77.

13 Naremore, *More than Night*, pp. 199–200.

14 Elizabeth Cowie, "Film Noir and Women," in *Shades of Noir*, ed. Joan Copjec (London: Verso, 1993), p. 131.

15 Leo Enticknap, *Moving Image Technology: From Zoetrope to Digital* (London: Wallflower Press, 2005), p. 95. See also Alan Nadel's "God's Law and the Wide Screen," in *Containment Culture: American Narratives, Postmodernism, and the Atomic Age* (Durham, NC: Duke University Press, 1995), pp. 90–116.

16 Enticknap, *Moving Image Technology*, p. 91.

17 For a discussion of these lesser-known color noirs, see Naremore, *More than Night*, pp. 187–189.

18 Enticknap, *Moving Image Technology*, p. 94.

19 See Kathrina Glitre, "Under the Neon Rainbow: Color and Neo-noir," in *Neo-noir*, ed. Mark Bould, Kathrina Glitre, and Greg Tuck (London: Wallflower Press, forthcoming).

20 Hoberman borrows this phrase from Mike Davis's chapter "Sunshine or Noir?" in *City of Quartz: Excavating the Future in Los Angeles* (London: Verso, 2006). Where Davis uses this phrasing to capture both the utopic myths and the noir anti-myths (of capitalist exploitation, empty commodity culture, etc.) of Los Angeles, Hoberman omits the "or" and takes seriously the possibility that "noir" and "sunshine" may be compatible aesthetic terms, especially for films noir that describe the decaying, decrepit, capitalist culture of blue-sky LA and Hollywood.

21 J. Hoberman, "A Bright, Guilty World," *Artforum* 45:6 (February 2007), pp. 260–267.

22 James M. Cain, "Double Indemnity," in *The Postman Always Rings Twice, Double*

Indemnity, Mildred Pierce, and Selected Stories (New York: Everyman's Library, 2003), p. 124.

23 Borde and Chaumeton, *A Panorama of American Film Noir*, p. 17.

24 Ibid., p. 17.

25 Ibid., p. 18.

26 Quoted in Frank Krutnik, *In a Lonely Street: Film Noir, Genre, Masculinity* (London: Routledge, 1991), p. 41. For more on the cinematic technique of the inter-war American novel, see Claude-Edmonde Magny, *The Age of the American Novel: The Film Aesthetic of American Fiction between the Wars*, trans. Eleanor Hochman (New York: Frederick Ungar, 1972). For a reading of Magny's study within the French visual culture of its production, see Justus Nieland, "French Visual Humanisms and the American Style," in *A Companion to the Modern American Novel*, ed. John T. Matthews (Chichester, UK: Wiley-Blackwell, 2009), pp. 116–140.

27 Krutnik, *In a Lonely Street*, p. 42.

28 See J. P. Telotte, *Voices in the Dark: The Narrative Patterns of Film Noir* (Urbana: University of Illinois Press, 1989), pp. 1–40.

29 Fredric Jameson, "The Synoptic Chandler," in *Shades of Noir: A Reader*, ed. Joan Copjec (London: Verso, 1993), pp. 36–37.

30 Jason Loviglio, *Radio's Intimate Public: Network Broadcasting and Mass-Mediated Democracy* (Minneapolis: University of Minnesota Press, 2005), pp. 104–107.

31 Ibid., p. 117.

32 Ibid., p. 110.

33 This is Michael Denning's phrase in *The Cultural Front: The Laboring of American Culture in the Twentieth Century* (London: Verso, 1996), p. 402. As Denning read it through Welles's own explanation, Vargas is inexperienced at using such recoding devices, and is, at this moment, guiding by the apparatus rather than guiding it himself.

34 Loviglio, *Radio's Intimate Public*, p. 107.

35 Jonathan Sterne, *The Audible Past: Cultural Origins of Sound Reproduction* (Durham, NC: Duke University Press, 2003), p. 290.

36 A great neo-noir that takes up the recorded voice and anxieties over its com-modification is Jean-Jacques Beineix's French, New Wave-inspired *Diva* (1981), based on the novel by Daniel Odier.

37 Mark Bould, *Film Noir: From Berlin to Sin City* (London: Wallflower Press, 2005), p. 112.

38 Ibid.

39 Ibid.

40 "Data toward the Irrational Enlargement of a Film: *The Shanghai Gesture*," in *The Shadow and its Shadow: Surrealist Writings on Cinema*, ed. Paul Hammond (London: BFI, 2000), p. 122.

41 Ibid., p. 122.

42 Paul Willemen, "Through the Glass Darkly: Cinephilia Reconsidered," in *Looks and Frictions: Essays in Cultural Studies and Film Theory* (Bloomington: Indiana University Press, 1994), p. 227.

43 Ibid., p. 236.

44 Godard, quoted in *Godard on Godard*, ed. Tom Milne (New York: Viking, 1972), p. 129.

45 Christian Keathley, *Cinephilia and History: Or, the Wind in the Trees* (Bloomington: Indiana University Press, 2006), pp. 17–18.

46 Godard, quoted in Keathley, *Cinephilia and History*, p. 84. All of these pieces – "Dossier: Nicholas Ray," Rivette's "The Essential," Chabrol's "Evolution of the Thriller," and Bazin's "The Death of Humphrey Bogart" – are included in the collection *Cahiers du Cinéma: The 1950s: Neo-realism, Hollywood, New Wave*, ed. Jim Hillier (Cambridge, MA: Harvard University Press, 1995), pp. 134, 158.

47 Willemen, "Through the Glass Darkly," p. 227.

48 On the changed status of cinephilia in the film culture of the 1970s and 1980s, especially as exemplified in what came to be called screen theory, see Thomas Elsaesser, "Cinephilia or the Uses of Disenchantment," in *Cinephilia: Movies, Love, and Memory*, ed. Marijke de Valke and Malte Hagener (Amsterdam: Amsterdam University Press, 2005), pp. 27–41. For an assessment of Melville's style as fully ideological, see Jean-Louis Comolli and Jean Narboni's landmark 1969 essay "Cinema/Ideology/Criticism," in *Narrative, Apparatus, Ideology: A Film Theory Reader*, ed. Philip Rosen (New York: Columbia University Press: 1986).

49 Serge Daney and Jean-Pierre Oudart, quoted in Ginette Vincendeau, *Jean-Pierre Melville: An American in Paris* (London: BFI, 2003), p. 177.

50 Claude Chabrol, quoted in Ginette Vincendeau, "France 1945–1965 and Hollywood: The Policier as International Text," *Screen* 33:1 (Spring 1992), p. 55.

51 Colin Crisp, *The Classic French Cinema: 1930–1960* (Bloomington: Indiana University Press, 1993), p. 73.

52 Vincendeau, *Jean-Pierre Melville*, p. 185.

53 Ibid., p. 184.

54 Willemen, "Through the Glass Darkly," p. 227.

55 Shinoda, quoted in Chris D., *Outlaw Masters of Japanese Film* (London: I. B. Tauris, 2005), p. 122.

56 Ibid., p. 122.

57 In a fit of cinephilic pique, William Preston Robertson has offered a brilliant "short history of bowling noir," stretching from Double Indemnity to The Big Lebowski, another cinephilic masterpiece, and a wild counter-genealogy of noir, not unlike Jarmusch's own. On "bowling noir," see Robertson's The Big Lebowski: The Making of a Coen Brothers Film (New York: W. W. Norton & Co., 1998), pp. 94–101. For solid reckoning with Lebowski's cinephilia, see The Year's Work in Lebowski Studies, ed. Edward P. Comentale and Aaron Jaffe (Bloomington: Indiana University Press, forthcoming).

58 Mark Schilling, No Borders, No Limits: Nikkatsu Action Cinema (Godalming, UK: FAB Press, 2007), p. 5.

59 David Chute, "Branded to Thrill," in Branded to Thrill: The Delirious Cinema of Suzuki Seijun, ed. Simon Field and Tony Rayns (London: Institute of Contemporary Arts, 1994), p. 17.

60 Woo, quoted in Lisa Odham Stokes, City on Fire: Hong Kong Cinema (London: Verso, 1999), p. 39.

61 Ibid., p. 39.

62 "Things I Felt Were Being Lost: John Woo Interviewed by Maitland McDonagh," Film Comment 29:5 (September 1993), pp. 51–52.

63 Woo, quoted in Stokes, City on Fire, p. 39.

64 John Woo, "The Melville Style," originally published in a 1996 special issue of Cahiers du Cinéma dedicated to Melville; reprinted in the supplementary material to the Criterion Collection's 2005 DVD release of Le Samouraï.

65 Woo, quoted in Stokes, City on Fire, p. 39; Woo, quoted in "Things I Felt Were Being Lost," p. 50.

66 Jinsoo An, "The Killer: Cult Film and Transcultural (Mis)Reading," in At Full Speed: Hong Kong Cinema in a Borderless World, ed. Esther Yau (Minneapolis: University of Minnesota Press, 2001), p. 105.

67 Ibid., pp. 106, 107.

68 Ibid., p. 108.

69 For a thoughtful critique along these lines, see Julian Stringer, "Problems with the Treatment of Hong Kong Cinema as Camp," Asian Cinema (Winter 1996/1997), pp. 44–65.

70 The critic is Jillian Sandell, who recounts this exchange with Woo in her essay "Reinventing Masculinity: The Spectacle of Male Intimacy in the Films of John Woo," Film Quarterly 49:4 (Summer 1997), pp. 23–34, p. 12. Woo was responding to her earlier essay "A Better Tomorrow? American Masochism and Hong Kong Action Movies," Bad Subjects 13 (April 1994), pp. 8–13.

71 On the Citroën DS, whose name puns on the French word for "goddess" (*déesse*), as the mythical spiritualization of the exploding French bourgeoisie's relationship to the world of things, the "best messenger of a world above that of nature," see Roland Barthes, "The New Citroën," in *Mythologies*, trans. Annette Lavers (New York: Hill & Wang, 1972), p. 88.

72 Juan A. Suárez, *Jim Jarmusch* (Urbana and Chicago: University of Illinois Press, 2007), p. 134.

73 Ibid., p. 134.

74 Ibid., p. 136.

4

FRAGMENTS OF ONE
INTERNATIONAL NOIR HISTORY

What follows is a fragmentary chronology of the international picture of film noir we have assembled in this book. The chronology is meant to be representative only of the limited scope of this book. In other words, it is not meant to be comprehensive, definitive, or exemplary. It is a product of our own cinephilia and scholarly interests, and – following the "precinematic" portion – is loosely structured by four key rubrics in noir's production around which our history pivots: global history, local culture, film history, and noir culture. We seek to stress the interdependence of local production with international and global phenomena, while reminding readers that film (even at times and places where its passport is revoked) has always been a global enterprise and mode of transnational communication. Most of the items in the chronology are central to the story we've presented here; others are threads we haven't been able to pursue here, but might be suggestive to future scholars, students, and lovers of film noir seeking a more complete story of its international scope.

For more comprehensive filmographies, we recommend Silver and Ward's Film Noir: *An Encyclopedic Reference to the American Style* and Spicer's *European Film Noir*.[1]

PRECINEMATIC NOIR

1764: Horace Walpole writes what is arguably the first gothic novel (roman noir), *The Castle of Otranto*.

1841: Edgar Allan Poe's "The Murders in the Rue Morgue" is published, featuring C. Auguste Dupin, perhaps the first modern fictional detective in the West.

1842: Eugène Sue's *The Mysteries of Paris* is published in installments.

1866: Dostoevsky's *Crime and Punishment* is published.

1867: Émile Zola's *Thérèse Raquin* is published, a naturalist novel whose plot James M. Cain adapted for *The Postman Always Rings Twice*.

1894: German dramatist Frank Wedekind's play *Earth Sprit* (*Erdgeist*) is published starring the femme fatale Lulu, which will later be adapted in G. W. Pabst's *Pandora's Box* (1929).

1900: British novelist Joseph Conrad publishes *Heart of Darkness* (1900), at once an indictment of the dehumanizing violence of British colonialism in Africa and a modernist experiment in perception.

NOTE

1 Alain Silver and Elizabeth Ward, eds., *Film Noir: An Encyclopedic Reference to the American Style* (Woodstock, NY: Overlook Press, 1992); Andrew Spicer, ed., *European Film Noir* (Manchester: Manchester University Press, 1997).

GLOBAL HISTORY	LOCAL CULTURE	FILM HISTORY	NOIR CULTURE
1910s			
The Mexican Revolution begins (1910–1920).		*Musketeers of Pig Alley* (Griffith, USA, 1912)	*Fantômas* (Feuillade, France, 1913)
World War I (1914–1917).		*The Cabinet of Dr. Caligari* (Weine, Germany, 1919)	*The Cheat* (DeMille, USA, 1915)
1920s			
1920			
			The pulp magazine *Black Mask* is founded by H. L. Mencken and George Jean Nathan, featuring the famous early private eye stories of Carroll John Daly and his detective Race Williams. *Black Mask* would publish the work of hard-boiled writers like Dashiell Hammett, Raymond Chandler, and Erle Stanley Gardner.

GLOBAL HISTORY	LOCAL CULTURE	FILM HISTORY	NOIR CULTURE

1921

The Japanese poet and short-story writer Ryunosuke Akutagawa publishes the short story "In a Grove" about seven conflicting accounts of the murder of a samurai. The story will later be adapted in Akira Kurosawa's *Rashomon*.

1922

Annus mirabilis of "high modernism" with the Paris publication of James Joyce's *Ulysses* and, in London, T. S. Eliot's "The Wasteland" and Virginia Woolf's *Mrs. Dalloway*.

Metropolis, Fritz Lang (Germany)

GLOBAL HISTORY	LOCAL CULTURE	FILM HISTORY	NOIR CULTURE
1925			
		The Joyless Street, G. W. Pabst (Germany)	
1927			
			"The Killers," Ernest Hemingway
			Underworld, Josef von Sternberg (USA)
1928			
			Détective magazine is founded in France.
			Edogawa Rampo publishes the Japanese detective novel Injū (*Devil in the Shadow*).
1929			
Stock market collapse in US; onset of global economic depression.		*Asphalt*, Joe May (Germany)	*Red Harvest*, Dashiell Hammett
		Un chien andalou, Luis Buñuel and Salvador Dalí (France)	*Pandora's Box*, G. W. Pabst (Germany)
1930s **1930**			
		M, Fritz Lang (Germany)	Dashiell Hammett publishes *The Maltese Falcon*.

GLOBAL HISTORY	LOCAL CULTURE	FILM HISTORY	NOIR CULTURE
		The Blue Angel, Josef von Sternberg (Germany)	
1931			
		La Chienne/ The Bitch, Jean Renoir (France)	Georges Simenon publishes the first Inspector Maigret novel, *Pietr-le-Letton*.
		The Public Enemy, William A. Wellman (USA)	
		The Maltese Falcon (first Hollywood adaptation)	
1932			
		Shanghai Express, Josef von Sternberg (USA)	
1933			
	The term "poetic realism" is coined to describe Pierre Chenal's *Nameless Streets*.	Future noir talent (Siodmak, Lang, Bernhardt, Tourneur, Wilder) begin to leave the German industry for France and then the US as Hitler is elected to power.	James M. Cain publishes the essay "Paradise," a critique of LA's rootless culture.
	FDR initiates New Deal economic programs to aid in economic recovery from the Depression.		*Woman of the Port*, Arcady Boytler (Mexico)

GLOBAL HISTORY	LOCAL CULTURE	FILM HISTORY	NOIR CULTURE
1934			
		Hollywood Production Code, adopted by the Motion Picture Association of America as a form of self-censorship, starts to be actively enforced.	*The Postman Always Rings Twice*, James M. Cain
			The Goddess, Yonggang Mingyou (China)
1935			
		Becky Sharp (USA), first Hollywood feature filmed in three-strip Technicolor.	
		The Thirty-Nine Steps, Alfred Hitchcock (UK)	
1936			
The Spanish Civil War begins, setting the geo-political stage for WWII.	A Popular Front coalition elects the left-wing Léon Blum as the first Jewish prime minister of France.	Fury, Fritz Lang (USA)	*Le Crime de Monsieur Lange*, Jean Renoir (France)
	Over at the Big Ranch, Fernando de Fuentes (Mexico), first major international		

GLOBAL HISTORY	LOCAL CULTURE	FILM HISTORY	NOIR CULTURE
1936 (continued)	success of Mexican cinema.		
1937	*The Shadow* begins as a stand-alone primetime radio show on CBS (USA).	*Pépé le Moko*, Julien Duvivier (France)	
1938 Adolf Hitler moves through Austria to attack Czechoslovakia, a French ally.	Léon Blum's Popular Front government falls in Paris.	*La Bête humaine*, Jean Renoir (France) Port of Shadows, Marcel Carné (France) *Algiers*, Cromwell (USA), a US remake of *Pépé le Moko*	
1939 The USSR and Nazi Germany sign a treaty of non-aggression.		*Le jour se lève*, Carné (France)	*Le Dernier tournant*, Chenal (France), first international adaptation of Cain
1940s **1940**	The Nazi occupation of France begins.		The surrealist *Anthologie de l'humour noir*/*Anthology of Black Humor* is published by

GLOBAL HISTORY	LOCAL CULTURE	FILM HISTORY	NOIR CULTURE
			André Breton in France.
1941			
	In December, Los Angeles is blacked out in the aftermath of Pearl Harbor.	*The Maltese Falcon*, John Huston (USA)	
		The Shanghai Gesture, Josef von Sternberg (USA)	
	The shah of Iran is installed by Great Britain and America.		
1942			
	Allied forces land in Sicily and begin moving inward on the peninsula.	*This Gun for Hire*, Frank Tuttle (USA)	Jean-Pierre Grumbach, master of the French film noir, takes the name "Melville" as a member of the French Resistance, and is jailed for two months in Spain.
		The Banco Cinematográfico is founded in Mexico, devoted to funding national productions.	
1943			
	On July 25, Mussolini's government falls; the German occupation of Italy begins.	*Ossessione*, Luchino Visconti (Italy)	Avant-garde filmmaker Maya Deren makes the "sunshine noir" *Meshes of the Afternoon* (USA).
		Distinto Amanecer, Julio Bracho (Mexico)	

1944

The Bretton Woods conference establishes the postwar international economic order, inaugurating the "golden age of controlled capitalism" and laying the groundwork for the founding of the IMF, the World Bank, and GATT.	Paris is liberated by the Allies in August.	*Double Indemnity*, Billy Wilder (USA) *Laura*, Otto Preminger (USA)	Raymond Chandler publishes his famous essay on the art of detective fiction, "The Simple Art of Murder," in the *Atlantic Monthly*.

1945

The US drops atomic bombs on Hiroshima and Nagasaki. Emperor Hirohito capitulates in Japan; occupation forces enter Japan. The Nuremberg War Crimes Tribunal convenes in Germany to prosecute captured Nazi military leaders; and the International Military Tribunal for the Far East is formed	Chester Himes, an African American noir novelist and later sensation of the French Série noire, publishes *If He Hollers Let Him Go* in the US. FDR dies.	*Detour*, Edgar G. Ulmer (USA) *Rome: Open City*, Roberto Rossellini (Italy)	Jean-Paul Sartre publishes "American Novelists in French Eyes" in the *Atlantic Monthly*. A former surrealist and Renoir collaborator founds the Série noire – a series of French translations of American and British crime novels and thrillers – at

GLOBAL HISTORY	LOCAL CULTURE	FILM HISTORY	NOIR CULTURE
1945 (continued)			
to try Japanese war criminals.			Gallimard, a prestigious French press.
1946			
	First French screenings of *The Maltese Falcon*; *Double Indemnity*; *Laura*; *Murder, My Sweet*; and *The Lost Weekend*.	Blum–Byrnes Agreement: the US forgives the French war debt in exchange for favorable trade agreements, opening French screens to US imports.	In August, the first writings on American film noir appear in French journals (Frank's "The Crime Adventure Story: A New Kind of Detective Film" in the socialist *L'Écran français*, and Chartier's "The Americans Are Making Dark Films Too" in the more conservative *Revue du cinéma*).
	Ango Sakaguchi publishes the essay "A Discourse on Decadence," an example of the postwar *kasutori* worldview.	*The Killers*, Robert Siodmak (USA)

The Big Sleep, Howard Hawks (USA) | |
| | President Alemán is elected in Mexico, and begins energetic modernization efforts. | *Gilda*, Charles Vidor (USA)

Shoeshine, Vittorio De Sica (Italy) | Siegfried Kracauer, "Hollywood's Terror Films: Do They Reflect an American State of Mind?"

The Spiral Staircase, Robert Siodmak (USA) |

GLOBAL HISTORY	LOCAL CULTURE	FILM HISTORY	NOIR CULTURE
1946 (continued)			
			Staudte's *The Murderers Are among Us* is the first post-WWII German feature and noir rubble film to be produced in the Soviet-occupied zone.
			The Bandit, Alberto Lattuada (Italy)
1947			
The US establishes the Marshall Plan (European recovery program) to rebuild Western Europe following World War II.	HUAC investigations begin.	Ronald Reagan, then president of the Screen Actors Guild and committed anti-communist, testifies before Congress.	*Between Yesterday and Tomorrow* (Braun, Germany) is the first post-WWII German feature film and film noir to be produced in the American-occupied zone.
The partition of India into the sovereign states of India and Pakistan takes place.	Britain agrees to 30% screen quota, and opens to US markets.		
	Jawaharlal Nehru is elected as the first prime minister of independent India.	*Crossfire*, Edward Dmytryk (USA)	
		Out of the Past, Jacques Tourneur (USA)	
		Nosotros los Pobres, Ismael Rodríguez (Mexico), example of *cine de arrabal* (slum film)	

GLOBAL HISTORY	LOCAL CULTURE	FILM HISTORY	NOIR CULTURE
1948			
	The Italians elect the Christian democrats to power; Italy's "economic miracle" begins.	In the Paramount Decision, the Hollywood majors are ordered to divest themselves of theaters.	*Without Pity*, Alberto Lattuada (Italy)
			Bílá tma, Frantisek Cáp (Czechoslovakia)
		The Bicycle Thief, Vittorio De Sica (Italy)	*Drunken Angel*, Akira Kurosawa (Japan)
		Rope, Alfred Hitchcock (USA)	*Foreign Affair*, Billy Wilder (USA)
		Call Northside 777, Henry Hathaway (USA)	*Puce Moment* (Kenneth Anger, USA) anticipates *Sunset Boulevard*.
		Berlin Express, Jacques Tourneur (USA)	
		The Live by Night, Nicholas Ray (USA)	
		The Naked City, Jules Dassin (USA)	
		The Lady from Shanghai, Orson Welles (USA)	

1949

Communist takeover of China.	Federal Housing Act of 1949, inciting "white flight" to suburbs.	*Border Incident*, Anthony Mann (USA)	*Stray Dog*, Akira Kurosawa (Japan)
		The Third Man, Carol Reed (UK)	John Alton, celebrated noir photographer (of *Boomerang*, *T-Men*, *Raw Deal*, *He Walked by Night*), publishes *Painting with Light*.
			Lost Youth, Pietro Germi (Italy)

1950s
1950

		Gun Crazy, Joseph H. Lewis (USA)	*The Blue Lamp*, Basil Dearden (UK)
		The Asphalt Jungle, John Huston (USA)	*Aventurera*, Alberto Gout (Mexico)
		In a Lonely Place, Nicholas Ray (USA)	*Criminal Brigade*, Ignacio F. Iquino (Spain), example of the Spanish *cine negro*
		Sunset Boulevard, Billy Wilder (USA)	
		Los Olvidados, Luis Buñuel (Mexico)	
		Story of a Love Affair, Michelangelo Antonioni (Italy)	

GLOBAL HISTORY	LOCAL CULTURE	FILM HISTORY	NOIR CULTURE
1951			
General Franco is given US aid in exchange for military bases in Spain.			The surrealist group performs an "irrational enlargement" of *The Shanghai Gesture*.
1952			
	India hosts its First International Film Festival, introducing audiences to Italian neorealism and postwar Kurosawa.	*Bienvenido, Mr. Marshall*, Luis García Berlanga (Italy) *Angel Face*, Otto Preminger (USA)	*Él*, Luis Buñuel (Mexico)
1953			
			Cyd Charisse and Fred Astaire perform the Technicolor-noir dance sequence in Vincente Minelli's *The Band Wagon*. Playing a femme fatale, Charisse revives her role from the Broadway Melody sequence in *Singin' in the Rain*, 1952.

GLOBAL HISTORY	LOCAL CULTURE	FILM HISTORY	NOIR CULTURE
1955			
American films command roughly half the screening time in most countries in the world.		*Kiss Me Deadly*, Robert Aldrich (USA) *Killer's Kiss*, Stanley Kubrick (USA) *House of Bamboo*, Samuel Fuller (USA), the first Hollywood film to be shot on location in Japan	First book-length study of film noir is published, Etienne Borde and Raymond Chaumeton's *Panorama du film noir américain*. Patricia High-smith publishes *The Talented Mr. Ripley*. Claude Chabrol, "The Evolution of a Thriller" *The Criminal Life or Archibaldo de la Cruz*, Luis Buñuel (Mexico) *Death of a Cyclist*, Juan Antonio Bardem (Spain)
1956		Humphrey Bogart stars in his final film, *The Harder They Fall* (Robson, USA).	*CID* (India)

GLOBAL HISTORY	LOCAL CULTURE	FILM HISTORY	NOIR CULTURE
1956 (continued)			
		Uncondamné à mort s'est échappé ou Le vent souffle où il veut / *A Man Escaped* (Bresson, France)	
1957			
	Chester Himes publishes *A Rage in Harlem* in France.		André Bazin writes a eulogy for Humphrey Bogart, "The Face of Humphrey Bogart."
			Manny Farber's essay "Under ground Cinema," on American genre movies, is published.
1958			
		Touch of Evil, Orson Welles (USA)	
		Underworld Beauty, Seijun Suzuki (Japan)	
1959			
		Odds against Tomorrow, Robert Wise (USA)	Boris Vian, author of *J'irai cracher sur vos tombes* / *I'll Spit on your Graves* (1946), dies in Paris.

GLOBAL HISTORY	LOCAL CULTURE	FILM HISTORY	NOIR CULTURE
1960s			
1960			
		Breathless, Jean-Luc Godard (France)	*Naked Youth*, Nagisa Oshima (Japan)
		Shoot the Piano Player, François Truffaut (France)	
		The Bad Sleep Well, Akira Kurosawa (Japan)	
1962			
		The Manchurian Candidate (USA)	
		High and Low, Akira Kurosawa (Japan)	
1963			
	The shah of Iran institutes the reforms of the "White Revolution."	*Le Doulos*, Jean-Pierre Melville (France)	
1964			
		Pale Flower, Masahiro Shinoda, (Japan)	
1966			
		Bonnie and Clyde (Penn) and the	*The Pornographers*, Shohei Inamura

GLOBAL HISTORY	LOCAL CULTURE	FILM HISTORY	NOIR CULTURE
1966 (continued)			
		start of the "Hollywood renaissance."	*Harper*, often considered the first American "neo-noir."
1967			
		Point Blank, John Boorman (UK)	
		Le Samouraï, Jean-Pierre Melville (France)	
1968			
	May, student revolt and general strike in Paris.	Langlois affair.	Charles Higham, *Hollywood in the 1940s*, the first English-language text to use the term "film noir."
1969			
		L'armée des ombres/Army of Shadows, Jean-Pierre Melville (France)	*Gheishar*, Masud Kimiai (Iran)
1970s			
1970			
		British critic Raymond Durgnat publishes "Paint it Black: The Family Tree of Film Noir" in London.	

GLOBAL HISTORY	LOCAL CULTURE	FILM HISTORY	NOIR CULTURE
1971			
		The French Connection, William Friedkin (USA)	
		Klute, Alan Pakula (USA)	
1972			
			American screenwriter and later noir director Paul Schrader publishes "Notes on Film Noir" in *Film Comment*.
1973			
		The Long Goodbye, Robert Altman (USA)	Bruce Lee's *Enter the Dragon* opens to phenomenal success.
1974			
		The Conversation, Francis Ford Coppola (USA)	Schrader publishes his essay "Yakuza-eiga: A Primer," which distinguishes the yakuza film firmly from American noir.
		Chinatown, Roman Polanksi (USA)	

GLOBAL HISTORY	LOCAL CULTURE	FILM HISTORY	NOIR CULTURE
1975			
		The Yakuza, a Hollywood–Japan coproduction starring Robert Mitchum and Ken Takakura, co-written by Schrader.	*Deers*, Masud Kimiai (Iran)
		Laura Mulvey publishes "Visual Pleasure and Narrative Cinema," helping to establish the theoretical terms of feminist film theory's interest in film noir.	
1976			
		Taxi Driver, Martin Scorsese (USA)	
1977			
		The American Friend, Wim Wenders (Germany)	

GLOBAL HISTORY	LOCAL CULTURE	FILM HISTORY	NOIR CULTURE
1978			
	John Woo works for Golden Harvest studios as an assistant director of the martial arts epic *Last Hurrah for Chivalry*.	E. Ann Kaplan's foundational collection of essays *Women in Film Noir*.	
	The Rex Theater in Iran is destroyed, helping to spark the Islamic revolution.		
1979			
	The Islamic revolution.		
1980s			
1980			
Ronald Reagan, still a committed anti-communist, is elected US president.			
1981			
	Body Heat, Lawrence Kasdan (USA)	*Film Noir: The Other Side of the Screen*, Foster Hirsch	
	The Postman Always Rings Twice, Bob Rafelson (USA)	*Film Noir: An Encyclopedic Reference to the American Style*, ed. Silver and Ward	

GLOBAL HISTORY	LOCAL CULTURE	FILM HISTORY	NOIR CULTURE
1983			
		Hammett, Wim Wenders (Germany)	
1984			
	Fredric Jameson's "Postmodernism: Or, the Cultural Logic of Late Capitalism" is published in the *New Left Review*.		French noir novelist Didier Daeninckx publishes *Murder in Memoriam*, a novel about the German occupation that helped pressure the French government to try Nazi collaborators.
1985			
The Sino-British Joint Declaration states that Hong Kong will be returned to China in 1997.			Japanese novelist Haruki Murakami publishes *Hard-boiled Wonderland and the End of the World*.
1986			
			Blue Velvet, David Lynch (USA)
1988			
		Stormy Monday, Mike Figgis (USA/UK)	

GLOBAL HISTORY	LOCAL CULTURE	FILM HISTORY	NOIR CULTURE
1989			
Tiananmen Square Massacre/June Fourth Incident		*The Killer*, John Woo (Hong Kong)	
1990s			
1991			
	India is bailed out by the IMF, catapulting the country into a globalized economy and culture.	*Nargess* (Iran) wins first prize at the Fajr Film Festival (its director is the first woman to win the award).	
1993			
			Enter the Wu-Tang: 36 Chambers is released, containing samples from RZA's personal collection of Hong Kong cinema.
1994			
		Chungking Express, Wong Kar-wai (Hong Kong)	*Pulp Fiction*, Quentin Tarantino (USA)
1995			
		Foreign Land, Walter Salles and Daniela Thomas (Brazil– Portugal)	*Devil in a Blue Dress*, Carl Franklin (USA)

GLOBAL HISTORY	LOCAL CULTURE	FILM HISTORY	NOIR CULTURE
1996			
	Bombay is renamed Mumbai.	*Lone Star*, John Sayles (USA)	
1997			
Hong Kong is returned from the UK to China.		*Insomnia*, Erik Skjoldbjærg (Norway)	Japanese detective fiction writer Natsuo Kirino's novel *Out* wins the Grand Prix for Crime Fiction, Japan's top mystery award.
			Deep Crimson, Arturo Ripstein (Mexico)
1998			
		Run Lola Run, Tom Tykwer (Germany)	*The Big Lebowski*, Joel and Ethan Coen (USA)
			Shark Skin Man and Peach Hip Girl (Japan)
1999			
		Ghost Dog, Jim Jarmusch (1999)	
		Nowhere to Hide, Lee Myung-see (Korea)	

**Twenty-first
century noir**
2000

GLOBAL HISTORY	LOCAL CULTURE	FILM HISTORY	NOIR CULTURE
		Amores Perros, Alejandro González Iñárritu (Mexico)	
		Snatch, Guy Ritchie (UK)	
		Sexy Beast, Jonathan Glazer (UK)	
		City of Lost Souls, Miike Takashi (Japan)	
2001 9/11: the US is attacked by Islamic terrorists. President George Bush orders the bombing of Afghanistan; the US invades Iraq, deposes Saddam Hussein, and attempts to install a democratic government.		*The Man Who Wasn't There*, Joel and Ethan Coen (USA)	
2002		*Insomnia*, Christopher Nolan (USA)	*Company*, Ram Gopal Varma (India)

GLOBAL HISTORY	LOCAL CULTURE	FILM HISTORY	NOIR CULTURE
2002 (continued)			
			The first annual "Lebowski Fest" is held in Louisville, KY, and a new mode of noir cinephilia is born.
2005			
		Sin City, Frank Miller and Robert Rodriguez (USA)	
2006			
		The Good German, Steven Soderbergh (USA)	Inland Empire, David Lynch (USA) The Host, Joon-ho Bong (South Korea)
2007			
		Boarding Gate, Olivier Assayas (France)	Canadian journalist Naomi Klein publishes The Shock Doctrine: The Rise of Disaster Capitalism, a noir history of neoliberalism.

APPENDIX

Suggestions for further reading, watching, discussing

1 COLONIAL NOIR

Another important challenge to concepts of French national culture in the interwar period was the status of its African colonies. This lesson plan encourages students to consider how this colonial relationship is also taken up both in an important poetic realist film from the period, *Pépé le Moko* and in a French neo-noir, Bertrand Tavernier's *Coup de torchon / Clean Slate*. These films are also of interest because they take up themes of mobility and displacement, and they do so as displaced translations of American genres – the American gangster film of the 1930s in *Pépé le Moko* and the American pulp novel in *Clean Slate*. Tonally, *Clean Slate*'s noir humor is an interesting stylistic counterpoint to *Pépé le Moko*'s powerful nostalgia.

Suggested Supplementary Screenings

Pépé le Moko (1937)
Director: Julien Duvivier
Principal cast: Jean Gabin (Pépé), Mireille Balin (Gaby), Lucas Gridoux (Inspector Slimane), Line Noro (Inès), Fréhel (Tania), Gabriel Gabrio (Carlos)

Summary: This masterpiece of French poetic realism tells the story of a doomed love affair between a dapper French gangster, exiled in the Algeria Casbah, and a lovely French tourist, attracted to exotic locales and dangerous creatures like Pépé.

Coup de torchon/Clean Slate (1981)

Director: Bertrand Tavernier

Principal cast: Philippe Noiret (Lucien Cordier), Isabelle Huppert (Rose)

Summary: This French neo-noir is an adaptation of American pulp master Jim Thompson's 1964 novel *Pop. 1280*. Tavernier deftly transfers Thompson's cynical novel about race relations in the American south to French colonial Senegal in 1938, where a corrupt, hapless cop suddenly decides to engage in acts of subversive violence against an absurd colonial regime.

Secondary Reading

Ginette Vincendeau, "Noir Is also a French Word: The French Antecedents of Film Noir," in *The Movie Book of Film Noir*, ed. Ian Cameron (London: Studio Vista Books, 1994), pp. 49–58.

Ginette Vincendeau, *Pépé le Moko* (London: BFI, 1998).

Janice Morgan, "In the Labyrinth: Masculine Subjectivity, Expatriation, and Colonialism in Pépé le Moko," *French Review* 67:4 (March 1994), pp. 627–647.

Discussion Questions

1 In "Noir Is also a French Word," Ginette Vincendeau explores the noirness of the French cinematic tradition of "poetic realism." How does Vincendeau define "poetic realism" and what is noir about its preoccupations? What particular attributes of *Pépé le Moko* might be considered "realist" and which "poetic"? What are the political implications of poeticizing the real in these ways?

2 Both *Pépé le Moko* and *Clean Slate* offer noir portraits of French

national culture; however, in these films the integrity of national culture is challenged by the historical reality of French colonialism in Africa. How do these films depict the local spaces and cultures in which their white, masculine heroes navigate their psychological turmoil? What is the relationship between the displaced male protagonists of these films and the local, colonial communities in which they find themselves situated?

3   As Janice Morgan's essay suggests, *Pépé le Moko* is acutely invested in the workings of memory and nostalgia. Tavernier's *Clean Slate* might be considered a critique of colonial nostalgia. How is the films' thematic interest in nostalgia connected both to their noirness and to their investigations of French national identity? Who, in these films, is at home in French national culture and what does it mean to share a memory of home, either idealized or ironic?

2 THE WEIMAR CONNECTION

There is an important connection between American film noir and Weimar cinema from the 1920s and 1930s. This lesson plan explores the continuity between Weimar and Hollywood noir through two films by Fritz Lang: M made in Germany, and Fury made in the US. In this context, students may not only consider the Weimar–Hollywood connection, but also take up the question of exile and film noir's critique of American society.

Suggested Supplementary Screenings

M (1931)

Director: Fritz Lang

Principal cast: Peter Lorre, Ellen Widmann, Inge Landgut, Otto Wernicke, Theodor Los

Summary: Peter Lorre plays Hans Beckert, a psychologically tortured serial killer of children. The police investigation, coupled with the hysterical civic response to the murders, proves to be bad for the business of the Berlin criminal underground. Thus the criminals mobilize to carry out an investigation of their own. Comparing the similarities between the police and the gangsters, both of which hunt Beckert, Lang's film is also a meditation on the seriality of mass culture and the culture of the masses. M is considered to be an important precursor to American film noir for its portrait of urban geography, deranged criminality, and the limits of justice.

Fury (1936)

Director: Fritz Lang

Principal cast: Sylvia Gibbons, Spencer Tracy, Walter Abel, Edward Ellis

Summary: Joe Wilson (Spencer Tracy), wrongly accused of kidnapping, is locked up in a small mid-western town. The locals, over-eager for justice and thrilled by the spectacle of mob violence, storm the jail and burn it down. The town then stands trial and, thanks to newsreel footage of the mob and evidence submitted by a "secret source," the guilty townsfolk are sentenced to death. At the last minute, Joe reveals that he is still alive (and the source of the most incriminating evidence), and thus saves his persecutors from their sentence. But the experience has transformed him from a hard-working everyman to an embittered misanthrope.

Secondary Reading

Anton Kaes, "A Stranger in the House: Fritz Lang's Fury and the Cinema of Exile," New German Critique 89, Film and Exile (Spring–Summer 2003), pp. 33–58.

Anton Kaes, M (London: BFI Publishing, 1999).

Siegfried Kracauer, "Hollywood's Terror Films: Do They Reflect an American State of Mind?," New German Critique 89, Film and Exile (Spring–Summer 2003), pp. 105–111.

Tim Bergfelder, "German Cinema and Film Noir," in European Film Noir, ed. Andrew Spicer (Manchester: University of Manchester Press, 2007), pp. 138–163.

Discussion Questions

1 In "Hollywood's Terror Films," Siegfried Kracauer suggests that in film noir the psychological dynamics "peculiar to the atmosphere of life under Hitler now saturates the whole world." In what ways does *Fury* comment on the psychological and social dynamics of "Hitlerism" (as Kracauer understands it) in the American context?

2 Anton Kaes argues for the centrality of the "experience of exile" in American film noir, and in the films of Fritz Lang in particular. How does *Fury* serve as a reflection on the experience of exile in the terms provided by Kaes?

3 In "Stranger in the House," Anton Kaes argues that Lang's *Fury* resonates with *M*'s representation of mob violence, legal evidence, and justice. How may we compare these films, and what do these similarities tell us about the instability of American democracy in the 1930s?

4 What is Bergfelder's argument for a uniquely German postwar noir? How does he situate postwar German filmmaking within the context of Weimar and Nazi cinema? What explains the German resistance to Hollywood noir?

To explore noir's culture of political exile further, consider the films made by Americans forced to leave the US in the wake of HUAC and Hollywood's Red Scare: Charlie Chaplin's *Monsieur Verdoux* (1947); Jules Dassin's *Night and the City* (1950) and *Rififi* (1955); and Joseph Losey's *Time without Pity* (1957).

3 THE SURREALISM OF INTERNATIONAL NOIR

As James Naremore has argued, the sensibility of the surrealist avant-garde helped to invent the American film noir in postwar France, and the first book-length study of film noir was influenced by surrealist fascination with criminality, fatal passion, and the eroticization of violence. This lesson plan involves films noir from France, Mexico, and the US, and allows students to consider the nature of their surrealism, as well as the way the surrealist fascination with cinematic excess helps us to understand noir cinephilia.

Suggested Supplementary Screenings

Le crime de Monsieur Lange / The Crime of Mr. Lange (1936)
Director: Jean Renoir
Principal cast: René Lefèvre, Florelle, Jules Berry
Summary: An idealistic, mild-mannered young Amédée Lange (René Lefèvre) forms a vibrant, socialist writing collective, printing a successful American-style serial named "Arizona Jim." In a fit of passion, he shoots and kills his nefarious capitalist employer, Batala (Jules Berry), who seeks to disrupt his enterprise, and is later acquitted of his crime by an informal jury.

Gun Crazy (1950)
Director: Joseph H. Lewis
Principal cast: Peggy Cummings, John Dahl
Summary: The gun obsession of young Bart (John Dahl) causes him to fall for Annie Laurie Starr (Peggy Cummings), the fetching sharpshooter in a local circus, and the two embark on a violent crime spree, chased by the police. The pursuit ends when Bart, clinging to his memory of a more innocent life, shoots his lover Peggy before they are both shot by the police.

Él (1952)
Director: Luis Buñuel
Principal cast: Arturo de Córdova, Delia Garcés, Luis Beristáin, Manuel Dondé
Summary: Francisco (Arturo de Córdova) is the seemingly upstanding Catholic gentleman and scion of an aristocratic Mexican family who is, in fact, a fetishist and paranoid schizophrenic convinced of his wife's infidelity and obsessed with the restoration of his family's land, lost during the Mexican Revolution. Francisco is overwhelmed by madness and violence, and tries to kill his wife (in

hallucinations and actuality). His insane jealousy finally drives her away, and he ends up, quite mad, living in a monastery.

Secondary Reading

Ernesto R. Acevedo-Muñoz, Buñuel and Mexico: The Crisis of National Cinema (Berkeley: University of California Press, 2003).

James Naremore, "The History of an Idea," in More than Night: Film Noir in its Contexts (Berkeley: University of California Press, 1998).

Jonathan Eburne, Surrealism and the Art of Crime (Ithaca, NY: Cornell University Press, 2009).

Paul Hammond, ed. and trans., The Shadow and its Shadow: Surrealist Writing on Cinema (San Francisco: City Lights Books, 2002). See especially the essays "On Décor," "The Marvelous is Popular," "As in a Wood," "Data toward the Irrational Enlargement of a Film: The Shanghai Gesture," "The Film and I," and "Hands off Love."

Raymond Borde and Etienne Chaumeton, A Panorama of American Film Noir, 1941–1953, trans. Paul Hammond (San Francisco: City Lights Books, 2002).

Robin Walz, Pulp Surrealism: Insolent Popular Culture in Early Twentieth-Century Paris (Berkeley: University of California Press, 2000).

Discussion Questions

1 How might you describe the surrealist writings collected in The Shadow and its Shadow as a theory of cinematic spectatorship, and why might this way of understanding cinematic pleasure produce a specific interest in film noir?

2 As Hammond and Walz explain, part of the surrealist interest in cinema can be explained by its very lack of cultural prestige, its status as "low" or "popular" culture. How would you compare the different attitudes expressed in these three films noir toward the nature of "popular" and "elite" culture? How has film noir, as it circulates internationally, been reinvented through a process of converting seemingly "low" cultural materials into something more highbrow?

3 As Eburne and Walz suggest, surrealism admires stories of criminal violence and mad love (l'amour fou). What different attitudes do

these films noir take toward (sexual) violence, murder, and criminality? How do these films use criminal psychology to mount a social critique?

4 THE BORDERS OF FILM NOIR

Film noir, itself a borderline genre, is thematically drawn to narratives of international border crossing, especially between the US and Mexico. In *Border Incident* and *Touch of Evil*, both made by progressive filmmakers, we see a different iteration of noir's racial politics. Students may consider these films in connection with our discussion of: noir and race; noir ontologies (since both films may be seen as "western noirs"); Mexican noir and Mexico in film noir.

Suggested Supplementary Screenings

Border Incident (1949)
Director: Anthony Mann
Principal cast: Ricardo Montalban, George Murphy, Owen Parkson, Juan Garcia
Summary: To shut down illegal border crossing by the Mexican *braceros* and the American farmers who exploit them, a Mexican federal agent (Ricardo Montalban) and his American counterpart (George Murphy) go undercover in this noir procedural. While they expose the crime circuit, the American agent is brutally murdered, and the Mexican agent is almost swallowed in quicksand.

Touch of Evil (1958)
Director: Orson Welles
Principal cast: Orson Welles, Charlton Heston, Janet Leigh, Joseph Calleia, Akim Tamiroff
Summary: Mexican drug controller Miguel Vargas (Charlton Heston) is about to honeymoon in the US with his bride (Janet Leigh) when an American industrialist is killed with a car bomb as he

crosses the US/Mexican border. Vargas delays his honeymoon in order to investigate this crime. In the process he uncovers the illegal planting of evidence by the American detective (Orson Welles), whom Vargas, in turn, takes down.

Secondary Reading

Dominique Bregent-Heald, "Dark Limbo: Film Noir and the North American Borders," *Journal of America Culture* 29:2 (June 2006), pp. 125–138.
Donald Pease, "Borderline Justice/State of Emergency: Orson Welles' Touch of Evil," *New Centennial Review* 1 (2001), pp. 75–105.
Jonathan Auerbach, "Noir Citizenship: Anthony Mann's Border Incident," *Cinema Journal* 47:4 (Summer 2008), pp. 102–120.
Michael Denning, *The Cultural Front: The Laboring of American Culture in the Twentieth Century* (New York: Verso, 1996).

Discussion Questions

1   Both of these films are considered noirs, and yet both share mise-en-scène and plot lines with the Hollywood western. How might these films problematize the borders of film noir?
2   For both Auerbach and Pease, the two noirs above dramatize the stakes of citizenship and the violence of the law. What is "noir citizenship" and why is this "genre" perhaps best equipped to convey the structures of American and Mexican national belonging and dispossession?
3   Welles's choice to "brown-face" Heston is both curious and highly racialized. How does Pease explain this decision in terms of the film's politics? Why, given Vargas's extra legal means, might it be necessary to code him as "not quite" Mexican?
4   Pease and Denning offer very different readings of Quinlan's character based on the social and political history through which they read the film. Explain how they both make use of Welles's biography and his Popular Front political activism, but come to rather different conclusions about the character he plays.

Another great Anthony Mann western noir that also takes up questions of citizenship and land rights is *The Furies* (1950). For more recent noir films about the arbitrariness of national borders, and their deadly consequences, see John Sayles's *Lone Star* (1996) and Tommy Lee Jones's *The Three Burials of Melquiades Estrada* (2005).

5 ON "FOREIGN" FEMMES FATALES

American noir is not the only film movement in which the fatal woman is connected to foreignness. We offer a few films below in which other national cinemas similarly code their evil, alluring, or fallen woman as being foreign or tainted by westernization.

Suggested Supplementary Screenings

À bout de souffle/Breathless (1960)

Director: Jean-Luc Godard

Principal cast: Jean-Paul Belmondo, Jean Seberg, Richard Balducci, Daniel Boulanger

Plot summary: This most famous of the New Wave films casts Jean-Paul Belmondo as a petty, Bogart-imitating thief on the run who is finally turned into the Parisian police by his American girlfriend, Patricia (Jean Seberg).

Die Büchse der Pandora/Pandora's Box (1929)

Director: G. W. Pabst

Principal cast: Louise Brooks, Fritz Kortner, Francis Lederer, Carl Goetz, Alice Roberts

Plot summary: Based on Frank Wedekind's play, this film casts the American actress Louise Brooks as Lulu, the alluring and charismatic femme fatale who flees Germany when she is sentenced for killing her husband. Through bribery and sacrifice, she and her raggedy friends reach England, where she breathes her last in the arms of Jack the Ripper.

Shen nu/The Goddess (1934)

Director: Yonggang Mingyou

Principal cast: Ruan Lingyu, Li Kend, Junpan Li, Huaigu Tang, Zhizhi
  Zhang

Summary: Set in modern Shanghai, *The Goddess* stars Ruan Lingyu at the
  height of her celebrity. Here she plays a single mother who must
  prostitute herself in the streets of Shanghai in order to support her
  child. An outcast, she must hide from the police and so finds herself involved with a gambling, alcoholic pimp, whom she kills at
  the end of the film. Tragically, she is sentenced to prison. She is victim of both the westernization and the modernization of Shanghai
  (which explains her prostitution). But she is also a victim of a lingering notion of class immobility. Made during the heyday of the
  May 4th movement, this film is a wonderful answer to the orien-
  talized visions of Shanghai in Sternberg's films and in film noir. It
  also shows the transnational cosmopolitan appeal of the "street
  film" we associate with Weimar cinema.

Secondary Reading

Ginette Vincendeau, "France 1945–65 and Hollywood: The Policier as
  International Text," *Screen* 33:1 (Spring 1992), pp. 50–80.
Mary Ann Doane, "The Erotic Barter: Pandora's Box," in *Femmes Fatales: Feminism,
  Film Theory, Psychoanalysis* (London: Routledge, 1991), pp. 142–162.
Miriam Bratu Hansen, "Fallen Women, Rising Stars, New Horizons:
  Shanghai Silent Film as Vernacular Modernism," *Film Quarterly* 54:1 (Fall
  2000), pp. 10–22.
William Rothman, "The Goddess: Reflection on Melodrama East and West,"
  in *Melodrama and Asian Cinema*, ed. Wimal Dissanayake (Cambridge, UK:
  Cambridge University Press, 1993), pp. 59–72.

Discussion Questions

1 *The Goddess* features Ruan Lingyu in a role as "the new woman"
   who is caught between a modern, urban, capitalist economy and

traditional notions of class and feminine virtue. How does *The Goddess* direct its political and social critique, and how might we compare the main character to Weimar and noir's fallen women?

2   Hansen situates *The Goddess* in the context of vernacular modernity. How might we trace the cinematic and transnational origins of the femme fatale through the circulation of cinema during the interwar period?

3   How may we compare Lulu and Patricia? What is the connection between these "images" of women and cinephilia, and how might the fact that both these characters are played by American actresses be relevant to the film's gender politics? That is, how do gender, desire, and foreignness signify in these two films made on either side of World War II?

4   Vincendeau's essay "France 1945–65 and Hollywood" discusses the complex reception of the cultural products of America in the context of France's postwar modernization. Vincendeau suggests that this reception troubled easy binaries between authentic Americanness and authentic Frenchness. How is this tension at work in *Breathless*?

Another excellent recent global noir about the transnational femme fatale is Olivier Assayas's *Boarding Gate* (2007).

6 CIRCUITS OF INTERNATIONAL CINEPHILIA: TRANSATLANTIC RIPLEYS

Film noir is especially given to international cinephilia, and to transnational cultures of literary translation, adaptation, and homage. This lesson plan invites students to consider the cinephilic circuit opened up through the cinematic afterlife of Patricia Highsmith's apt serial killer Tom Ripley: from France, René Clément's *Plein Soleil/Purple Noon* (1960); from Germany, Wim Wenders's *Der amerikanische Freund/ The American Friend* (1977), discussed in Chapter 2; from the US, Anthony Minghella's *The Talented Mr. Ripley* (1999), and Liliana Cavani's international coproduction *Ripley's Game* (2002). Here we encourage instructors to pair the films with one of their noir source novels, *The Talented Mr. Ripley* or *Ripley's Game*.

Secondary Reading

Patricia Highsmith, *The Talented Mr. Ripley* (1955).
Patricia Highsmith, *Ripley's Game* (1974).

Discussion Questions

1   Why has the character of Tom Ripley proven such an enduring object of cinephilic fascination? How do Highsmith's novelistic meditations on Tom's psychology and mutable identity relate to her interest in Tom's international mobility and travel?

2   How do the Ripley adaptations themselves comment on Tom's Americanness, or not? What is the status of Tom's nationality in these films, and what does Tom's attitude toward local culture and art suggest about national "authenticity"?

3   Do the novelistic and cinematic treatments of Tom – a deadly man – reflect a characteristically noir interest in sexuality? What is the nature of Tom's gender and sexual identity in these films, and how is this related to his criminality and violence?

INDEX

Blum, Leon 10, 38
Blum–Byrnes Accord 38
Boarding Gate 274
Bogart, Humphrey 32, 200, 201
Bollywood 97–8
Bonnie and Clyde 132
Borde, Raymond 18, 79, 86, 128,
    147, 183–4, 190–1, 269
border crossing 270–1
Border Incident 66, 270
*Boudu sauvé des eaux / Boudu Saved from
    Drowning* 9
Bould, Mark xiv n1, 196
Braun, Harald 47
Breu, Christopher 157–8, 165
Brigada Criminal / Criminal Brigade 92
Buai-laju laju / Swing High, My Darling x
Buñuel, Luis 73, 78–86

cabaretera musical 70, 72, 139
*Cabinet des Dr. Caligari, Das / The Cabinet of
    Dr. Caligari* 44
Cahiers du Cinéma 132, 147, 202–6,
    210, 222
Cain, James M. ix–xi, 2–7, 26, 20, 31
Call Northside 777 43
Camus, Albert 30
capitalism: American fiction's
    critiques of 31; and colonialism
    197; corporate 157; film noir's
    critique of 37–8, 41, 47, 58,
    60, 128; Hong Kong 109, 218;
    and the New Deal 36; and
    postmodernism 135–6; and
    uneven development 68–70; *see
    also* democracy; "economic
    miracle"; Hollywood; "Market
    Empire"; modernity
Cavani, Liliana 274–5
censorship: in Germany 41, 45–6,
    48; Hollywood Production Code
    x, 37, 125, 154, 164, 185,
    190–1; in Iran 104; in Italy 20,
    23, 27–8, 29; in Japan 41, 50,
    52, 53, 54; in Spain 90, 92, 104

Cercle rouge, Le / The Red Circle 208
Chandler, Raymond 2
Chaplin, Charlie 53, 267
Chartier, Jean-Pierre 37, 126–7
Chaumeton, Etienne 18, 79, 86, 128,
    147, 183–4, 186, 190–1
Cheat, The 185
Chenal, Pierre 8, 10
Chien andalou, Un / An Andalusian Dog 78
Chienne, La / The Bitch 9
Chinatown 132, 188
Chow, Yun-fat 216, 218–19, 220
Chung Hing sam lam / Chunking Express
    109–15, 140, 147, 218
cine de arrabal 72, 80
cine negro español 92
Cinema magazine 19, 28
cinephilia: as historical practice
    146–7, 183–4, 197–9; of
    Jarmusch, Jim 220–9; and
    neo-noir 131–6; in postwar
    France 29, 199–210; of Woo,
    John 214–20
Clément, René 274–5
Cold War 130, 156, 212
colonialism 97, 102, 110, 263–5
comedia ranchera 70, 72
communism 22, 40; *see also* popular
    front
concentration camps 30
consumer culture 40, 58–60, 89,
    112, 115
Conversation, The 132, 188
Corber, Robert J. 153, 156
cosmopolitanism: definition of xi–ii;
    "emergency" 20; and film noir
    style 78, 213; of Hollywood
    39; of the Hong Kong New
    Wave 126; imposed by
    occupation 42; and Japanese
    detective fiction 52; of
    Kurosawa, Akira 53; modernist
    2–3; and the Weimar street film
    273; of Visconti, Luchino 21–8;
    see also modernism

Halloween, noir style.